TURKISH AND OTHER MUSLIM
MINORITIES IN BULGARIA

ALI EMINOV

Turkish and other Muslim Minorities in Bulgaria

ROUTLEDGE
New York

Published in the United States of America in 1997 by
ROUTLEDGE
29 West 35th Street
New York, NY 10001

Printed in England

ISBN 0-415-91976-2

Cataloging-in-Publication data available from the Library of Congress

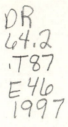
*Respectfully dedicated to the memory of
my father, Mümün Emin Bilâl (1917-80),
my mother, Hayriye Bayram Idriz (1916-96),
and my brother, Aptullah Mümün Emin (1952-89)*

PREFACE AND ACKNOWLEDGEMENTS

The idea for this book dates to early 1985 when the Bulgarian authorities made several extraordinary claims: first, that there were no Turks in Bulgaria; second, that all Muslims in Bulgaria were the descendants of Bulgarians who had been forced to convert to Islam during the Ottoman period; third, that over the years the descendants of "forcibly Islamized Bulgarians" had become aware of their true identity as Bulgarians and reclaimed their original identity by voluntarily and spontaneously replacing their Muslim names with conventional Bulgarian ones. The authorities characterized the several waves of assimilation campaigns against Muslims during the 1960s, 1970s and 1980s as the culmination of a "process of national revival" among Muslims which, the authorities said, had been under way since Bulgarian independence from Ottoman rule in 1878. From March 1985 until 29 December 1989, the Bulgarian authorities continued to insist that Bulgaria was a single-nation state; that with the exception of a small number of Armenians and Jews, the population of the country was entirely Bulgarian. Even after the methods used to assimilate Turks and other Muslim minorities became widely known outside of Bulgaria and the Bulgarian government came under international criticism, the authorities insisted that such criticism was nothing more than malicious rumors spread by the enemies of Bulgaria, mainly Turkey, in an attempt to besmirch the reputation of the country in the international arena. Finally, on 29 December 1989, more than a month after the ouster of Živkov from power, the new leaders of the Bulgarian Communist Party acknowledged that the assimilation campaign had been a grave political error and announced its termination.

In response to the claims of Bulgarian authorities in early 1985, I wrote two articles, "Are Turkish speakers in Bulgaria of ethnic Bulgarian origin?", and "The status of Islam and Muslims in Bulgaria", which were published in *JIMMA* (1986, 1987). Dr. Syed Abedin, then director of the Institute of Muslim Minority

vii

Affairs (IMMA) and editor of its Journal suggested that I prepare a short monograph on Muslim minorities in Bulgaria based on these articles for publication in the mongraph series of the Institute. The monograph was ready at the end of 1987 and plans were made to publish it in 1988. However, several unforseen circumstances – the illness of Dr Abedin, momentous developments in Eastern Europe and the Soviet Union, and the death of Dr Abedin in 1993 – made publication impossible. Since I didn't hear from the Institute for several years after 1987, I gave up on the project, although I continued to do research on the plight of Muslim minorities in Bulgaria. Then, in the winter of 1994 the new director of the Institute of Muslim Minority Affairs and chief editor of the IMMA book series, Dr Saleha Mahmood, expressed an interest in publishing a revised and expanded version of the original monograph. I agreed to undertake such a revision. The present monograph is the result of that effort.

If this monograph is mostly about the experience of Turkish Muslims in Bulgaria, this is not only because the Turks make up the overwhelming majority of Muslims, but also because much has been written about them by scholars within and outside of Bulgaria. The considerable literature, mostly in Bulgarian, that exists on Bulgarian Muslims (Pomaks) is largely propagandistic in nature, devoted to prove the Bulgarian origins of this population, to recount their tragic experience under the "Turkish yoke", and to describe the progress they have made toward recovering their authentic identity as Bulgarians since 1878. The literature on Gypsies is even more sparse. Little of value was published in Bulgaria about Gypsies until after 1989. In fact, during the last two decades of communist rule, the word Gypsy disappeared entirely from the language of official discourse. It is only since 1989 that numerous articles and several books have appeared describing the Gypsy experience under communist rule and their problems under the transition from communism to post-communism.

At this point I wish to acknowledge the help of a number of individuals for making this monograph a reality. I thank the late Dr Abedin for his original inspiration for this project, and Dr Saleha Mahmood, who revived the project and personally followed up the production of the manuscript through its various stages, her efforts leading to its publication as part of the IMMA Book

Series. An anonymous reviewer of the first draft made numerous and valuable comments and suggestions. Prof. Catherine Rudin carefully read the entire manuscript and made numerous suggestions and comments. Whenever possible I have incorporated their suggestions into the text of the monograph. Prof. Randy Bertolas prepared the maps on the distribution of Turks and Muslims. Before 1985, during several visits to Bulgaria, when standard anthropological research, especially on ethnic issues, was not permitted, many Muslim informants, both friends and strangers, provided me with valuable information. I'd like to thank them for their generosity and courage. Between 1985 and 1989, when visiting Bulgaria was impossible for me and there was an almost total news blackout concerning the plight of Muslims, my main sources of information about events in Bulgaria were Turkish refugees from Bulgaria in Turkey and the United States. I would like to thank them. Any shortcomings of the monograph are my sole responsibility.

Wayne, Nebraska   ALI EMINOV
October 1996

CONTENTS

TABLES

MAPS

GLOSSARY

Akçe	Silver coin long used in the Ottoman Empire.
Allah	The core of the Islamic faith is monotheism. Allah is simply the Arabic word for God.
Alevi	Shi'ite; follower of Ali.
Ali	Cousin and son-in-law of Prophet Muhammad.
Baba	Head of a dervish sect; elder of a Kızılbaş community.
Bayram	Turkish term used to refer to the two Muslim festivals: Büyük Bayram or the Major Festival and Küçük Bayram or the Minor Festival.
Bektashi	A Sufi order named for its founder, Hacı Bektaş Veli. Arose in Asia Minor about 12-13th centuries and spread throughout Turkey and the Balkans. The order was closely associated with the Janissaries and remained influential until the disbanding of the Janissaries in 1826; dervish of the Bektaşi order.
Bogomil	Balkan follower of the Albigensian heresy.
Caliph	Literally, one who comes after Muhammad. Muhammad's successors as leaders of the Muslim community. Title implied continuation by its holder of Muhammad's leadership over the Muslim community, but without direct, divine revelation.
Cizye	Poll/head tax on non-Muslims (*zimmis*) living in Muslim lands.
Cizye defterleri	Poll tax registers.
Defter	A register or account book used by administrative officials.
Defterdar	Keeper of the *defter* (account book); Minister of Finance.
Dervenci	Guard of militarily important mountain passes or roads; they were Muslims in Muslim areas and Christians in Christian areas.
Dervish	A member of a Muslim mystical order; a sufi.

Devşirme	Periodic levy of Christian youths to serve in the palace, Janissary corps, and other branches of government.
Dhimmi/zimmi	Christians and Jews who have a revealed book and have entered into special relationship with a Muslim community and are permitted religious freedom in return for payment of the *cizye*.
Eyalet	Province; principality.
Firman/ferman	Ottoman imperial edict.
Fetva/fatwa	A formal legal opinion or decision by a religious leader on a matter of religious law.
Gazi/ghazi	Warrior fighting for Islam/for the Faith; later became a title of honor.
Hafiz	A person who has memorized the entire Koran.
Hacı	A person who has made the pilgrimage to Mecca.
Hacı Bektaş Veli	Founder of the Bektaşi order of dervishes.
Hadith	A saying of the Prophet Muhammad or a saying about him or his teachings by contemporaneous sources which form one of the cornerstones of Islamic law.
Hajj	The pilgrimage to Mecca that all Muslims are obliged to make at least once in their lives, if they are physically and financially able to do so. Also, the month of the Islamic calendar in which pilgrimage takes place.
Hanafi	One of the four major schools of Sunni religious thought.
Hane	Household, constituting the smallest Ottoman tax unit, estimated to average five persons in size; "hearth".
Hatip	A religious person who reads the hutba in the mosque during the Friday prayers and during religious holidays.
Hoca	Religious teacher; tutor and chaplain; community leader.
Ijma	Consensus of a scholarly community of believers on religious regulation.
Icmal defteri	Register of fief holdings.
Ilk okul	Primary/elementary school.

Imam	Leader of community prayers. Also among Shi'ites, the first twelve leaders of their community were given the this title. For the Shi'a, the imam is the necessary, divinely guided, infallible, sinless political/religious leader.
Islam	Submission to Allah and accepting Muhammad as His Messenger.
Janissary	A corruption of the Turkish *yeni çeri* (new troops); refers to the Ottoman infantry recruited through the *devşirme*.
Kadı	Muslim judge learned in the *sharia*, whose decisions were legally binding.
Kanun	Laws issued by Ottoman sultans, based on their right of custom, as opposed to laws based on the *sharia*.
Kanunname	Collection of *kanuns* regulating a particular subject (pl. *kanunnameler*).
Kaza	Smallest administrative unit in the Ottoman Empire.
Kızılbaş	Name generally used to refer to Shi'ites in Bulgaria meaning "Red Head" from their traditional head gear with twelve red stripes representing the twelve *imams*.
Koran	The Muslim Holy Book; considered divine, contains God's revelations as given in Arabic to Muhammad, and is the basis for the Islamic way of life.
Kurban bayramı	Muslim holiday of sacrifice celebrated 70 days after Ramazan; also known as *Büyük Bayram* (Major Festival) in Turkish.
Mahalle	Residential quarter; borough.
Medrese/madrasa	Religious college; originally a Sunni school teaching the *sharia*, term later applied to most secondary schools that taught the Islamic sciences, usually attached to a mosque.
Mevlid	A poem celebrating Muhammad's birth; ceremony when this poem is read, usually on the fortieth day after a person's death, either at the mosque or at the home of the deceased.
Millet	An internally autonomous religious community in the Ottoman Empire; the three major *millets* were: Armenian Orthodox, Greek Orthodox and Jewish.
Milletbaşı	Ethnarch; leader of a *millet* in the Ottoman Empire.

Minaret	The spire of a mosque from which the muezzin traditionally calls the faithful to prayer fiver times a day. In modern times, loudspeakers often broadcast recordings instead.
Muezzin	One who sings or chants the call to prayer.
Mosque	A place of Muslim worship. It may be a simple room or a magnificent marble edifice.
Muslim	Literally, one who submits to God's will and laws.
Mufti	Person trained in the *sharia*, who gives a non-binding legal opinion (*fetva*) in response to questions submitted to him; Muslim religious leader; provincial director of religious affairs.
Nahiye	Subdivision of a *kaza*.
Nüfus defteri	Summary household register.
Oba	Nomad family; a large compartmented nomad tent.
Ocak	"Hearth"; Yürük military company or platoon.
Osmanlı	An Ottoman, i.e., one who was a Muslim, knew Ottoman ways, and, originally, in theory, a "slave of the Sultan".
Pasha, paşa	Turkish title of very high rank, normally military, under the Ottomans.
Qiyas	Process of juridical reasoning by analogy.
Ramazan	The ninth month of the Muslim calendar, during which Muslims fast from dawn to dusk; one of the Five Pillars of Islam; according to Muslim tradition it was during this month that Muhammad received the first of many revelations from Allah.
Ramazan bayramı	Celebration that follows the ending of the month of fasting, also known as *Küçük Bayram* (Minor Festival) in Turkish.
Reaya, rayah	In the Ottoman Empire initially meant all non-Ottomans, but eventually came to refer only to non-Muslim tax payers.
Rum	First the Byzantine (Roman) Empire, then Anatolia, particularly under Seljuk rule.
Rumeli	Ottoman territories in Europe.
Rüştiye	High school.
Sainame	Statistical yearbook.
Şalvar	Pantaloons worn by Muslim women.

Sancak/sanjak	Ottoman military or administrative district; the number of *sancaks* varied in different periods.
Şeyh, sheikh	Used as a title to refer variously to: head of a tribe/leader of a village/head of a sufi order/head of a Muslim guild.
Şeyhülislam	Title of leading religious figure aside from the Caliph in a Muslim state; under the Mamluks he was a *qadi* while, eventually, the Ottomans, appointed the mufti of Istanbul to the office; Grand Mufti.
Sharia	Islamic law based on the Koran, *hadith* (words or actions of Prophet Muhammad and his companions), *qiyas* (process of juridical reasoning by analogy), and *ijma* (consensus of a scholarly community of believers on religious regulation).
Shi'ite	Adherents to the Islamic faction that arose in the seventh century in a split over who should be caliph, or successor, to Muhammad. The 'Shiat Ali', or partisans of Ali, Muhammad's cousin and son-in-law, believed that Ali was the legitimate successor and that the leadership should stay with Muhammad's descendants.
Sicil	Register kept by a *kadi*.
Sipahi	Ottoman cavalry; horseman.
Sublime Porte	European translation of Bab-i Ali (high gate); term stood for the Ottoman Grande Vezir's office and, eventually, Ottoman government.
Sultan	Title that came to mean "supreme secular ruler"; primarily associated with rulers of Turkish origin.
Sunna	The traditions of the Prophet Muhammad. Those things that He did Himself, or approved by Him, or that were done in His presence without earning His disapproval.
Sunni	Orthodox sect of Islam (cf. Shi'ite); "One who follows the way (Sunna) of Muhammad", particularly those who accept one of the four schools of law, as opposed to Shi'i sects; the majority sect among Muslims.
Sürgün	Exile, banishment; one of the methods used by Ottoman administrators to settle strategic areas in the Balkans by Turks from Asia Minor and Anatolia.
Tahrir defterleri	Population census registers.

Tarikat	"Way", "path", "method" laid down by the founder of a Sufi order for its devotees.
Tekke	Dervish lodge.
Timar	Ottoman grant of income from a tax source, usually land, in return for services, in particular, for the Ottoman cavalry, the *sipahis*.
Timara, timariot	The holder of a *timar*.
Turcoman	Turkic-speaking nomads brought over from Anatolia to the Balkans by the Ottomans.
Ulema/ulama	A body of religious scholars who interpret Islamic law for the commuity.
Vakf/waqf/vakıf	Trust established with a grant of land or other income-producing property to support a pious foundation. In the Balkans it often meant the property of a Muslim community and included socially beneficial property of various kinds.
Vilayet	An Ottoman administrative unit of varying size and number,
Vezir	Advisor to a ruler, who, under the Ottomans, was the equivalent of a Prime Minister.
Voynuk	A Bulgarian serving as a horsegroom in the Ottoman army.
Yörük/yürük	Nomad, tribesman; Turkish pastoralists in the Balkans.
Zaviye	A small dervish lodge with a hostel.
Ziamet/zeamet	Large *timar*.

NOTE ON TRANSLITERATION
AND PRONUNCIATION

For transliteration of Bulgarian letters I have followed the system used by the editors of *Slavic and East European Journal*. Most Bulgarian letters are pronounced as in English except for the following.

Ž, ž	Ж, ж	pronounced *s* as in trea*s*ure
J, j	Й, й	pronounced *y* as in *y*es
S, s	С, с	pronounced *s* as in *s*oon
U, u	У, у	pronounced *oo* as in br*oo*m
X, x	Х, х	pronounced *ch* as in Ba*ch*
C, c	Ц, ц	pronounced *tz* as in quar*tz*
Č, č	Ч, ч	pronounced *ch* as in *ch*urch
Š, š	Ш, ш	pronounced *sh* as in *sh*ould
T, t	Щ, щ	pronounced *shed* as in wa*shed*
Ŭ, ŭ	Ъ, ъ	pronounced *u* as in *u*rgent
Ju, ju	Ю, ю	pronounced *you* as in *you*th (but shorter)
Ja, ja	Я, я	pronounced *ya* as in *ya*rd (but shorter)

Most Turkish letters are pronounced as in English except for the following:

C, c	pronounced *j* as in *j*am
Ç, ç	pronounced *ch* as in *ch*urch
ğ	not pronounced; serves to lengthen slightly the preceding vowel
I, ı	pronounced *u* as in *u*rgent
J, j	pronounced *j* as in the French *j*olie
Ö, ö	pronounced *ö* as in the German K*ö*nig
Ş, ş	pronounced *sh* as in *sh*ip
Ü, ü	pronounced *u* as in the French t*u*

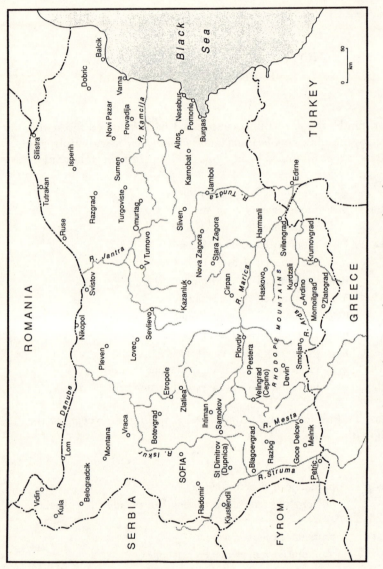

Bulgaria, showing places mentioned in the text

1

BULGARIAN NATIONALISM AND MUSLIM MINORITIES

The idea of nationalism

Of the many secular ideologies that have moved people to political action during the last two centuries, nationalism has been the toughest survivor and remains the most widespread today. Although in a few instances nationalism has been a force for unity, more often it has led to the disintegration of multi-ethnic states and empires and an increase in tension and conflict between different ethnic groups. Attempts to transcend nationalism and to organize the political universe on some other principle have generally failed (Hoffman 1993: 101). For example, orthodox Marxists in formerly communist countries used class as the pivotal concept in defining various types of social relations. All other differences were reduced to class differences. To them ethnic divisions were superficial and did not reflect the most important kinds of social divisions in society. Orthodox Marxists prided themselves on their success in substituting the class principle for the national one, thereby eliminating ethnic antagonisms. However, by overemphasizing class and power distinctions and minimizing the importance of ethnic and other social divisions, they failed to appreciate the actual character of self-identity in the modern world. The collapse of communism and the reemergence of nationalist quarrels in formerly communist countries is proof that the apparent ethnic peace in these countries was an imposed one.

For the purposes of this chapter we define nationalism as a "theory of political legitimacy which requires that ethnic boundaries should not cut across political ones and, in particular, that ethnic boundaries within a given state should not separate the power-holders from the rest" (Gellner 1983: 1). That is, the rulers and

1

the ruled should belong to the same group. Nationalists are people who espouse such an ideology.

We can look at nationalism in the abstract and in practice. Nationalism in-the-abstract espouses an ethical "universalistic" spirit. People who subscribe to this form of nationalism do not show any biased "favour of any special nationality of their own". Their motto is "let all nations have their own political roofs, and let all of them refrain from including non-nationals under it" (Gellner 1983: 1-2). This territorial-political or liberal nationalism has its roots in the French Revolution. The main pillar of liberal nationalism is the citizen. The citizens constitute the state and there is complete equality between citizens. Liberal nationalism envisages an open society where citizens are free to participate fully in the life of society. In practice, nationalists have not followed the reasonable and rational principles enshrined in liberal nationalism. Instead, they have tried to organize the political universe in terms of a second type of nationalism, romantic-ethnic nationalism, with roots in nineteenth-century German romanticism. Romantic nationalists claim that each state belongs to a particular ethnic nation; that the ethnic nation occupies a privileged position within the state. Historically there has been a tendency "to make exceptions on one's own behalf or one's own case" (Gellner 1983: 25); national sentiment has almost always engendered egoistic or chauvinistic nationalism. Romantic nationalists reject the Enlightenment and French rationalism. They deny the workability of the liberal idea of citizenship because, to them, authentic communities are not held together by constitutions but by organic, semi-mystical folk ties that precede and transcend the political. As Kohn (1973: 327) has written, romantic nationalists envisage "a perfect national community, in which the individual could be fully himself only as an integral part of the nation; in such a case individual and society were no longer in need of legal or constitutional guarantees". He goes on to note:

> This nationalism rejected individual liberty as its foundation; it stressed the belief that every individual was determined by the organic national or ancestral past, fundamentally unaltered and unalterable, forward into the future. . . . The concept of an organic and unique personality was transferred from the individual to the nation. The latter was no longer primarily a legal society of individuals entering into union according

to general principles and for mutual benefit; it was an original phenomenon of nature and history, following its own laws. This national personality, alive, striving, and growing, often stirred by desires for power and expansion, appeared as a manifestation of the divine, entitled and called upon to explore all its dynamic potentialities for the rights of other nations (Kohn 1973: 327).

Romantic nationalists argue that the existence of multiple ethnic communities within a single state is a source of tension and instability, and therefore undesirable. Cultural diversity is a threat to the integrity of the nation-state. Therefore, ways must be found to culturally homogenize the nation so that the state and the nation come to coincide with one another (Gellner 1983: 45). Unfortunately, a rigid adherence to romantic nationalism has often led to hypernationalism and xenophobic extremism and to the use of force as an instrument to eliminate undesirable minority ethnic communities. Nazism in Germany, "ethnic cleansing" in the former Yugoslavia, expulsion of Turks from Bulgaria, armed confrontations between various ethnic groups in former Soviet republics and the rise of extreme nationalist groups and parties in Western Europe are just a few examples of the consequences of hypernationalism in the twentieth century.

Nationalism holds that the nation and the state "were destined for each other; that either without the other is incomplete, and constitutes a tragedy" (Gellner 1983: 6). Nationalism does not recognize the contingent nature of the nation and the state. However, according to Gellner (1983: 3), a historical analysis of the rise of nations and states reveals that both "are a contingency and not a universal necessity . . . before they could become intended for each other, each of them had to emerge, and their emergence was independent and contingent." Therefore, the "coincidence between the nation and the state arises from deliberate political action, but that action may proceed in two directions. The state, defined by its administrative apparatus, may become or drive toward becoming a nation-state by promulgating a single language, a single culture, and a single set of symbols for the people within its borders" or a nation may seek to become a nation-state by "agitating for a political apparatus to match its cultural boundaries. In this process, local sentiments and group solidarity are capitalized on and given a political cast." (Woolard 1989: 10).

As Denich (1993: 45-6) observes, in South Slavic languages (Bulgarian, Macedonian, Serbo-Croatian, and Slovene) "the word '*narod*' means both 'people' and 'nation'. Thereby, the 'nation-state' is attached to a specific 'nation,' or 'people,'conceived as an ethnic population." Such a conception does not allow the possibility that nationality can be "an attribute of citizenship, and can even be chosen, regardless of ancestry. To define the 'state' further as an attribute of a 'nation' means that there is also no way to separate the issue of control over the state from ancestry . . ."

In Bulgaria, as in other formerly communist countries, ethnic categories were often "employed as an instrument of the power system, variable according to changing definitions of the state quite apart from how people 'felt' about themselves. Definitions of ethnic identity were not left to personal choice, but employed as an instrument of state policy, variable with the changing definitions of what constitutes the state" (Denich 1993: 47).

Bulgarian nationalism and Muslim minorities, 1878-1989

Since Bulgarian independence from Ottoman rule in 1878 political action in Bulgaria has been directed toward the creation of a territorially, culturally and linguistically unified nation-state by eliminating cultural diversity through assimilation/migration of the country's ethnic minorities. Although the language of political discourse about nationalism has gone through various phases, reflecting the particular preoccupations of Bulgarian leaders over the years, the goal has remained the same. Bulgarian ideologues took "for granted that *nation = language = territory = state . . .* Because the territory is Bulgarian, the dogma goes, the people who inhabit it are Bulgarians. *Because* they are Bulgarians, they must speak the Bulgarian language and *should* be in a single nation-state" (Lunt 1986: 729; emphasis in original).

Todorova (1992: 28) identifies four phases of Bulgarian nationalism since 1878. During the first two phases, 1878-1918 and 1918-44, large numbers of texts were published which focused on the problem of the national ideal pivotal to romantic nationalism, "the correlation between nation and territory, or, in other terms, between ethnicity and the state".

"Bulgaria" was being used both as a synonym for the Bulgarian people, and as designating the territory of the state. The national ideal . . . held that a nation could develop fully and adequately only within independent national borders which would encompass all members of the nation (Todorova 1992: 29).

The continuity of historical tradition from the medieval period, when Bulgaria reached its greatest territorial expansion, was invoked as an argument for the establishment of the "natural" national borders of the Bulgarian nation-state. These borders were briefly established by the San Stefano Treaty ending the Russo-Turkish War in 1878 but were revoked by the Treaty of Berlin the same year. Bulgaria considered the provisions of the Treaty of Berlin a grave injustice. Its failure to reunite the nation-state within the San Stefano borders during the Balkan wars and the First World War led to an emergence of defensive nationalism reflected in numerous works "based on a martyrological approach, painting a victimized nation, isolated and on the sidelines of world attention . . ." (Todorova 1992: 34). After the establishment of communist dictatorship in Bulgaria, a brief period (1944-56) of non-national experiment quickly gave way to communist nationalism, which "appropriated important elements of the Marxist doctrine . . . thus legitimizing its claims on the basis of Marxist discourse . . . The so called 'Communist nationalism' was nothing else but a transvestite 'ordinary' nationalism" (Todorova 1992: 35-6).

During the period of international experiment between 1944 and 1956 the existence of minorities in Bulgaria was constitutionally recognized and their rights were guaranteed and protected. The government, for a while, even encouraged and supported the development of minority cultural institutions. This was especially true for the Turkish minority. The party ideologues believed that the class interests of workers, regardless of their ethnic affiliation, would, over time, overcome their parochial interests and identities, which would be given up voluntarily and replaced with the Bulgarian socialist identity. It did not take long for these ideologues to realize that encouraging and supporting the development of minority cultural institutions, albeit within a socialist framework – "national in form, socialist in content" – was strengthening rather than weakening parochial identities. Also, by the mid-1950s a more worrisome problem for the government had emerged: significant numbers of Pomaks (Bulgarian-speaking Muslims), Gypsy Muslims, and Tatars were identifying themselves as Turks. The authorities felt that a radical corrective to existing policies was necessary if Bulgaria was to become a homogeneous, single-nation state. The April 1956 Plenum of the Central Committee (CC) of the Bulgarian Communist Party (BCP) seems to have been a watershed event. After the Plenum, the government issued and implemented a series of decisions that not only eliminated the rights of minorities but forced the members of the country's largest minorities, mostly Muslim, to replace their original names with Bulgarian ones. These groups were henceforth identified as Bulgarians. We briefly and chronologically mention the most important of the decisions that impacted adversely on the status of minorities in the country. Most are discussed in more detail in the following chapters.

The first group to experience the impact of communist nationalism were the Macedonians of the Pirin region of southwestern Bulgaria. They were issued new passports in 1956 in which they were identified as Bulgarians. By administrative fiat the number of Macedonians was reduced from 187,789 in the 1956 census to 8,750 in the 1965 census (King 1973: 262). A decree in December 1956 recommended that nomadic Gypsies be settled and engage in socially beneficial labor and that the rest of the Gypsies be more fully integrated into Bulgarian society (Helsinki Watch 1991: 61-7). In October 1958 the CC of BCP approved plans not only to intensify the party's ideological work among the Turkish population but also to reorient its official policy by introducing a corrective "regarding this population which until then incorrectly been labeled as a 'Turkish national minority.' The party directives contained the following recommendation: '. . . starting gradually in the 1958/9 academic year, the instruction of Turkish youth in the secondary educational establishments, teacher-training institutes and higher educational establishments shall be carried out in Bulgarian'" (Kertikov 1991: 83). This decision was implemented between 1960 and 1972 when all Turkish-language schools were merged with Bulgarian schools and Turkish-language instruction came to an end. As Mutafchieva (1994: 33) notes:

> [After 1958] the Bulgarians began to be brainwashed *en masse* with fresh arguments about "the otherness" of Turks and Pomaks. Compared to the "internationalism", a new conception developed: they were not only "the others", they were moreover dangerous for our state because they strove to cut off a part of the national territory and to annex it to Turkey.

In 1962 the government took steps to counteract "the trend of Turkification" among Gypsy Muslims, Pomaks, and Tatars. The document entitled "Endorsement of measures against the Turkish self-identification of Gypsies, Tatars, and Bulgarians professing the Mohammedan religion" identified the reasons for this trend and recommended specific steps to reverse it. To minimize or eliminate the influence of Turks within these communities, the party recommended "a campaign of public persuasion" to change their identities to Bulgarian by replacing their Turco-Arabic names with Bulgarian ones. Force or other forms of pressure were not to be used in this effort. In practice, however, abuses of power were widespread. Local authorities used brutal methods to force Pomaks in southwestern Bulgaria to replace their Muslim names with Bulgarian ones in 1962, which generated considerable resistance. In 1964 the Politburo in its "Work among the Bulgarian Mohammedan population in the Blagoevgrad district and its abuses" condemned such abuses of power and allowed some Pomaks to restore their Muslim names. However, a few years later, in 1970, the Politburo reconfirmed the necessity of changing Turco-Arabic names and the name-changing campaign was renewed (Kertikov 1991: 83-4). Between 1971 and 1973 all Pomaks were forced to replace their Muslim names with Bulgarian names.

Constitutional language and political discourse after 1970 reflected the new ideological requirements. The 1971 Constitution dropped any mention of national minorities or the word minority itself. In fact, after 1971 references to "national minorities" or "ethnic groups", were purged from official discourse. Instead, there were only "Bulgarian citizens", "normal ones, on the one hand, and those of 'non-Bulgarian ancestry' on the other". For the latter, the decisive factor was not their ancestry, "which concerns only the past, but rather their membership in a collective 'unitary Bulgarian socialist nation,' a term which was frequently employed after the consecration of the concept during the February 1974 party plenum" (Baest 1985: 22).

After the approval of the 1971 Constitution, the creation of a nation-state with a single language and a homogenous culture became an explicit government policy. This official policy was reflected in the language of political discourse of the time. Party ideologues began frequently to declare that Bulgaria was well along the way to becoming a unified single-nation state. The

BCP platform for 1971 notes that "the process of development of the socialist nation will expand further" and "citizens of our country of different national origins will come closer together" (*Rabotničesko Delo* 1971). After the February 1974 party plenum the use of the term "unified Bulgarian socialist nation" began to appear in the official press. In 1977 an article in the Party daily, *Rabotničesko Delo*, claimed that Bulgaria was "almost completely of one ethnic type and [was] moving toward complete national homogeneity." In 1979 Party leader Todor Živkov claimed: "The national question has been solved definitively and categorically by the population itself . . . Bulgaria has no internal problems with the nationality question" (*Rabotničesko Delo* 1979). Bulgarian history was revised in order to bring it in line with ideological requirements.

By 1973 all Pomaks and most Gypsy Muslims had been forced to assume Bulgarian identity. However, the members of the country's largest minority, the Turks, were unwilling to voluntarily fall in line with the demands of the party ideology and assume a Bulgarian identity. Over the next several years the Turks would feel the heavy-handed pressure tactics of the government to force them to give up their Turkish identity and to reclaim their original Bulgarian identity. Between December 1984 and March 1985, all Turks in Bulgaria were forced to assume Bulgarian names. The effort began in the Turkish villages in the eastern Rhodope region but quickly spread to central and northeastern Bulgaria. The campaign capped a twenty-five-year government effort to assimilate the country's largest minorities, the Macedonians, Pomaks, Gypsies, and Turks.[1] In early March 1985 the government would confidently announce that Bulgaria was a homogenous one-nation state.

Until the late 1970s Bulgarian historians not only acknowledged the existence of a sizable Turkish minority in Bulgaria but also located the origins of this minority outside the Balkan Peninsula. They noted that Turkish colonists from Asia Minor and Anatolia were settled in large numbers along important commercial and military routes in Bulgaria and the Balkans between the fourteenth and nineteenth centuries (Kosev, Xristov, and Angelov 1966: 83; Bŭlgarska Akademija na Naukite 1969: 197). Moreover, Bulgarian

---

[1] A discussion of this campaign and its consequences is found in Amnesty International (1986), Helsinki Watch (1986, 1987), Eminov (1990), and Poulton (1993: 119-51).

scholars noted that the Turkish minority was the largest national group after Bulgarians and lived "in large concentrations in the eastern Rhodopes, Gerlovo, Dobrudža and Slannik. They are primarily workers in agricultural cooperatives. Bulgarians and Turks live amicably and together with all other nationalities participate in the building of socialism" (Dinev and Mišev 1969: 136; see Živkov 1964a). In 1980, in his discussion of the achievements of socialist culture, Hristov (1980: 240) notes the contributions of minority nationalities to the development of socialist culture, and the complete equality of minorities in all spheres of life:

> Along with Bulgarians, all the ethnic minorities, including Turks, Gypsies, Tartars, Wallachians and others, are involved in its creation and development. With the exception of the first two, the other minority groups are small. In socialist Bulgaria all nationalities and ethnic minorities enjoy equal rights both in the sphere of material production and in socio-political life, on the one hand, and in the sphere of culture, on the other.

After 1980, however, the Turks disappear from Bulgarian territory and are written out of Bulgarian history. Petrov (1981: 145) writing in 1981 claimed: "Bulgaria is a uninational state. The population throughout is Bulgarian. Only in the northeastern part – Shoumen, Turgovishte and Rasgrad districts – are there communities of Bulgarian Turks." Turks living in the Rhodopes and other parts of Bulgaria disappear at the stroke of a pen! In another work written in 1982, the existence of Turks in the entire Balkan Peninsula is denied:

> In terms of ethnic and linguistic affiliation, the population of the Balkan states as a whole belongs to the Indo-European group. In the Balkans there also live Russians, Armenians, Jews, Gypsies, Tatars and other ethnic groups (Dimitrov 1982: 14).

The Bulgarian government enlisted the aid of scholars from various fields to collect evidence in support of this new version of Bulgarian history and place Turks and other minorities in that history as "pure-blooded" Bulgarians. Most Bulgarian scholars readily obliged and found the required "evidence" everywhere they looked, it seems. During the 1960s and 1970s they collected evidence to prove the Bulgarian origins of the Pomaks.[2] Similar research was undertaken in the 1980s to prove the Bulgarian origins of ethnic Turks and again Bulgarian scholars produced volumes of pseudo-scientific "evidence". In these works the authors played fast and loose with facts or manufactured "evidence" from thin air. Xristov's (1989: 100-1) discussion of the spread of Turkish in Bulgaria during Ottoman rule is one example where political correctness substituted for fact:

> Anatolian Turkish and other Turkic languages from Anatolia were spread through various means. The carriers of Turkish language were Ottoman administrators, the military, and the religious establishment. The representatives of these groups married Bulgarian women, and the children and grandchildren of these families spread Turkic dialects in Bulgaria, which were called Turkish later on. To these groups must be added Janissaries and other units in the Ottoman army which consisted of Islamized Christian children. Sent back to the Bulgarian lands, they not only spread Turkish dialects but also established families with Bulgarian women who were converted to Islam. In these families the Turkish language gradually assumed ascendancy. . . . The Islamized Bulgarian slaves, Bulgarian women in harems, and young men and women employed as domestics in Turkish families were also important in spreading Turkish in Bulgarian lands.

The impression is given that most Turks who settled in Bulgaria were single men, and that they then married Bulgarian women who converted to Islam. The children born to such unions were brought up as Turks and as Muslims. Everything mentioned in the statement indeed happened. However, the statement ignores the fact that Turkish families, both pastoralists and peasants, were settled in large numbers in Bulgaria during and following the Ottoman conquest, a fact that Bulgarian historians freely acknowledged into the late 1970s. Here partial truth is expanded into a sweeping generalization.

Xristov (1989: 101) also claims that specific Ottoman policies

---

[2] A Commission to study the history, customs and cultures of the Rhodope population was established in the late 1950s. The members of the Commission were charged to collect evidence on the Bulgarian origins of the Pomaks. The results were published in *Rodopski Sbornik*, a periodical especially established for this purpose.

toward Orthodox Christians in Bulgaria contributed to the spread of Turkish in Bulgaria:

> There [was] the Ottoman policy of imposing upon the Islamized population the language of the ruling ethnic group. The new Muslims and non-Muslims were required to speak Turkish. From many parts of Bulgarian lands there are stories of old people which tell that during "Turkish times" various sanctions and tortures were used, including the cutting off of the tongues of those who refused to speak Turkish.

Again, this claim is not supported by the historical evidence. It was not official Ottoman policy to require that converts to Islam give up their native languages as a precondition for conversion. On the contrary, many converts in the Balkans could and did preserve their native languages: Pomaks in Bulgaria, Bosnian Muslims, and Albanian Muslims are examples.

Why such cavalier disregard of evidence? As Todorova (1992: 37) observes, during the 1960s and increasingly during the 1970s "there was a continuous escalation in the national feelings of all groups within the intelligentsia but primarily among the liberal arts, and particularly acute among historian and writers." Bulgarian scholars collected and presented "evidence" in support of the thesis that the Bulgarian nation had taken shape during the Middle Ages from a blending of Proto-Bulgarians, Thracians, and Slavs and ever since had remained pure and uncontaminated. In the political discourse of the time, this thesis "served as an endorsement of the principle of the unitary state with no accommodation for ethnic or other minorities" (Todorova 1992: 38). The main character in the revival of generic memories of Bulgarians was the stereotype of the Turk, but with a "new accent: he had been a Bulgarian forcibly converted to Islam! The theme so elaborately treated in the Lives of the 'new saints' in the sixteenth and seventeenth centuries about the cruelties that Bulgarians forcibly converted to Islam suffered appeared in modern renditions. The idea of voluntary conversion of the once subjugated peoples was entirely discarded: violence and only violence described with puzzling masochism" (Mutafchieva 1994: 34).

Long-discarded racial theories from the 1920s and 1930s were resurrected in support of the racial purity of the Bulgarian nation. For example, an article published in *Otečestven Front*, a national daily, summarized the "findings" based, according to the article, on "anthropological tests" carried out "over the last 30 years by anthropologists from the Sofia Institute of Morphology" in three ethnically mixed districts. A commentary in the *Newsletter of the East European Anthropology Group* (1988: 16-17) summarizes these "findings":

> The Bulgarian nation is pure and uncontaminated, and has remained unchanged since the Middle Ages. According to the anthropologists, the Bulgarian people took shape in the ninth and tenth centuries as a blending of Slavs, Thracians, and Asiatic tribes. This mixture evolved into a homogeneous entity, the people now called Bulgarians.[3] The foreign invasions of the past 1,000 years left no racial mark, it seems. The implication is that members of the Turkish minority are merely Bulgarians who happen to speak Turkish.

There is a glaring contradiction between the claim of purity of the Bulgarian nation and Xristov's claim of widespread practice of Turks marrying Bulgarian women mentioned previously. The biological consequence of such marriages is a hybrid population whose gene pool contains genes from both populations. The ideology of nationalism triumphed over such contradictions and overcame biology.

The notion of the purity of the Bulgarian nation figured prominently in the speeches of party leaders following the official conclusion of the assimilation campaign among Turks in early 1985. On 2 March 1985 and subsequent days, high-ranking party officials and government representatives were sent to ethnically mixed areas to brief local party officials about what had happened and why it had happened. Prime Minister Griša Filipov briefed local party officials of the Sliven district in the village of Novačevo. The meeting was attended by the President of the National Assembly, Stanke Todorov, and other high-ranking party officials. On 6 March, Milko Balev, member of the Politburo and close Živkov confidant, traveled to Haskovo; Dimitŭr Stojanov, the Minister of Internal Affairs, to Veliko Tŭrnovo, and Dimitŭr Stanišev, Secretary of the Central Committee, to the village of Dupnica in the Blagoevgrad district. On 14 March Stojan Mihailov, Secretary

---

[3] Several articles in English on this topic are found in Yankov (1989). This collection also includes articles presenting "evidence" for the Bulgarian origins of Pomaks and Turks.

of the Central Committee, went to Silistra; and Todor Božinov, deputy Prime Minister, traveled to Ruse. Lower-level party and government functionaries were sent to other ethnically mixed areas. Their message in every district was the same: "There are no Turks in Bulgaria. The case is closed."

They all gave essentially the same speech, indicating that the speakers were repeating official theses previously adopted by the Politburo and accepted as the official policy of the government.[4] Their speeches were published in provincial newspapers only and parts were excerpted in the English-language weekly, *Sofia News*, for foreign consumption.[5] Newspapers with national distribution remained largely silent about the events taking place in Bulgaria at the time. The following quote from the speech given by Politburo member Milko Balev in Haskovo and reported in *Haskovska Tribuna* on 9 March 1985 gives a sense of the tone of these speeches:

> Comrades! A fundamental, historic achievement of the April line of the Bulgarian Communist Party is the qualitatively new level of moral-political unity and national resolve of the Bulgarian people. In the sixties, and especially in the seventies, there took place in a number of districts in the Rhodope (mountains) a process of national rebirth. Recognizing historic truth, a large number of the descendants of forcibly Islamized Bulgarians in the Smoljan, Pazardjik, and Blagoevgrad districts reconstituted their Bulgarian names [refers to Pomaks]. The positive results of this process is known to all . . . The economy of these areas grew quickly, the culture and education of the population rose, the cadres of the future grew up. The working people shed their Islamic fanaticism, freed themselves from the influence of conservatism in their daily lives, and strengthened their Bulgarian patriotic consciousness. At the close of 1984 and the beginning of 1985, there arose throughout our land a newly strengthened, spontaneous and all embracing process of the reconstitution of Bulgarian names among our countrymen with Turco-Arabic names. This process was an avalanche in the strictest sense of the word, completed throughout the country in two or three months, in some areas inside a matter of

---

[4] The full text of the speech delivered by Stanišev in the village of Dupnica, Blagoevgrad district in southwestern Bulgaria on 6 March 1985 is found in Rajkin (1990).

[5] The full texts of these speeches are found in *Südost-Europa* (1985).

days [refers to Turks]. How did this occur so spontaneously, so comprehensively? Above all because the process is a striking expression of a new historical awareness . . . With wisdom and foresight, these people have made a historic choice and reconstituted their Bulgarian names. Because they trust the Bulgarian Communist Party, convinced that its greatest concern is for the welfare of the broad masses in our country. Everyone has clearly understood that changing names is an historical act, a rebirth, opening up limitless space for the all-round development of the worker, for his complete self-realization in our society; it opens the path to happiness and good fortune for his children, grandchildren, and great-grandchildren.

Comrades! The People's Republic of Bulgaria is a one-nation state, her borders incorporate no foreign territory, and not a single part of the Bulgarian people belongs to any other people or nation . . . (quoted in Baest 1985: 24).

The themes developed in these speeches would be repeated over and over again for almost five years. One theme was that Pomaks and Turks had been descendants of Bulgarians who were forcibly converted to Islam during the Ottoman period. The former had been forced to accept Islam but had preserved their native Bulgarian language, while the latter not only had been forced to accept Islam but also had been Turkified. Another theme was that since Bulgarian independence from Ottoman rule in 1878 there had been a process of national rebirth among Bulgarian and Turkish Muslims; that over the years they had become aware of their true identity as Bulgarians.[6] This process of national rebirth had gained speed during the second half of the twentieth century, culminating in a voluntary and spontaneous change of names, first among the Pomaks, then among the Turks:

The rudiments of a process of resurgence of the national identity of Muslim Bulgarians can be traced back to as early as the second half of the 19th century and especially in the 20th century. *It is based on the traditions common of the Bulgarian nationality*

---

[6] After January 1985, reference to "the Turks of Bulgaria " or, "the Muslims of Bulgaria", which was still in practice until fall 1984, was purged from official vocabulary. Instead terms such as "Bulgarian citizens", "our fellow citizens who reverted to their Bulgarian names", "our fellow countrymen who had Turkic-Arabic names" or "Muslim Bulgarians" replaced previous designations.

(regardless of religion) in the domains of language, folklore, ethnography and others which, as is known, are the most conservative and enduring elements of the ethnic psychology and they are the chief influences of the so-called ethnocentrism (*Sofia News* 1985a: 1,12; emphasis added).

The same editorial asserted further that the growth of awareness of original Bulgarian identity among Turks had intensified during the second half of the twentieth century:

The 1960s witnessed the first big wave of resurgent national self-consciousness among Muslim Bulgarians [Pomaks] which found expression in the renunciation by tens of thousands of people of the once assumed personal names of Arabic and Turkish origin. This virtually uninterrupted process continued into the 1970s too, and by the end of last year [1984] it had assumed the nature of a truly massive popular movement (*Sofia News* 1985a: 12).

During a press conference for foreign journalists in April 1985, Ljubomir Šopov, chief of the Balkan Department of the Ministry of Foreign Affairs, more or less repeated the points made in the *Sofia News* editorial. However, he went further and suggested that there was no connection between Turks in Turkey and Turks in Bulgaria, that "Turkey had no historical rights and no other grounds whatsoever to claim some 'Turkish national minority' or 'compatriots' in Bulgaria" (*Sofia News* 1985b: 3). Therefore, he concluded, the affairs of the Muslim community in Bulgaria were a purely internal matter. Šopov went on to reiterate the latest government position on the status of the Turks in the following words:

The forcibly converted part of the population has become aware of the historical truth about their national identity and has been regaining their national self-consciousness [as Bulgarians] in the whole course of a century after Bulgarian liberation in 1878 . . . *All this has found a final and categorical expression in the process of the restoration of Bulgarian names by the Bulgarian Muslim citizens of their own free will and on their own initiative* (emphasis added).

Bulgaria categorically denied any use of force or terror to coerce Turks to assume Bulgarian names. The government insisted that the entire name change process had been voluntary. The idea that during the bitter cold winter months hundreds of thousands of Turks flocked to police stations throughout Bulgaria in droves and stood in line to change their names is absurd to say the least. Šopov also claimed that all Turkish Muslims had left Bulgaria during and immediately after the Russo-Turkish War of 1878. Those "Bulgarians with Turkish ethnic consciousness" who had remained in Bulgaria after Bulgarian independence had also emigrated to Turkey by 1978. Hence, in 1985 there were no Muslim Bulgarians with any connection with Turkey or anyone in Turkey.

Dimitŭr Stojanov, Minister of Internal Affairs, was even more intransigent, claiming that:

All our countrymen who reverted to their Bulgarian names are Bulgarians. They are the bone of the bone and the flesh of the flesh of the Bulgarian nation; although the Bulgarian national consciousness of some of them might still be blurred, they are of the same flesh and blood; they are children of the Bulgarian nation; they were forcibly torn away and now they are coming back home. *There are no Turks in Bulgaria* (Radio Free Europe Research, 1985: 5; emphasis added).

Deputy Prime Minister Todor Božinov reiterated this point even more forcefully. His response to suggestions that Turks be allowed to emigrate to Turkey was:

There will be no emigration to Turkey, either now or in the future! This is not subject to negotiation, now or in the future! There is no one to negotiate with, because no part of the Bulgarian people belongs to any other nation This is the unshakable position of the People's Republic of Bulgaria, of her party and state leaders. Out countrymen who have reconstituted their Bulgarian names are Bulgarians . . . they are flesh and blood of the Bulgarian people. Bulgarian blood flows in their veins, even if their national consciousness is beclouded . . .

Božinov went further and claimed that the change of names among Turks would serve the cause of peace in the world and contribute to better relations between Bulgaria and Turkey!

The reconstitution of Bulgarian names is an extraordinarily

important historic step, a revolutionary act of liberation for those of our countrymen who only recently found themselves in a serious dilemma. The completion of this process has put an end to this situation once and for all. But the process is not exclusively patriotic, but contains a class content as well. *It serves the objective of peace in Europe and good relations in our region, in Europe, and in the world, creating a solid basis for the further development of our bilateral relations with the Turkish Republic* (in Baest 1985: 24; emphasis added).

Vasil Canov, a secretary of the Central Committee, expressed similar sentiments. He characterized the name-changing

.... as a revolutionary act, which dealt a strong blow to bourgeois nationalism [Turkish nationalism] and rendered powerless its ceaseless attempts to confuse and poison the consciousness of some Bulgarian citizens [Turks], to alienate them from the socialist motherland, and to turn them into tools of reactionary anti communist forces [Turkey] (Radio Free Europe Research 1985: 6).

As Baest (1985: 24-5) observes, "It is difficult to imagine what might have led the Bulgarian leadership to think they could manage all the domestic and international repercussions of their new policy with statements like these, but they continued to push the new line" for almost five years. However, the name-changing campaign proved easier to accomplish than the more far-reaching plan of the government to assimilate the Turks linguistically by prohibiting the use of Turkish in daily intercourse and to eradicate Islamic rituals associated with important life-cycle events by banning them. In this the government badly miscalculated: the assault on Turkish ethnic and religious identity strengthened the resolve of Turks to cling to their ethnic and religious identities even more tenaciously. The continuing campaign against the Turkish ethnic and religious identity would lead to widespread rebellion in May 1989 which would hasten the downfall of Živkov later that year. If the Bulgarian leaders had remembered the lessons of Bulgaria's own history of stubborn cultural survival in the face of oppression, they would have had second thoughts about their campaign to obliterate the identity of Turks and other Muslims and avoided needless suffering.

Bulgarian nationalism and Muslim minorities since 1989

During the entire communist period the language of political discourse avoided the word "nationalism" in describing government policies toward minorities. On the contrary, any manifestation of nationalism was to be discouraged and fought against. Instead, the explanations of the assimilation campaigns against Muslims resorted to pseudo-scientific, pseudo-Marxist clichés such as "the coming together of different nationalities", ethnic "unification", "the operation of natural historical laws", and during the 1970s and 1980s a "process of national revival". Even the expulsion of Turkish leaders and the mass migration of Turks from Bulgaria to Turkey in 1989 was euphemistically called a "grand excursion".

However, the developments in Bulgaria since 1989, where political parties and other interest groups appeal openly to nationalism to further their political and personal interests, are not something new but a continuation of the national ideal since 1878. The "transvestite communist nationalism" has shed its clothes and appears in its full nakedness. According to Todorova (1992: 40), three things have happened in Bulgaria since 1989. First, nationalism today has no need for the dominant pseudo-Marxist jargon of the communist period. The same individuals who not so long ago resorted to Marxist clichés have now appropriated the language of democracy in articulating the same nationalist discourse. Today they speak "in the name of the people", "national unity", "common national ideals and interests" and so on, but the underlying message is the same – to create a culturally and linguistically unified Bulgaria. Secondly, the end of the Cold War left a power vacuum in the Balkans leading to a perception among various states in the region that they can realize their nationalist goals without serious risks. Third, the serious economic, political, and cultural crisis under the transition from communism to post-communism and the resulting frustration provides a fertile ground for nationalism and scapegoating of minorities.

The potential political usefulness of nationalism became apparent soon after the ouster of Živkov from power on November 10, 1989. The results of a sociological survey on attitudes toward the assimilation campaign, the so-called "revival process", carried out among salaried party workers in December 1989, proved prophetic by identifying the most problematic aspects of the "Turkish problem" that could be used to manipulate public opinion. This survey found that support for several aspects of the revival process had been very high among party workers. For example, 77.3 per cent said they approved the idea of changing the names of Muslims; 75.9 per cent approved the limitation and prohibition of the official use of Turkish; 52.7 per cent approved limiting such practices as circumcision, traditional burial rituals and the wearing of traditional clothes (Petkov and Fotev 1990: 218). In the same survey party workers were asked whether they thought the party apparatus would approve an eventual change in ethnic politics concerning the free choice of name, language, religion and religious rituals, and emigration to another country. Almost three-quarters of respondents, 74.2 per cent, were against the restoration of Turkish/Muslim names; 56 per cent were against lifting the prohibition on the use of Turkish; and 49.6 per cent were against the free emigration of Turks. More tolerance was expressed concerning freedom of religion and religious and cultural practices; over 80 per cent thought that the party apparatus would approve such changes in the future (Petkov and Fotev 1990: 224).

When the new leadership of the Bulgarian Communist Party reversed the forced assimilation policy of the Živkov regime on 29 December 1989, a nationalist backlash was not long in coming. Two days later, on 31 December, nationalist unrest flared up in Turkish areas. In Kŭrdžali, the seat of a predominantly Turkish district in southeastern Bulgaria, Bulgarian nationalists set up a Committee for the Defense of National interests to protest the government's decision to restore the rights of Turkish and other Muslims. They vehemently objected to its decision to allow Muslims to restore their names and its plan to reintroduce Turkish-language classes in schools in ethnically-mixed areas. They organized demonstrations and strikes and called for a national referendum on the issue. To them there was no place in Bulgaria for Turks, Gypsies and other minorities. Minorities should either assimilate or emigrate. The platform of the Radical National Party declared its intentions more openly: to drive the Turks out of Bulgaria and to replace them with Bulgarians from Moldova and elsewhere. Over the next several days nationalist demonstrations spread to other ethnically mixed areas of the country such as Plovdiv, Haskovo, Pleven, Šumen, Ruse, Tŭrgovište and Sliven, and to Sofia itself. The nationalists raised a number of mostly unfounded fears: that the restoration of the human and civil rights of Muslims would inevitably lead to demands by them for cultural autonomy which would weaken Bulgarian culture; that Turkey would invade Bulgaria and divide Bulgarian territory between Turks and non-Turks, making Bulgaria another Cyprus; that high birth-rates among Muslims would overwhelm the Bulgarian population, which would quickly lead to the "Turkification" or "Islamization" of Bulgaria, and so on. These strikes and demonstrations ended temporarily when the government held a national conference of the Social Council of Citizens from 8 to 12 January 1990 in Sofia to discuss the issue. The conference issued a compromise document which tried to satisfy both the opponents and the proponents of the government revocation of assimilation. It condemned the abrogation of the rights of Muslims under the Živkov regime and reaffirmed the rights of Muslims to choose their own names, practice Islam and observe traditional customs, and of Turks to speak Turkish in everyday life. The document also tried to appease the nationalists by affirming Bulgarian as the official language of the country and by opposing groups and organizations who advocate autonomy or separatism (see Ashley 1990: 4-11, Perry 1991: 5-8).

The government took concrete action to implement the restoration of the rights of Muslims soon after. On 6 March 1990 the parliament enacted a law on the Names of Bulgarian Citizens as a step toward national unity and concord. The law condemned forcible name changes and the restrictions imposed on Turkish and other Muslims as gross violations of the equality of citizens before the law as guaranteed by Article 35 of the 1971 Constitution. Article 17 of the Law on Names stipulated that "Threat, coercion, violence, fraud, abuse of power or other illicit action in choosing, keeping, changing or restoring a name is punished under the Penal Code" (Sofia Press 1990: 8). This law also declared that "Bulgarian citizens whose names have been forcibly changed may, of their own free will, restore their former names", and spelled out the procedures by which names could be restored (Sofia Press 1990: 8-9). In the mean time, Turks and other Muslims were taking initiatives on their own: reopening Islamic schools closed during the Živkov regime and founding new Islamic schools, planning to publish Turkish newspapers, and preparing for the reintroduction of Turkish-language classes in municipal schools in ethnically mixed areas. These developments provoked renewed nationalist agitation. The nationalists characterized government actions as anti-Bulgarian or as a betrayal of national interests. Plans to reintroduce Turkish-language classes in schools in ethnically mixed areas became an especially contentious issue. Government promises to begin such classes as quickly as possible provoked nationalist strikes and boycotts of classes by Bulgarian parents. The government's response of postponing such classes provoked strikes and boycotts of classes by Turkish parents.

The nationalist appeals of major political parties during the first two multi-party elections in 1990 and 1991 were relatively muted because the memory of the brutal assimilation campaigns was still too fresh. But such appeals have become more prominent with each passing year. The mass media have not only given wide coverage to nationalist appeals, but have collaborated with nationalists to fan the flames of ethnic hatred. An unfettered press has become an irresponsible press when it comes to discussions of the nationality problem in Bulgaria.

Journalists often manufacture evidence, expand rumors into major stories, or create rumors themselves, and these stories are given wide play in both print and broadcast media. Journalists promise to back their allegations with concrete evidence but evidence is never provided because there is none. The sources are always unidentified because they do not exist. Dimitrova (1994: 332), in analyzing the contents of the print media concerning the nationality problem in Bulgaria, mentions several headlines that frequently appear in the print media. Among other titles we find the following: "The demographic invasion of minorities", "The sinister wave of Turkish separatism is swelling", "The declaration of a Turkish Republic in the Rhodopes is in preparation", "Turks want to redraw the ethnic map of Bulgaria"; "Turkey is secretly training Janissaries for the Bulgarian army." Or the sinister plans of Muslims for Bulgaria: "Bulgarian Muslims are subjected to forced Turkization"; "Islamic fundamentalists are crisscrossing Bulgaria"; "Emissaries from the Middle East are scuttling through the Rhodopes". The conspiratorial approach of journalists to the nationality problem extends to building mosques. The journalists keep track of the number of new mosques built and under construction (by 1994, 129 new mosques had been built and 200 additional ones were under construction). In their comments no mention is made of the fact that under communist rule many mosques were closed down or destroyed and that new mosques are needed to minister to the needs of the faithful. Rather, according to the journalists, mosques are used by Muslim leaders to inflame anti-Bulgarian passions among Turks and Muslims and to hatch diabolical plots to destroy the Bulgarian state and nation. The goal of Islamic missionaries, together with Muslim leaders in Bulgaria (often meaning Turks), is said to be nothing less than the "consolidation of the Muslims under the banner of Islamic fundamentalism", and "to create an Islamic state from China to the Adriatic Sea", so that the "forefront of Islam could pass through Bulgaria" (Dimitrova 1994: 333-4). Any attempts by Turks and Muslims to form organizations to articulate their interests and concerns are considered conspiratorial. When the veracity of people who report such stories is challenged, the government does little or nothing to investigate. The BSP itself and other political parties have increasingly resorted to such conspiratorial theories in their election campaigns. There is little movement toward establishing laws or rules to make people who spread unfounded and incendiary propaganda accountable.

The strong irrational fear such stories generate among Bulgarians strengthens their negative attitudes toward minority populations. A survey on inter-ethnic relations carried out by a sociological collective in June 1992 found a high level of ethnic prejudice among Bulgarians towards Turks and other minorities. For example, 51.1 per cent of Bulgarians considered the Turkish minority a real danger to national security, 83.8 per cent thought Turks were religious fanatics, 61.7 per cent thought that Turks occupied an excessive number of crucial positions in the government, and 36.5 per cent felt that all should be done for more Turks to emigrate to Turkey (Kŭnev 1992a: 47). Another disconcerting finding of this survey was that even after the repudiation of the assimilation campaign and its excesses by major political parties since 1989, many Bulgarians still felt that the campaign was right or necessary. Even though 62.2 per cent of Bulgarians felt that the revival process was a gross violation of the rights of minorities, and 49.5 per cent considered it a crime, still 35.2 per cent felt that it was necessary for the unification of the Bulgarian nation, 56.2 per cent felt that it was needed to help the offspring of "Turkified Bulgarians" to recover their true Bulgarian identity, and 60 per cent thought the goals of the revival process were right, although they had reservations about the specific methods used to accomplish them (Grekova 1992: 75)

Such findings are discouraging, to say the least, for the possibility of establishing ethnic peace in the country any time soon. The BSP government does not seem to be in a hurry to establish the conditions necessary for such a peace. One would hope that the desire of Bulgaria to join the European Union and NATO will moderate Bulgarian nationalism. Such membership will require Bulgaria to recognize the existence of minorities in unambiguous language; to amend Article 11 (4) of the Constitution prohibiting the formation of political parties based on ethnic or religious affiliation or, at least, pass *ad hoc* laws to facilitate the participation of ethnic and/or religious parties in the political process; to pass and enforce laws against discrimination on the basis of ethnic or religious affiliation; and to curb the activities of individuals and groups whose sole purpose is to inflame ethnic hatreds. All of this is a small price to pay for ethnic peace within the country and for membership in the community of democratic nations.

2

THE STATUS OF ISLAM AND MUSLIMS IN BULGARIA

Introduction

This chapter discusses the status of Islam and Muslims in Bulgaria within three broad historical periods; from the middle of the fourteenth century to Bulgarian independence from Ottoman rule in 1878; from 1878 to the end of the Second World War; and from the end of the Second World War to the present. Although the primary focus is on the experience of Turkish Muslims, the findings are applicable to the experience of Gypsy and Bulgarian Muslims (Pomaks) as well.

The present ethnic and religious mosaic in the Balkans is the product of millennia of migratory invasions. The central location of the Balkans between Europe and Asia and the existence of a well-developed road system for the carrying of military, administrative, commercial and cultural traffic since Roman times encouraged such movements.[1] Like other conquerors before them, Muslims entered the Balkans by using these well-established arteries and by securing them consolidated their control of the region.

The Marica, Tundža and Iskŭr river valleys and the open plains of Dobrudža have served as natural routes for a number of Turkic-speaking groups to invade Bulgaria, as a refuge for those pushed out by their rivals from the Asian steppes, and as transit points between Europe and Asia. Turkic groups which have passed through or settled in Bulgaria include the Huns, Avars, Bulgars, Peçenegs, Oguz, Uz, Cumans, Circassians, Tatars, and

---

[1] Description of this road system and discussion of its historical importance is found in Browning 1975: 24–5; Fine 1983: 3; Spiridonakis 1977:59–65; and Obolenski 1971 among others.

Turks (Browning 1975: 26-45; Inalcik 1965: 610-13).[2] Most of these groups made little long-term impact upon the cultural and religious landscape of Bulgaria and the Balkans. The Cumans and Peçenegs played an important political role in the early history of Bulgaria, while the Tatars and Circassians were to play a similar role in the later history of the country.

The Cumans and Peçenegs, who entered Bulgarian lands during the eleventh century, for a time posed a serious military threat to Byzantine hegemony in the Balkans. Toward the end of the eleventh century, in spite of mutual animosities, Cumans and Peçenegs formed a brief but powerful federation (1089-91) that controlled large areas of western Thrace, Macedonia, and Bulgaria. However, instead of presenting a united front against the Byzantines, they turned against one another. The Peçenegs were utterly defeated in 1091; those who were left retreated northward to Romania, Austria, Czechoslovakia, and Hungary, converted to Christianity, assimilated and disappeared from history. After 1091 most of the Cumans also left, but scattered communities remained in the Rhodope and Pirin mountains of Bulgaria. Here they came in contact with Muslim missionaries from North Africa and the Middle East and converted to Islam sometime before the beginning of Ottoman conquests in the Balkans during the fourteenth century. Later, the Cumans are said to have helped Muslim Yürük, Tatar, and Turcoman settlers to adjust to the unfamiliar environment of the Rhodope and Pirin mountains. For this they were called *pomagač* (helper) by their Christian neighbors, which was later abbreviated to Pomak, a general designation for Bulgarian Muslims to the present day (Memişoğlu 1991). Today, the Bulgarian-speaking Muslim residents of several villages in the Blagoevgrad district of southwestern Bulgaria continue to identify themselves as Turks, in an attempt to keep the historical memory of their Turkic origins alive.

The Bulgars founded an independent state north of the Balkan mountains toward the end of the seventh century to which they gave the name Bulgaria. Within two centuries, the Bulgars conquered most of the Balkan Peninsula and established a Greater Bulgaria stretching from the shores of the Adriatic to those of the Black Sea (Runciman 1930). Because of their small numbers

---

[2] Gürün (1981: 135-50, 255-62) discusses the history of these and other Turkic groups in some detail; see also Kafesoğlu (1983) and Moškov (1904).

and lack of reinforcements, the Bulgars were rapidly assimilated into the indigenous Slavic population. The adoption of Christianity by the Bulgar rulers in 864 accelerated the pace of assimilation. By the end of the ninth century, the Bulgars had become thoroughly Slavicized and Christianized (Gyuzelov 1976). The Turks, of course, were the major players in reshaping the ethnic, religious, and politico-economic landscape of Bulgaria and the Balkans from the fourteenth through the nineteenth centuries, which will be discussed in more detail later on.

The Muslim presence in the Balkans dates to pre-Ottoman times. Muslims from North Africa and the Middle East made sporadic contact with Balkan populations, especially coastal ones, from the end of the seventh century on, but such contacts had little long-term impact on local populations. It was during the early Ottoman period, beginning in the mid-fourteenth century, that Islam and Muslims gained a permanent foothold on the Balkan Peninsula and within a short period of time achieved a dominant position in the region which lasted until the Russo-Turkish War of 1877-8. Islam and Muslims in Bulgaria came under periodic attack between the independence of Bulgaria from Ottoman rule in 1878 and the Second World War. After the consolidation of power by the Communist Party in Bulgaria following the Second World War, and especially after 1956, the Bulgarian government engaged in a wide-ranging and systematic attack upon Islamic institutions and persecution of Muslims in the country. Under communist rule all Muslim groups in Bulgaria – Turks, Gypsy Muslims, Pomaks, and Tatars – became targets of government efforts to eliminate all evidence of the historical presence of Islam and Muslims in the country. During the early 1970s Muslim Gypsies, Pomaks, and some Turkish Muslims living in or close to Pomak villages were forced to replace their Muslim names with conventional Bulgarian names. During the winter of 1984-5 hundreds of thousands of Turks were forced to do the same.

Islam and Muslims in Bulgaria to 1878

Although small groups of Muslims had already settled in Bulgaria and the Balkans, the more permanent settlement of Muslims in Bulgaria dates from the second half of the fourteenth century. Significant changes in the religious landscape of the Balkans were brought about by the Ottoman conquests in the Balkans begun at that time. A significant Muslim presence was established in the region, which has continued into modern times. The Ottoman conquests in the Balkans were facilitated by rivalries among Byzantine royal families. The Cantacuzenus and Paleologus families, rivals to the Byzantine throne, used Turkish mercenaries in their struggles with one another. The Turks were allowed to establish a temporary base at Tzympe on the European side of the Dardanelles near Gallipoli. Instead of honoring repeated requests by the Byzantines to evacuate the base, the Turks fortified and reinforced it with fresh troops from Anatolia and laid siege to Gallipoli itself. The destruction of the walls of Gallipoli and other fortresses in the region by an earthquake in 1354 led to the occupation of Gallipoli by Turkish troops, who turned it into a permanent European base (Charanis 1955: 113-17; Inalcik 1973: 9; Pitcher 1968: 30-51). Within a century the Ottomans would use this European bridgehead to conquer most of the Balkans and, with the conquest of Constantinople in 1453, put an end to the Byzantine Empire.

The conquest of the Balkans by the Ottomans set in motion important population movements, which modified the ethnic and religious composition of the conquered territories. This demographic restructuring was accomplished through colonization of strategic areas of the Balkans with Turks brought over from Anatolia and Asia Minor, establishing a firm Turkish-Muslim base for further conquests in Europe. The Ottomans used colonization as a very effective method to consolidate their position and power in the Balkans (Barkan 1942). The colonizers that were brought to the Balkans consisted of diverse elements, including soldiers, nomads, farmers, artisans and merchants, dervishes, preachers and other religious functionaries, and administrative personnel. Among the earliest arrivals were large numbers of pastoral peoples such as the Yürüks and Tatars from Anatolia. As the Ottomans expanded their conquests in the Balkans, "they brought nomads from Anatolia . . . and settled them along the main highways and in the surrounding mountain regions . . . Densely populated Turkish colonies were established in the frontier regions of Thrace, the Maritsa and the Tundzha valleys" (Inalcik 1973: 11). The colonization policies already begun under Orhan were continued by his successors Murat I (1360-84) and Bayezid I (1389-1402). Additional colonists, mostly nomads again, were established along key transportation and communication routes in Thrace, Macedonia, and Thessaly.

The Ottoman authorities maintained these nomads in their tribal organization through the sixteenth century and began to settle them only during the seventeenth century (Gökbilgin 1957).

In addition to voluntary migrations, the Ottoman authorities used mass deportations (*sürgün*) as a method of control over potentially rebellious elements in the Balkans and in Asia Minor and Anatolia. Far away from their home bases, the potential threat of such elements was considerably reduced. Deportations in both directions occurred throughout the fourteenth, fifteenth, and sixteenth centuries (Barkan 1949-50: 108-19; Inalcik 1954: 122-6).

After the defeat of Bayezid I at the battle of Angora by the forces of Tamerlane in 1402, the Ottomans abandoned their Anatolian domains for a while and considered the Balkans their real home, making Adrianople (Edirne) their new capital. The Timurid invasions and other upheavals in Anatolia and Asia Minor brought additional Turkish settlers into the Balkans. Numerous Turkish colonists were settled as farmers in new villages. "*Waqf* deeds and registers of the fifteenth century show . . . that there was a wide movement of colonization, with western Anatolian peasantry settling in Thrace and the eastern Balkans and founding hundreds of new villages" (Inalcik 1976: 36). Some other settlers came in search of military and administrative service, and still others to establish Islamic religious institutions (Vryonis 1972: 165). Muslims were settled densely "along the two great historical routes of the Peninsula, one going through Thrace and Macedonia to the Adriatic and the other passing through the Maritsa and Tundja valleys to the Danube. The *Yürüks* were settled mostly in the mountainous part of the area" (Inalcik 1954: 125). By the early sixteenth century the Muslims constituted about a quarter of the Balkan population.

The greatest impact of Ottoman colonization in the Balkans, however, was felt in the urban centers. Many towns became major centers for Turkish control and administration, with most Christians gradually withdrawing to the mountains. Historical evidence shows that the Ottomans embarked on a systematic policy of creating new towns and repopulating older towns that had suffered significant population decline and economic dislocation during the two centuries of incessant wars preceding the Ottoman conquest, as well as the ravages of the Ottoman conquest itself. Often recolonization of old towns and the establishment of new towns were accomplished by bodily transplanting settlers from other areas of the Empire or with Muslim refugees from other lands (see Sahin, Emecen, and Halaçoğlu 1990). There are two main competing interpretations of urbanization in Bulgaria during the Ottoman period. These are what Kiel (1990: 81) calls the "Todorov thesis" representing the Bulgarian view, and the "Barkan thesis" representing the Turkish view. According to Todorov (1963), urbanization patterns in Bulgaria during the Ottoman period were not something new but a continuation of trends already well-established during pre-Ottoman times. Barkan (1955), on the other hand, claims that the Ottomans created brand new towns along militarily and commercially important arteries in the Balkans and populated these towns exclusively with Turks brought over from Asia Minor and Anatolia. The process of urbanization in Bulgaria during the Ottoman period was more varied than represented in either view.

Kiel's (1990: 83-4) analysis of relevant Ottoman archival materials shows that some pre-Ottoman towns in Bulgaria were developed further by the Ottomans. These towns include Silistra, Nikopol, Vidin, Loveč, Tŭrnovo, Varna, Nesebŭr, Pomorie, Sozopol, and Melnik. Other towns developed around pre-Ottoman Bulgaro-Byzantine castles, such as Provadija, Aitos, Karnobat, Ruse, Pleven, Vraca, Montana, Belogradčik, Samokov, Ihtiman, and Petrič. Although Turks settled in these towns in large numbers, their populations remained mixed throughout the Ottoman period. Kiel calls these "Todorov thesis" towns.

The Ottomans also rebuilt and repopulated a number of towns which had been destroyed and/or depopulated during the more than two centuries of wars preceding the Ottoman conquest and the conquest itself. These include Sofia, Plovdiv, Stara Zagora, Jambol, Šumen, and Kjustendil. Their populations were largely Turkish. The Ottomans also built brand new Turkish towns that grew around important government-sponsored buildings, such as Herazgrad (Razgrad), Eski Cuma (Pazardžik), Mustafa Paşa (Svilengrad), Harmanlı, and to some extent Kazanlık, and Zağra Yenicesi (Nova Zagora). Kiel Calls these "Barkan thesis" towns.

Two additional sets of towns which developed in Bulgaria during the Ottoman period do not fit either thesis. There were towns that grew out of villages, some very rapidly, others over many decades, that were populated largely by Turks. These include Hacıoğlu Pazarcık (Dobrič), Osman Pazar (Omurtag), Eski Džumaja

(Tŭrgovište), Yenice-i Çirpan (Čirpan), Dupnica (St. Dimitrov), Yeni Pazar (Novi Pazar), and Selvi (Sevlievo). There were also villages established by Bulgarian artisans, craftsmen, and merchants during the fifteenth and sixteenth centuries that by the seventeenth and eighteenth centuries had developed into thriving towns: Drjanovo, Elena, Etropole, Gabrovo, Kalofer, Koprivštica, Kotel, Panagurište, Teteven, Trjavna, and Žeravna. These towns were centers of Bulgarian national life and played an important role in the preservation of Bulgarian religious and cultural institutions.[3]

The expansion of Islam in the Balkans was accompanied by the spread of Turkish throughout the region. Turkish became the spoken language of the majority of people in some areas, particularly in towns and administrative centers. Along with Greek, Turkish became the major *lingua franca* for trade and communication among Muslims and Christians alike.

During the Ottoman period many urban centers in the Balkans experienced fundamental demographic restructuring. As Stavrianos writes,

> There was a common tendency among the Balkan Christians to move out of urban centers in order to avoid Turkish officials and garrisons. As a result the towns became denationalized. During most of the Ottoman period they reflected the nationality of those who held political and economic power. Accordingly, the towns, regardless of their location, consisted largely of Turkish artisans, administrators, and soldiers, and the Greek and Jewish traders and artisans (1958: 98).[4]

Major Balkan towns, especially those on or near major transportation and communication routes, were the focal point of Ottoman colonization in the Balkans. The Muslim population, whether of indigenous origin or brought there from outside the Peninsula, was concentrated in urban centers and garrison towns.[5] Most urban centers in the Balkans, especially in Thrace, Macedonia,

---

[3] Kiel (1990: 86-129) discusses the development of some of the towns mentioned above in some detail.

[4] See especially Barkan (1955: 292-3).

[5] Todorov (1983) argues that conversion of indigeneous Christians to Islam played a greater role than migration of Muslims from outside the Balkan Peninsula in the growth of the Muslim population of Bulgarian towns during the early period of Ottoman rule. This view is controversial and is not shared by most historians of the Ottoman period in Bulgaria.

Thessaly, and Bulgaria, achieved Muslim majorities or substantial minorities soon after the completion of the conquest and remained overwhelmingly Muslim in composition into the eighteenth century, and in some areas such as Macedonia and Bulgaria well into the nineteenth century. Ottoman statistics for the decade 1520-30 show that major cities in the Balkans already had substantial Muslim majorities (see Table 2.1).

Table 2.1. RELIGIOUS COMPOSITION OF
BALKAN TOWNS, ca. 1520-35

	Muslims	*Christians*	*Jews*
Sarajevo	100.0	–	–
Larissa	90.2	9.8	–
Edirne	82.2	12.8	5.0
Istanbul (1478)	58.2	31.6	10.2
Monastir	75.7	20.3	4.0
Skopje	74.8	23.7	1.5
Sofia	66.4	33.6	–
Serres	61.4	32.7	5.9
Nikopolis	37.7	62.3	–
Trikala	36.5	41.6	21.2
Salonica	25.3	20.3	54.4

Source: Barkan 1970: 1700.

Because of the proximity of Bulgaria to Istanbul and its strategic location in the European portion of the Ottoman Empire, the Muslim proportion of the population remained high until late in the nineteenth century. The 1866 census figures for the Danubian province of the Ottoman Empire (which included most of present-day Bulgaria, Romanian Dobrudža, and parts of Macedonia, eastern Thrace and Serbia) shows that Muslims were in the majority in most cities; Nikopol, H. Pazarcik (Dobrič), Zlatica, Osman Pazar (Omurtag), Balčik, Provadija, Belogradčik, Eski Džumaja (Tŭrgovište, Silistra, Loveč, Gorna Džumaja (Blagoevgrad), Vidin, Ruse, Šumen, Kjustendil, Dupnica (St. Dimitrov), Sofia (see Table 2.2). Muslims formed substantial minorities in other Bulgarian cities – Berkovica, Ihtiman, Kula, Lom Orjahovo, Pleven, Radomir, Sevlievo, Svištov, Tŭrnovo, Tutrakan, and Varna – accounting for from 30 to 50 per cent of the population. According to the 1866 census, several cities in Romanian Dobrudža had clear Muslim majorities: Medžidije 98.5 per cent; Mangalia 93.3; and Babadag 70.4 per cent (Todorov 1969: 38); and according to the *Salname* of 1875, Kjustendža 88.1 per cent, Harsovo 72.9 per cent, the *nahiye* of Isakča 62.9 per cent and the *nahiye* of Mahmudije 48.4 per cent (Todorov 1969: 33).

The demographic equilibrium that had existed in Bulgaria since the early sixteenth century began to be reversed only after the Russo-Turkish War of 1877-8. During and following the war, large numbers of Turks and other Muslims (most of the Tatars and almost all of the Circassians), especially from among the urban population, left with the retreating Ottoman armies. This was especially true for Muslims living in areas directly in the path of war. The Muslims living in the eastern parts of the Danubian province, especially in rural areas, being remote from the war zone, did not experience a general exodus. Consequently, the eastern Danubian province remained strongly Muslim following the war. For example, the first census carried out by the Bulgarian government, on 1-3 January 1881, shows that in five of the seven eastern districts Muslims made up a clear majority (Eski Džumaja 82 per cent; Razgrad 68.6 per cent; Šumen 67.9 per cent; Silistra 71.1 per cent; and Provadija 62.3 per cent). In the district of Ruse they constituted more than half of the population and in the district of Varna 44.9 per cent (Şimşir 1966: 9). In the country as a whole, the Principality plus Eastern Rumelia, Muslims accounted for about one-third of the entire population in 1881. But we are getting ahead of our story.

Conversions to Islam: voluntary or forced?

Historical evidence indicates that a significant portion of the Muslim element in Bulgaria originated outside the Balkan Peninsula. The rest was made up of converts from among the indigenous populations. However, there are serious disagreements over the number of Orthodox Christians who converted to Islam and also over the nature of the conversion process itself.

There is a well-established tradition in Bulgarian historiography which treats the Ottoman period in Bulgaria as a five-centuries-long dark age during which Ottomans deliberately attempted to

Table 2.2 RELIGIOUS COMPOSITION OF SELECTED TOWNS
IN BULGARIA AND DOBRUDŽA, 1866 CENSUS (%)

Town	Christians	Muslims	Jews
NORTHWEST			
Vidin	37.4	54.3	8.1
Vraca	73.3	24.8	2.0
Lom	58.3	37.0	4.7
Berkovica	57.5	38.6	4.0
Orjahovo	50.3	49.6	0.1
Belogradčik	31.5	68.5	–
Kula	62.5	37.5	–
Sofia	38.1	42.2	19.7
Kjustendil	37.8	51.5	10.7
Samokov	65.9	29.2	4.9
Dupnica	38.0	50.7	11.3
Radomir	55.2	44.8	–
Ihtiman	66.8	33.2	–
Gorna Dzumaja	40.4	59.6	–
NORTH-CENTRAL			
Pleven	49.3	48.3	2.4
Tŭrnovo	65.8	34.2	–
Svištov	59.5	40.5	–
Loveč	37.3	62.7	–
Sevlievo	68.3	31.7	–
Nikopol	7.2	92.8	–
Etropole	72.7	27.3	–
Orhanije	73.6	26.4	–
Ziatica	16.7	83.3	–
NORTHEAST			
Ruse	42.3	53.0	4.7
Šumen	54.2	52.6	2.2
Varna	57.4	41.9	0.7
Razgrad	29.3	69.6	1.1
Silistra	33.4	64.3	2.3
Tutrakan	56.8	42.3	0.9
Balčik	22.6	77.4	–
Provadia	24.5	71.4	4.1
Osman Pazar	18.8	81.2	–
Eski Džumaja	35.3	64.4	0.1
H. Pazardžik	15.3	84.7	–
DOBRUDŽA			
Babadağ	26.6	70.4	3.0
Mačin	58.0	41.5	0.5
Medžidije	0.8	98.5	0.7
Mangalia	6.7	93.3	–

Source: Todorov 1969: 38.[6]

[6] The figures for Muslims include Tatars and Circassians who were settled in Dobrudža

wipe out the Bulgarian nation and its culture by a combination of forced conversion of Orthodox Christians to Islam, assimilation, and massacres. The following quote from Hristov (1980: 63) is a representative sample that runs through most Bulgarian historiography:

> Bulgaria's fall under Turkish rule ushered in the grimmest period in the history of the Bulgarian people, a period of almost 500 years of foreign domination. During it, the very existence of the Bulgarians as a nationality was threatened as a result of their extermination, eviction and assimilation and the brutal oppression and exploitation to which they were subjected by the Turkish conquerors. Foreign domination held back the development of the country's productive forces, severed the Bulgarians' contacts with all other nations and put an end to their free cultural development.
>
> Bulgaria's conquest by the Turks was accompanied by the destruction of whole towns and villages and eviction of the population. Hitherto prospering towns and villages were reduced to ruins and the land was turned into a desert. The population of whole regions were forced to seek refuge in the mountains and in remote areas far away from any roads and communications. Turkish colonists and nomadic herdsmen from Asia Minor were settled in the most fertile regions thus vacated.

Such statements grossly misrepresent both the conquest itself and the policies followed by Ottomans toward the indigenous populations in Bulgaria and the Balkans. If violence against Orthodox Christians was a purposeful and consistent Ottoman policy over five hundred years, as the above suggests, then how do we explain the survival of Orthodox religious institutions and the Bulgarians as a people over such a long period? Mutafchieva's (1994: 11) observations on this question are to the point. She notes that such a policy

> . . . . could not help being successful in its intentions for whose realization it had sufficient forces and more than enough time. What could have hampered it? Balkan historians answer

during the mid-19th century and Muslim Gypsies; the figures for Christians include Eastern Orthodox Bulgarians, Catholics, Armenians, and non-Muslim Gypsies. Only those towns in which Muslims made up 25 per cent or more of the population are included on the table.

almost unanimously: the resistance of the Christians owing to their deep commitment to their traditional religion . . . [7] But they could hardly be successful in resisting an entire political system implemented through administrative and military measures; they could hardly be effective against official mass violence whose objective was to Islamize the population of the Peninsula.

Most Bulgarian historians, having committed themselves to the thesis of mass conversions achieved through systematic application of force, quoted fragments from unrelated documents in defense of this thesis. The kinds of questions Mutafchieva raises were not only ignored, but the critics of extreme historical revisionism of the 1970s and 1980s, including Mutafchieva herself, were professionally ostracized.

The approach of Bulgarian scholars to the problem of conversions to Islam in Bulgaria during the Ottoman period fits into what Kiel (1985: 33-5) calls "the catastrophe theory" as outlined in Hristov's quote above. The prevailing view of conversions to Islam by Orthodox Christians in Bulgaria, especially in the central and western Rhodopes, has been that these conversions were the result of a deliberate Ottoman policy of Islamization and absorption and were achieved through the systematic use of force and terror. The "evidence" for forced mass conversions to Islam of Orthodox Christians in the central Rhodopes consist of three chronicular notes purportedly describing eyewitness accounts of several brutal Ottoman military campaigns in the area during the 1660s (see Hupchick 1983). None of the three notes exist in the original, and all were published by Bulgarian nationalists in the late nineteenth century (1870, 1893, 1898) and promptly disappeared. Immediately after the publications of these notes serious questions were raised about their authenticity. However, for most of the twentieth century these chronicles were treated as authentic documents. During the communist period they acquired even greater

---

[7] The almost superhuman heroism of the Bulgarian people in the face of an overwhelming foe runs through most Bulgarian historical writings, literature, and folklore. Hristov (1980: 246-9) describes some of the characteristics of the Bulgarian people which make them unique in the world. The heroic people of Bulgaria not only triumphed over the powerful Ottomans, but, by so doing, they saved Western civilization. Moreover, "while fighting for their political and social liberation they have never forgotten their internationalist duty and have never harboured feelings of haughtiness, contempt and hatred for other nations."

importance because the information in the chronicles could be used, as it was in the government's anti-Turkish and anti-Muslim campaigns. Since 1989 it has once again become possible to subject the texts of these chronicles to an objective linguistic and ethnographic analysis and publish the results without fear of professional ostracism.

One such analysis is provided by Zeljazkova (1990a), who concludes that one of them was written during the early nineteenth century while the other two are late-nineteenth-century fakes. Zeljazkova gives two primary reasons for her conclusion: first, the lack of confirmation of the events described in the chronicles from any other source, and second, the special status of the central and western Rhodope populations within the Ottoman Empire (Zeljazkova 1990a: 107-9), which argues against forced conversions. She notes that the famous Turkish traveler Evliya Çelebi, who is known for his meticulous observations, passed through the region during the time in question, and does not mention any Ottoman military campaigns in the area. The seventeenth century was a period of intensive contacts between the West and the Ottoman Empire. "A number of special missions, travelers and observers crossed the Ottoman lands in the second half of the century, too. The majority of them being experienced observers, erudites, filled with sympathy towards the enslaved Christians in the European provinces of the Empire, those diplomats and travelers, performing the tasks they were set, carefully and scrupulously recorded everything they saw and heard. They had a special interest in the iniquities of the Ottoman regime, the lawlessness, the heavy tax system, the cases of violence involving Christian subjects, the decay of the economy and agriculture of the fertile Balkan regions" (Zeljaskova 1990a: 107). These observers who traveled through the Rhodopes during the 1660s do not mention anything about Ottoman military campaigns, "about violence, arson and mass bloodshed, accompanying the propagation of Islam" described in the chronicles. A comprehensive survey of seventeenth-century historiography of the Ottoman Empire, the history of Ottoman military forces published in Ankara during the 1970s, which describes in detail every battle, does not mention Ottoman military campaigns in the Rhodopes during the 1660s (Zeljazkova 1990a: 108).

The second reason to doubt the authenticity of these chronicles was the special status of many of the villages mentioned in the chronicles. Mutafchieva's (1965) analysis of poll-tax registers (*cizye defterleri*) from the period in question reveals that seven of the villages from Čepino district mentioned in the Draginov chronicle belonged to the *vakf* of the Süleymaniye mosque in Istanbul, and were not soldiers' (*voynuk*) villages as claimed in the Draginov chronicle. The claim that the inhabitants of these villages had refused to serve in the military, for which they were given the choice between execution or conversion to Islam, and that the villagers converted to Islam to escape punishment, is surely false. The inhabitants of *vakf* villages were under the personal protection of the Sultan, which meant that local authorities or military units had to exercise restraint in their dealings with them. They were not free to engage in the unrestrained violence and other outrages described in the chronicle. Unfortunately, such sober assessments of the evidence were ignored and the "catastrophe theory" prevailed.

Conversions to Islam were welcomed, but not enthusiastically sought by the Ottomans, especially mass conversions, because a significant portion of the Ottoman budget depended on the poll tax (*cizye*) collected from non-Muslim subjects of the Empire. According to Goodwin (1994: 29), "The government even had to discourage the proliferation of converts because of diminished revenues, as happened when Bosnia was taken in 1463 and Herzegovina in 1482." Kiel (1990: 71) notes: "The *cizye* was the backbone of Ottoman finances, providing a third to a half of the entire state budget. It was the single largest revenue for the Ottoman treasury, a fact which must be constantly kept in mind when interpreting demographic or religious changes shown in the records, as no state, past or present, can be expected to diminish voluntarily its principal source of income."

What was the purpose of these chronicles, then? According to Zeljazkova (1990a: 106),

> A heavy, unequal struggle was waged for cultural and political emancipation and the Bulgarian people needed a prompt answer to some questions, related to their remote and more immediate past. Among them were the questions of why Islam had spread in the Bulgarian lands; whether those fellow-countrymen who had accepted Islam should be considered as renegades, traitors and defectors, or as martyrs who suffered the ordeals of religious fanaticism? Who was to bear responsibility? . . . The answer

to these and other similar questions was to help the people muster their strength and encourage them in the struggle for national and political independence.

Although faking such documents out of patriotic duty at the time of their publication can be justified, the perpetuation in the twentieth century of the myth of coercive Islamization of Orthodox Christians cannot possibly serve such noble purposes. Lack of evidence corroborating the events described in the three chronicles has not stopped some unscrupulous Bulgarian historians from using these chronicles to build elaborate scenarios of brutal conversion of Orthodox populations to Islam. Some "revivalist" historians in Bulgaria have used the Metodi Draginov chronicle and other documents of dubious value to write numerous books on the forced conversion of Orthodox Christian populations in the Rhodopes to Islam (see Petrov 1964, 1975, 1977).

An objective analysis of archival sources preserved in Sofia by some Bulgarian historians shows that Islamization in the Rhodopes was a gradual process beginning in the early sixteenth century, perhaps earlier, and continuing through the seventeenth and eighteenth centuries (see Dimitrov 1965; Zeljazkova 1990b). According to Zeljazkova (1990a: 109), "The conversion to Islam in the Rhodopes was obtained not through direct coercion and mass campaigns, organized by the Sultan, but owing to economic reasons and personal choice of the individual, the family or the whole village, and, especially in the case of the population in the *vakif* villages, with the personal permission and imperial mercy of the Sultan." Like other Christians in Bulgaria and other areas of the Balkans who converted to Islam, Christians of the Rhodopes converted to Islam for material, political-legal, and social advantages, not as a result of deliberate Ottoman policy or as result of military campaigns expressly organized for this purpose.[8]

It is a well-established fact that by the early sixteenth century a significant Muslim presence was established in Bulgaria and the

---

[8] Even today, when there is no official compulsion to present a particular point of view, some Bulgarian scholars cannot free themselves from the firmly entrenched view of forced conversion of Orthodox Christians to Islam. For example, Nitzova (1994: 48), in an otherwise objective reappraisal of the history of Islam in Bulgaria, writes that "mass conversions to Islam was [sic] carried out in whole regions (the Rhodope mountains in southern Bulgaria and the Razgrad district in the north-eastern part of the country, for example) by brutal means and atrocities. Christians were compelled to adopt the new faith under the threat of death."

Balkans. The problem is to explain the origins of this population. According to Ottoman census statistics for the years 1520-30, Turkish nomads made up 19 per cent of the total Muslim population in the Balkans (37,435 nomad hearths out of a total of 194,958 Muslim hearths). There is scholarly agreement, even among some Bulgarian historians, that this population clearly originated outside the Balkan Peninsula. What was the origin of the rest of the Muslims? We have already seen that in addition to Yürüks and Tatars, many other Muslims were brought over or emigrated from Anatolia and Asia Minor to settle in Balkan cities and villages. Unfortunately, it is not possible to reliably establish the size of this population because of the limitations of Ottoman census methods. The Ottoman Empire was not organized along ethnic or linguistic lines. It was organized along confessional lines and religious identity was paramount. Therefore, Ottoman censuses provide information on religious affiliation but rarely on ethnic affiliation.[9] Consequently we are left to speculate about the proportion of the Muslim population that originated outside the Balkan Peninsula and the proportion that has indigenous origin through conversion. A conservative estimate is provided by Vryonis (1972: 165-6), who suggests that half of the total Muslim population of 1520-30 may have originated outside the Peninsula. It is very likely that the actual figure was somewhat higher. The remaining half of the Muslim population resulted from the conversion of part of the indigenous population to Islam beginning soon after the conquest of the Balkans and continuing throughout the five-hundred year Ottoman rule of the area.

According to Spridonakis (1977: 129), conversions to Islam in the Balkans seem to have had a limited objective, mainly to "reinforce the transplanted Anatolian colonies in order to contain more easily a potentially hostile population and thus provide a permanent policy supervision over the entire domain." Contrary to the claim of Bulgarian historians, Ottoman scholars with no ideological ax to grind generally agree that Ottoman policy in conquered territories was not oriented toward the creation of a homogeneous Turkish-Muslim society. As Inalcik (1991: 409; see

---

[9] For example, it is only possible to identify the new Muslims of the first generation; nomadic Muslims are clearly identifiable, but it is not possible to distinguish the other Muslims from the Turkish colonists. These issues are discussed in Karpat (1978, 1985); see also Thirkell (1979).

also 1954: 103-29) observes, prior to the formalization of the *millet* system Ottomans "maintained intact the laws and customs, the status and privileges, that had existed in the preconquest times, and what is more unusual, they incorporated the existing military and clerical groups into their own administrative system without discrimination, so that in many cases former *pronoia*-holders and seigneurs in the Balkans were left on their own fiefs as Ottoman timar holders." For a while they were able to maintain their Orthodox religion but since many entered a largely Muslim religious and social milieu they converted to Islam and over time became Turkified. After the fall of Constantinople in 1453, the formalization of the *millet* system ensured the maintenance of the religious heterogeneity of the Empire. Non-Muslim subjects of the Empire (Christians, Jews and Zoroastrians) came under the official protection of the Ottoman state, the Orthodox church was strengthened and conversions to Islam declined.

The conquest of the Balkans by the Ottomans was facilitated by local political, religious, and socio-economic conditions prevailing in the region at that time. By the middle of the fourteenth century when the Ottomans began to expand their rule into Anatolia and the Balkans, "the Christian world of Anatolia and the Balkans was in a state of anarchy precipitated by religious, national, and social conflicts. Islam seemed to offer a constructive alternative to chaos and misery; hence many Christians adopted it [Islam] voluntarily" (Vucinich 1969: 236). As Goodwin (1994: 29) notes, "In Bulgaria, for example, the choice lay between serfdom and brigandage or Ottoman order . . . The brutal feudal rule of the Bulgarian barons could win no hearts. Once they had bowed their heads to the conquerors, landowners as much as their peasantry were swift to escape the poll tax by being converted to Islam, making religion subservient to economics." According to Sugar (1978: 299), Ottoman conquests in Europe brought "law and order into a chaotic situation; religious strife ceased; insecurity caused by endemic wars and civil strife was ended." Most importantly, the majority of Balkan peasants welcomed the Ottomans for economic reasons as well, especially because of the proprietary rights offered them by the Ottoman *timar* system, which provided the peasants "security of tenure and property . . . something they did not enjoy before the Ottoman takeover" (Sugar 1978: 300). To be sure, there were times, especially during wars and times of tension, when some Ottoman officials and military leaders resorted to coercion to convert Christians; however, only a small percentage of the conquered were forced to adopt Islam. Most conversions, both of the individual and group varieties, were voluntary. According to Wittek (1952: 659), "In the Balkans conditions favored [the] acceptance of Islam with retention of language – witness the Muslim Bulgarians (the Pomaks), the Bosnian Muslims speaking Serbo-Croat, the Muslim Albanians." Moreover, the "conquered people of another religion were allowed a definite place under the direction of their own ecclesiastical authorities" (Jelavich 1983: 40). There were a number of additional reasons for a positive response to Ottoman conquest and the religion of Islam on the part of Balkan peoples. Vryonis (1972: 167-8) identifies material, religious, and social advantages of conversion:

> First, there were the real or material advantages which would ensue upon religious conversion. A change in religious status meant, in effect, a basic movement from an inferior to a superior class. As members of the triumphant religion, Muslims enjoyed a lighter tax burden and a favored legal position in all their economic and social relations in the eyes of the courts which judged these relations.

As Vryonis (1975a: 146) observes, "Muslim society was at all times accessible by religious conversion and, indeed, conversion was usually welcomed." Many of those who had the most to gain from conversion to Islam did so quite early. These included former government officials, tribal chiefs, landowners, artisans and merchants as well as members of dissatisfied or heretical Christian sects such as the Bogomils in Bosnia (See Cvetkova 1983). A sizable segment of the aristocratic class that survived the Ottoman conquests "made arrangements with the victors and received a satisfactory status in the new situation", even maintaining their Christian religion for a while (Vryonis 1975a: 146). But because the Christian *timar* holders entered a society that was essentially Muslim, they converted to Islam by the sixteenth century, although still carrying the Christian patronymic. At the time of their conversion, they must have brought their serfs into the fold of Islam as well.

Sometimes conversion and absorption of subject populations came about as a result of the activities of religious institutions, especially the missionary activities of dervish orders. Vryonis (1972: 168) continues:

> Second there were the successful appeal of religious preaching and social ministration of Muslim dervishes, *medreses* [theological schools], mosques, and *imarets* [public improvement associations]. These combined effective preaching with the economic affluence assured them by the fact that the Ottoman state was Muslim.

The dervish orders brought to the Balkans a version of folk-Islam which shared many elements with folk-Christianity, increasing the appeal of the new religion to segments of the local populations. Balkan Islam became a syncretistic religion, heavily affected by the Christian beliefs and practices of the converts, including baptism of infants, veneration of holy men and pilgrimages to the shrines of saints, certain types of animal sacrifice, celebration of certain Christian holidays, practices associated with the seasonal cycle, and iconolatry (Vryonis 1972: 172-4; 1975b: 139). This was due, to a considerable degree, to the way dervishes worked, lived, and were perceived by local populations. Sugar (1977: 53-4), who favors syncretism as a major factor in the conversion of Balkan peoples to Islam, writes:

> the dervishes wandered almost constantly, preaching and practicing their *tarikat* and numerous related ceremonies. They were the *babas*, a sort of combination holy man, miracle worker, medicine man, etc. and were often regarded as living saints. Their eclecticism and pragmatism knew practically no bounds. Given the numerous similarities between folk-Christianity and folk-Islam, they had no difficulty in fitting local customs into their *tarikats* . . . It was not difficult for Christians whose faith was of the superstitious folk variety to pass over to similar but more secure folk versions of Islam.

Sugar (1977: 54) feels that this explanation for early mass conversions to Islam is as valid as interpretations favored by other authors who attribute "such conversion either to the wish of the population to retain its landed possessions or to the desire of previously persecuted heretics (mostly Paulicians and Bogomils) to become the master of their oppressors." Mass conversion may have acted to insulate "the religious practices [of the Christians] from thorough penetration by Islamic practices and beliefs".[10] One may also assume that some of the sedentary Muslims of Anatolia who came to the Balkans as colonists were converts or the descendants of converts who had retained certain Christian elements in their version of Islam.

The dervish orders, in their willingness to equate comparable Christian and Muslim beliefs and practices and to adopt outright some Christian items, played an important role in the spread of Islam throughout the Balkans as well as in the preservation of pre-Islamic religious customs in Balkan Islam. Many Muslim villages "developed around a *zaviye* (a kind of hostel maintained by a dervish) or a pious foundation. These institutions enjoyed certain financial privileges which encouraged the formation of villages in their vicinity" (Inalcik 1954: 126). Finally, there was the element of fear, particularly in stressful times, which predisposed various Christian groups and individuals to convert.

In addition to conversion carried out through the administrative and military apparatus of the government and the religious institutions, the slave institution also played a role in the conversion process. The conversion of prisoners of war, renegades, and the best known example, that of the *devşirme* recruits that made up the Jannisary corps, swelled the ranks of Muslims of indigenous origin.

In traditional Bulgarian historiography the *devşirme* system is treated as an unmitigated demographic disaster for Balkan populations in general and for the Bulgarian population in particular. This is a gross exaggeration. Large segments of the population were exempt from the levy. According to Goodwin (1994: 34), Ottoman provisions for recruitment "forbade taking an only son from a widow or more than a percentage of the youth of a village [usually one boy from every forty households] . . . No levy was imposed on towns" because "Townsfolk were needed for their skills and were regarded as 'soft' when compared with countrymen. No married men might be taken, a provision which had the obvious result that boys were frequently married at the

---

[10] It is more than likely that the opportunity to insulate certain Christian beliefs and practices may have encouraged community-wide rather than individual conversions under certain circumstances. An individual convert entering the Turkish-Muslim community alone could hope to maintain his beliefs and practices only during his own lifetime, while an entire comunity was in a better position to perpetuate these beliefs and practices for generations.

age of 12." The Romanians, Wallachians, Moldavians, Jews, Gypsies, and to some extent Armenians were exempt. Greeks and Slavs made up the bulk of the *devşirme* recruits. The groups subject to the levy dreaded it and found various ways to avoid it. "This is evident from the searches for substitutes, the regulations about absentee youths and names that vanished from the parish registers [. . .] A trade in Muslim substitutes . . . had received recognition by the mid-sixteenth century" (Goodwin 1994: 34–5). Since the *devşirme* system was one of the few ways the non-Muslim subjects could hope to achieve high military and administrative posts in the Empire, it was not unknown for some Christian parents to volunteer their sons to Ottoman service. "The success of the levy is clearly shown by the rise of the best recruits to the highest offices of the state" (Goodwin 1994: 35).

The levy was not an annual affair. It "was supposed to follow a seven-year cycle but was more frequent in the sixteenth century since recruitment was inevitably related to the high command's hunger for heads in a period of great military activity" (Goodwin 1994: 35). The number of boys recruited was small, rarely exceeding 8,000 from the entire Balkans and Anatolia at any one time. If the Bulgarians and Greeks had been subject to the military draft their losses would have far exceeded those suffered through the *devşirme* system. Hence, the demographic impact of the system on the Bulgarian population was not that great.

Most conversions to Islam in Bulgaria were of the individual variety. A few large-scale conversions occurred during the 1660s and again in the beginning of the eighteenth century in the Rhodope mountain region of southeastern Bulgaria.[11] According to Vryonis (1972: 172), some 74 villages in the Rhodope region of Bulgaria converted to Islam. However, there is no reliable evidence to support the claim of Vryonis (1972: 168) that these conversions were "occasioned by the pressures of war and accompanied by the presence of expeditionary armies and heavy tax extortions."

In contrast to Anatolia and Asia Minor, where conquest had taken several centuries and conversion and assimilation of the

---

[11] Conversion *en masse* was not the normal pattern of Islamization in the Balkans. Islamization through conversion was a gradual process that resulted from the extension of the influence of largely Muslim urban centers to the surrounding communities. See Djurdjev (1960) for an excellent description of the process of Islamization in Bosnia and Hercegovina.

non-Muslim population was almost total, in the Balkans conquest was relatively rapid, and conversion and assimilation of the indigenous population into Turkish-Muslim society took place only in restricted areas that were strategically important for the control of the Balkan Peninsula (Vryonis 1971). In the Balkans the Ottomans were more interested in consolidating their gains than in converting and assimilating subject populations. Large numbers of compact Christian groups, especially those who lived in the hinterlands or had moved to the hinterlands to get away from the Ottomans, were not absorbed, and retained the administrative structure of their church.

Furthermore, even groups who converted to Islam, such as the Greeks of Crete, Bulgarians of the Rhodopes, Albanians and Bosnians, often retained their native languages. When conversion occurred during times of trouble or under direct or indirect duress there appeared "individuals and groups who, while publicly professing Islam, satisfied their conscience by practicing Christianity – Orthodox or Catholic – in private." Ottoman efforts

. . . . to implement equality among the religious communities of the Ottoman Empire in the nineteenth century caused many crypto-Christians to reveal themselves in an effort to have themselves registered as Christians rather than as Muslims, thereby demonstrating their imperfect absorption (Vryonis 1975a: 150).[12]

Although most urban centers in the Balkans became largely Muslim very quickly, the hinterlands remained overwhelmingly Christian. In contrast to Anatolia, where almost all of the non-Muslims were Islamized and assimilated into the Turkish-Muslim society, in the Balkans, for the most part, the relationship between the Ottomans and the Christian population was more symbiotic than absorptive (Vryonis 1975a: 150). The system of *dhimma* regulated the relationship between Muslim and non-Muslim communities in the Empire. As Lopasic (1979a: 49) explains, the *dhimma* relationship

. . . . guaranteed free performance of religion and preservation of traditional custom in return for payment of poll-tax [*cizye*] and recognition of suzerainty. It was an asymmetrical relationship between two partners [similar to a patron-client relationship],

---

[12] See especially Dawkins (1933), Hasluk (1921), and Skendi (1967).

one of whom [the non-Muslim community] acknowledged the supremacy of the other [the Muslim community] in return for religious and local autonomy within the limits of certain restrictions.

Outside the instances of conversion cited above, either carried out as part of Ottoman government policy, pursued by dervish orders as part of their proselytizing mission, or voluntarily entered into by groups and individuals from among the indigenous Christian population for perceived or real fiscal and social advantages, the Ottomans not only left local Christian populations and institutions essentially alone "but gave them legal status by issuing 'Kanunnameler', law codes for them" (Sugar 1969: 28).

After the conquest of Constantinople in 1453, the non-Muslim subjects of the Ottoman Empire were formally organized into the *millet* system. *Millets* were organized on the basis of a profession of faith alone, independently of any consideration of race or nationality. As originally established, *millets* enjoyed a large degree of autonomy. Each had its own leader (*milletbaşı*) chosen by the Sultan and given "full ecclesiastical powers and jurisdiction". He also "acquired legal powers in those areas, such as marriage, divorce and inheritance that were regulated by canon law" (Sugar 1977: 46; also pages 3, 5, 47-9, 252-9). As long as these ethno-religious communities fulfilled their political and economic obligations to the state, they were free, within limits, to organize their religious, cultural, and educational institutions in accordance with their own needs and desires. As Stavrianos (1958: 113) observes, the Ottoman Turks "ruled the Balkans as long as they did because they satisfied the needs of their subject peoples to an acceptable degree . . . . "

In the long run, Ottoman policies toward non-Muslims in the Empire strengthened group solidarity among the latter. The law codes together with the *millet* system were to be instrumental in preparing the groundwork for the development of nationalism in the Balkans, an ideology that was to be used very successfully by various groups to gain their independence from Ottoman rule. Sugar (1969: 28) explains:

In the beginning these *kanunnameler* did little more than recognize as binding the existing customs and conditions, leaving local administration in the hands of those who were responsible for it in the past. While placing numerous burdens on the population, these documents also assured the continuation of existing customs, economic establishments, political command chains, and so on, in short the legalized survival of the identity of nationalities. These *Kanunnameler* never achieved either the status or the influence of constitutions, but they assured differentiation among the various Balkan districts, gave them some, even if minimal, rights, and maintained the cohesion and assured the survival of certain institutions (*zadruga*, parish, and so forth), thus creating the framework within which modern nationalism could develop.

Although there could be no question about the equality between Muslims and non-Muslim subjects of the Empire, the rights of non-Muslim subjects were recognized and such communities were given considerable autonomy in organizing their own affairs in return for loyalty to the Empire. Such autonomy contributed significantly to the maintenance of the separate identities in the Empire ultimately used by these communities to gain their independence during the nineteenth and twentieth centuries.

Beginning in the eighteenth century, the Ottoman Empire entered a period of serious decline. Taking advantage of this, many foreign powers sought to use the *millet* system to their political and economic advantage by demanding that its privileges be granted to them. By 1875 the number of officially recognized *millets* had risen to nine and by 1914 to seventeen (Kinross 1977: 32ff, 527-93; Shaw and Shaw 1977: 55-272). Increasingly ethnic affiliation replaced the profession of faith as the primary criterion for membership in a *millet*. During the nineteenth and early twentieth centuries the *millet* system was used by revolutionaries among the non-Muslim subjects of the Empire to further their nationalist ideas and to gain their independence from Ottoman rule.

The Ottoman period in Bulgaria was not a golden age of toleration and equality, far from it. However, it was not a centuries-long dark age of unrelieved cruelty toward Bulgarians either. The Ottoman policies toward non-Muslim subjects and their institutions in the Empire, when analyzed within the broader context of European history, compare favorably with the policies of West European countries toward their minorities during the same period. Bulgarians as a people and their cultural and religious institutions survived, not through the superhuman efforts of Bulgarians but because the relatively benign Ottoman administration allowed them to survive. After the establishment of a stable Ottoman administration in the Balkans and the formalization of the *millet* system after 1453, Orthodox Christians were allowed to repair their churches and monasteries damaged during the conquest and to build new ones (See Gradeva 1994; Kiel 1985). They were allowed to maintain their cultural and religious institutions in return for their loyalty to the Ottoman Empire. This contrasts sharply with the actions of Bulgarians and other Balkan peoples toward Muslims during and after the various wars of independence that led to the establishment of independent Balkan states. For example, during and immediately after the Russo-Turkish War of 1877-8 Bulgarian soldiers, militias, and civilians engaged in indiscriminate killing of Muslim civilians, wholesale destruction of mosques, *medreses*, and other religious buildings, burning of Muslim villages, and the seizure of Muslim lands (Şimşir 1988: 12-20; Lory 1985: 36-7, 54-8). The killing of Muslim civilians and the destruction of mosques in "ethnically cleansed" areas of Bosnia and Herzegovina in the 1990s provides a sinister echo of what happened to Muslims in Bulgaria and elsewhere in the Balkans immediately after the Ottoman period. It is legitimate to ask if, when peace has been established in Bosnia and Herzegovina, Muslims will be allowed to return to their communities to repair the damaged mosques, to rebuild the ones that were destroyed and to reestablish their cultural and religious institutions. The policies of the communist regime in Bulgaria toward Muslim minorities from the end of the Second World War until 1990 was aimed at nothing less than the eradication of all traces of Muslim presence in Bulgaria. The regime almost succeeded in eliminating the Ottoman architectural legacy from the Bulgarian landscape.

Islam and Muslims from 1878 to 1945 [13]

The ebb and flow of Turkish and other Muslim emigration from Bulgaria between 1878 and 1944 was greatly influenced by changing political conditions. During and after the Balkan wars and the First World War, as the situation of Muslims worsened, Muslim emigration picked up. Another significant factor influencing the pace of Muslim emigration was the extent to which Bulgarian

---

[13] A discussion of post-Ottoman developments concerning Islam and Muslims in the Balkans is found in Popovic (1986a)

governments were willing to honor the provisions of international and bilateral agreements guaranteeing the rights of minorities in Bulgaria. Under the Agrarian government of Alexander Stambolijski, who was tolerant toward the country's Muslim minority, the situation of the latter was quite favorable. This favorable period was short lived. The overthrow of Stambolijski on 8-9 June 1923 ushered in a period of oppression against the Muslim minority. Its situation worsened under the leadership of a military junta that came to power in 1934. Between 1934 and 1944 large numbers of Turkish schools were closed and *vakf* properties were expropriated; many Turkish-language newspapers and periodicals were banned; Turkish intellectuals were exiled; and Muslims came under strong Christian missionary pressure. As a result, many Muslims were forced to emigrate to Turkey, so that by the beginning of the Second World War the proportion of Turks in Bulgaria had fallen to under 10 per cent.

As nation after nation gained its independence from Ottoman rule during the nineteenth and early twentieth centuries, the treaties establishing these independent states always provided for the protection of the rights of minority populations both within these new nations and those still remaining under Ottoman control. When Bulgaria gained independence from Ottoman rule in 1878, the rights of minorities were guaranteed by treaties establishing an independent Bulgaria. Later on, these guarantees were incorporated into the legal system of Bulgaria. Article 54 of Section IV of the Neuilly Peace Treaty of 1919 reads:

> Bulgarian nationals who belong to racial, religious or linguistic minorities shall enjoy the same treatment and security in law and in fact as the other Bulgarian nationals. In particular they shall have an equal right to establish, manage and control at their own expense, charitable, religious and social institutions, schools and other educational establishments, with the right to use their own language and to exercise their religion freely therein (quoted in Şimşir 1986b: 4).

The Law Concerning the Establishment and Administration of the Mohammedan Religious Community adopted by the Bulgarian government in 1919 followed closely this provision of the Neuilly Treaty. Moreover, this law followed closely the Ottoman laws governing the status of non-Muslim *millets*. It provided the Muslim community a substantial degree of "autonomy in religion, education and other cultural affairs, as well as authority over all aspects of family life" (Kostanick 1957: 80). Moreover,

> A "Grand Mufti" was established in Sofia in the ancient mosque of Banja-Bachi. Regional districts were authorized, among which Shumen was given a special position. Turkish schools were established . . . Two special schools of higher theology were maintained in Sofia and Shumen. A large number of "cultural societies" were also formed, many of which maintained close contact with similar organizations in Turkey (Kostanick 1957: 80).

Even though there were periods when Turks and other Muslims came under extreme discriminatory pressure after 1878, and especially during and following various wars in the Balkans, such pressures were not systematic but reflected the anti-Islamic and anti-Muslim sentiments of individual Bulgarian politicians. Overall, during most of this period the situation of Turks and other Muslims in Bulgaria was quite favorable. This is reflected in the fact that during most of the period under question Muslims' control of their educational, religious, and cultural institutions was interfered with very little. The patterns established during the long period of Ottoman rule remained in place. Muslims maintained their own private secular and religious schools. Even in secular schools the teaching of religion had a central place. Often primary schools were attached to the mosques, and teachers, whether in primary or high schools, were graduates of religious schools.

A Turkish religious college was established in Šumen in the early 1920s. Before that time higher education was available only in Istanbul. Many Turks from Bulgaria and elsewhere in the Balkans went to Istanbul to continue their education. Unfortunately, many of them also chose to stay in Turkey after completing their studies, which retarded Turkish education in Bulgaria and elsewhere in the Balkans considerably. There were also Koranic schools (*medreses*) where students were taught the Arabic language and the Islamic religion exclusively. In the town of Mecidiye in Romanian Dobrudža there was an Islamic Seminary which prepared Muslim preachers and other religious functionaries to serve the needs of the faithful (see Ülküsal 1966: 105-21).

During this entire period, in spite of Bulgaria's independence, its Muslim communities were still under the authority of the *Şeyhülislam*, an Ottoman official, who was responsible for all matters connected with canon law, religious schools and so on. His office was next in importance to that of the Grand Vizier, the highest civil authority, during Ottoman times. The *Şeyhülislam* delegated his authority to other experts in Islamic law (muftis) who were responsible for the administration of Islamic law (*sharia*) in different regions of the Balkans. Bulgaria, for example, was divided into several administrative regions, each headed by a mufti to administer the *sharia* and to oversee the proper functioning of other religious institutions, such as mosques, community schools, and Koranic schools, under their jurisdictions. These regional muftis were under the authority of a chief mufti.

Almost every Muslim village in Bulgaria, depending on its size, had one or more mosques, while in large towns almost every neighborhood had its own mosque. Wealthy Muslims bequeathed their estates to pious foundations (*vakfs*). The resources of these foundations were used to build and to maintain mosques, Koranic schools (*medreses*), and to pay the salaries of preacher-teachers (*hocas*), prayer leaders (*imams*), and experts in Islamic law (muftis).[14] However, after an anti-Islamic and anti-Muslim military junta came into power in 1934, many of these schools were closed. Even the schools that were allowed to continue functioning had a difficult time because of the determined efforts of Bulgarian authorities to limit the influence of Islam (Şimşir 1986b: 5-6).

Islam and Muslims from 1945 to the present

The deteriorating situation of Islam and Muslims during the years preceding the Second World War became still worse after the consolidation of power by the Communist Party in Bulgaria after the war. The rhetoric of equality of all citizens regardless of creed and national origin masked the real intentions of the Bulgarian authorities toward Islam and Muslims. Freedom of conscience and religion was an integral part of the Dimitrov Constitution adopted by the National Assembly in 1947. These freedoms were

---

[14] Ülküsal (1966: 129-45) provides a detailed description of the religious situation in Romanian Dobrudža before the First World War. He also discusses the changes that took place in the situation of Muslims between the wars as well as after the Second World War in Romania.

codified in the Law on Religious Denominations adopted by the Grand National Assembly in 1949. The Law provided for freedom of conscience and religion for all citizens of the People's Republic of Bulgaria. These guarantees were retained in the new constitution adopted in May of 1971. Article 53 of the new constitution stated that the citizens of Bulgaria "are guaranteed freedom of conscience and creed. They may perform religious rites and conduct anti-religious propaganda" (Sofia Press 1971: 19). Article 35 (2) stated that "no privileges or limitation of rights based on nationality, origin, creed, sex, education, social and material status is allowed", and subsection four of the same article prohibits "the propagation of hate or humiliation of man because of race, national or religious affiliation" (Sofia Press 1971: 15). Articles 164 and 165 of the Penal Code provided for punishment of persons preaching hatred on religious grounds. As we will see later on, in practice the provisions of the Law on Religious Denominations, the provisions of the Penal Code, and the constitutional guarantees of freedom of conscience and religion were not only ignored but violated with impunity. Only the provision for the right of citizens (read the government) to conduct anti-religious propaganda was fully enforced. All religious manifestations were interpreted as anti-state and/or bourgeois nationalist propaganda. This was especially true for non-Orthodox believers, in particular Muslims.

Soon after the adoption of the 1947 constitution, contrary to its provisions guaranteeing freedom of conscience and religion, the Bulgarian government initiated determined steps to counteract the influence of religion among the Muslim population. All Koranic schools were closed in 1949. Many mosques were closed and others fell into ruin due to neglect. Yet others were converted into museums, libraries, warehouses, shops, and restaurants. After 1952 teaching of religion in public schools was banned. Measures were taken to discourage the teaching and study of Islam in private. In fact, the teaching of religion became a serious crime. In the late 1940s all private Turkish schools were nationalized and a uniform curriculum was imposed on them. The cornerstone of this curriculum was patriotic, internationalist, and atheistic education. A wide-ranging propaganda campaign was launched against Islamic beliefs, practices, and rituals. Several reasons were given for the necessity of such a campaign, including the assertions that: (1) Islam was an alien religion which had been imposed on Bulgarians by force; (2) Prior to Bulgarian independence in 1878, Islam had played a reactionary role in Bulgaria, retarding the development of Bulgarian culture for centuries (see Snegarov 1958); (3) Since Bulgarian independence foreign reactionary elements from abroad (i.e., Turkey) have been using Islam in Bulgaria to promote bourgeois nationalism and religious fanaticism among Muslims in the country; and (4) Islam was an obstacle to the integration of Muslims into the Bulgarian socialist nation (Nitzova 1994: 101).

Initially, it was felt that atheistic education and anti-Islamic propaganda together would be enough the weaken the influence of Islam among Muslims without any need for coercion. Eventually the Islamic world view would be replaced with a scientific-atheistic world view. According to this scenario, as the number of young intelligentsia increased among the Muslim population, they would play their historical role in replacing the superstitious ideology of their elders with the scientific Marxist-Leninist ideology of the Communist Party. Vrančev (1948: 55), in his 1948 monograph on Bulgarian-speaking Muslims (Pomaks), claimed that this task would be accomplished without any resort to coercion not only because there was no need for it but also coercion would "*not be either expedient or in agreement with the principles of our contemporary democratic government*" (Vrančev 1948: 55; emphasis added). The author also stated unequivocally the stand the new government should take toward Islam among the Turkish-speaking population:

> But about one question we must be clear: the government is within its rights to pursue all those grand Turkish schemes which could be promoted through religion. *Every Turkish national aspiration must be condemned* (Vrančev 1948: 57; emphasis added).

By the mid 1950s it became apparent that the hold of religion among Turkish and other Muslims in Bulgaria was much more deep-seated and tenacious than policy-makers had expected. Atheistic education and anti-religious propaganda were not making appreciable inroads in weakening the hold of Islam among the Muslim population. Among the Turks, state support of Turkish-language instruction and the opportunities to develop Turkish culture, instead of weakening Turkish identity, were strengthening it even further. The Communist Party felt that it needed to take a much tougher stand on Islamic beliefs and practices.

The initial plan of action against Islam and Muslims was broadly outlined during the April plenum of the Central Committee of the Bulgarian Communist Party in 1956. From this date on the anti-Islamic propaganda apparatus of the government was organized and systematized. During 1958 the Central Committee of the party approved the "Theses for work among the Turkish population". The main goal of these "theses" was the waging of a determined and decisive fight against all forms of Islamic religious expression among Turks in particular and Muslims in general. Special programs were set up to prepare dedicated political cadres to work among Turkish, Gypsy, and Bulgarian (Pomak) Muslims as well as Orthodox believers. Affiliated with national, regional, and local party organs, these programs trained tens of thousands of young, ideologically committed cadres who were expected to lead conferences and seminars on scientific atheism among the Muslim population; they were also instructed to carry out propaganda against Islamic beliefs and practices. Throughout the 1960s and 1970s the party members were constantly reminded of the necessity of utmost vigilance against all religious expression among the Turks, Pomaks, and Gypsies.

Mizov (1965) in his *Islam in Bulgaria* assesses the impact of government policy toward Islam and Muslims immediately following the April plenum of the BCP in 1956. He notes that before the Second World War Turkish and Pomak villages in Bulgaria averaged between four and eight *hocas* (teachers of religion). Between the end of the war and 1956, there was a slight decline in the number of *hocas* in Muslim villages. In 1956 there were 2,393 *hocas* working among the Turkish population in Bulgaria, a ratio of one *hoca* for 170 Turks. During the same year there had been 322 *hocas* working among the Pomaks, a ratio of one *hoca* for 430 Pomaks. In 1961, after the new government policy had been in place only for three years, the number of *hocas* had decreased by a factor of 5.1, to 462, or one *hoca* for 1,397 Turks, and by a factor of 3.3, to 95, or one *hoca* for 1,459 Pomaks (Mizov 1965: 195). Even the remaining *hocas* were prohibited from teaching religion, so that, over the years, their role in their communities was transformed from teachers to prayer leaders (*imams*).

During the communist period several ideologically motivated sociological surveys were carried out to assess the extent of the impact of atheistic education on religious attitudes in the country, to identify the groups within which religious influence remained strong, to provide reasons for this, and to recommend additional ideological work among the members of these groups. Aliev (1980) discusses in detail the impact of atheistic education and anti-religious propaganda on the religious beliefs and practices of Muslims in Bulgaria. He provides a detailed analysis of the results of three such surveys carried out in 1962, 1967, and 1973. The results of these surveys indicated differences in religiosity by occupation, residence, level of education, gender, and age. In each of these categories, Turks were found to be more religious than non-Turks. According to the results of a sociological survey carried out by the Institute of Philosophy at the Bulgarian Academy of Sciences in 1962, for example, Turkish peasants (cooperative farmers) were 1.5 times more religious than non-Turkish peasants, Turkish blue-collar workers were 2.2 times more religious than non-Turkish blue-collar workers, and Turkish white-collar workers were 1.7 times more religious than non-Turkish white-collar workers (see Table 2.3).

Table 2.3. RELIGIOSITY AND OCCUPATION
AMONG TURKS

	Peasants	Blue-collar workers	White-collar workers
Religious	51.3	71.6	22.2
Not religious	48.4	28.4	77.8
No answer	0.3	–	–

Source: Aliev 1980: 41.

The results of this survey showed variation in religiosity according to age. Eighteen to twenty-three-year-old Turks were the least religious – 32.3 per cent – while those over sixty-nine were the most religious – 98.4 per cent (Aliev 1980: 50). Religiosity also varied according to educational level. The illiterate Turks were the most religious – 88.5 per cent – while those with high-school education were the least religious – 7.7 per cent (Aliev 1980: 46).

The study found differences in religiosity by ethnicity and gender. Turkish men and women were found to be significantly more religious than Bulgarian men and women. Among both Bulgarians and Turks, women were more religious than men (see Table 2.4).

Table 2.4. ETHNICITY, GENDER AND RELIGIOSITY

	Bulgarians		Turks	
	Men	Women	Men	Women
Religious	32.1	42.0	58.3	75.3
Not religious	76.8	57.9	41.6	24.7
No answer	0.1	0.1	0.1	–

Source: Aliev 1980: 47.

The surveys carried out in 1967 and 1973 confirmed the results of the 1962 study and showed further declines in religious attitudes along a number of dimensions. For example, according to the results of the 1973 survey in the district of Razgrad in northeastern Bulgaria, 46.2 per cent of Turks said they believed that their destiny was preordained by God; 46.3 per cent said life on earth was more important than the afterlife; 11.3 per cent read religious literature; 58.9 per cent preferred to consult non-religious authorities about their personal problems compared with 9.5 per cent who consulted religious authorities for such problems (Aliev 1980: 38-9). The question, "Do you go to mosque for Friday Prayers?" elicited the following responses: always – 9.1 per cent, only during religious holidays – 18.4 per cent, infrequently – 11.3 percent, and never – 58.2 per cent. Moreover, the overwhelming number of those who went to the mosque for Friday prayers were over fifty years old – 93.3 per cent (Aliev 1980: 55).

Nevertheless, 88.4 per cent of Turkish Muslims believed in the eternity of the soul. They also believed that proper burial was essential for entrance of the soul into paradise. Sociological surveys carried out between 1945 and 1962 showed that 91.5 per cent of burials among Turks were supervised by religious officials. Apparently this was a serious concern for government authorities because after 1962 new "socialist" burial rituals were devised to replace the traditional religious rituals (Aliev 1980: 81-2). After 1978 these became mandatory and were strictly enforced. These surveys indicate a general trend of the declining influence of religion in the daily lives of Turks and other Muslims. Over the years fewer Turks performed their daily prayers or visited the mosque for Friday prayers (see Table 2.5).

Table 2.5. TRENDS IN PERFORMANCE OF DAILY PRAYERS AND
FRIDAY PRAYERS AMONG TURKS, 1946-73

	1946	1956	1962	1967	1973
Daily prayers	100.0	56.3	32.2	15.8	9.1
Friday prayers	100.0	73.0	42.6	31.6	–

Source: Aliev 1980: 55.

On the basis of these survey results, Turkish Muslims were
divided into three groups: fanatical believers, moderate believers,
and those who waver between belief and atheism (Aliev 1980:
56-7). The members of the first group unquestioningly believed
in God, in the eternity of the soul, in the afterlife, prayed to
God regularly, fasted during Ramazan and fulfilled all other religious
obligations and duties. The members of this group did not believe
in science and sought the truth in the Koran and in other religious
texts. Some members of this group defended Islam openly, criticized
atheistic education and the anti-religious propaganda of the government, and actively disseminated the doctrines of Islam among the
rest of the population, especially among the members of the younger
generation. They also spoke out against the education of women,
and against women wearing modern clothes. There were others
in this group who were too timid to express their views openly.
They confined their activities to the members of their immediate
families, who they compelled to fulfill their religious duties and
obligations, and tried to limit the penetration of socialist culture
into their homes.

The second group of Turkish Muslims included more moderate
followers of Islam. Although their adherence to Islam was not as
strong as those of fanatical believers, nevertheless, religious beliefs
influenced their behavior. Even though they were aware of the
declining influence of Islam in their communities as a result of
atheistic education, they did not openly criticize such trends. To
them belief in God was a personal matter and they felt religious
belief was not an obstacle to the building of socialism in Bulgaria.
Even though the members of this group did not pray or attend
mosque regularly, they still continued to observe the fast during
Ramazan and fulfill what they considered to be the most important
religious duties.

The third group included people who were described as waverers between religion and atheism. They believed in God and often fulfilled some religious duties but they did so not out of deeply held conviction but because of the strength and influence of religious tradition. They did not have a very definite idea of God, had not thought about it, did not fast during Ramazan, did not believe in the revealed nature of the Koran, did not pray regularly, and visited the mosque occasionally during religious holidays, often at the urging of their parents. They preferred to go to movies and theaters instead.

The greater hold of Islam among the first two groups was the most worrisome for the authorities. The greater religiosity among Turks and other Muslims were attributed to the conservative and fundamentalist nature of Islam, the cultural and educational back-wardness of Muslims, and their isolation in rural areas. These factors made them susceptible to fundamentalist religious propaganda. Even though government efforts to weaken the influence of Islam over the years had achieved significant results, the authorities were not satisfied with the impact of atheistic education and anti-religious propaganda on religious attitudes among Muslims. The ultimate goal of the government was nothing short of stamping out religious beliefs and practices altogether.

During the 1970s and 1980s the authorities intensified their anti-religious propaganda and increasingly resorted to outright prohibitions of certain religious practices and rituals. A number of Islamic beliefs and practices came under wide-ranging attack in the mass media. Circumcision was portrayed as a barbaric and pagan rite, a holdover from the stone age, and prohibited. Fasting during the month of Ramazan was discouraged on two specific grounds: the authorities claimed that fasting lowered one's immunity to disease, and that it was economically wasteful, especially when it came during planting and harvesting seasons when workers who were fasting could not perform to full potential. Slaughtering of lambs during the Festival of Sacrifice (*Kurban Bayramı*) was attacked on similar grounds: eating a lot of fatty meat over a very short period of time, they claimed, led to serious gastrointestinal disorders, and the slaughtering of large numbers of lambs at the same time was economically wasteful because such a practice deprived the government of badly needed foreign currency. The two major religious festivals were banned. The wearing of traditional clothes by Turkish and other Muslim women, referred to as "religious clothes", came under attack because it was claimed that such clothes were a symbol of women's subservience to men. The traditional Muslim burial rituals were characterized as contrary to socialist practice and were replaced with a "socialist" burial ritual. Initially the performance of these rituals was voluntary, but compliance was not very high.

In May 1978 the Council of Ministers announced "an obligatory system of socialist rituals and holidays" to replace the traditional ones. The implementation of the new rituals was spelled out in "Guidelines for the Development and Perfection of the System of Holidays and Rituals in the People's Republic of Bulgaria" (Helsinki Watch 1991: 12). From then on, only those rituals that were allowed could be performed, and these had to conform to the guidelines spelled out in the above document. Party officials were sent to Muslim funerals to make sure that the new burial ritual was properly observed and prayers were said in Bulgarian only. Muslim leaders who protested these draconian measures were arrested and imprisoned.

All of these measures seriously threatened the long-term viability of Islam in Bulgaria. During the 1980s an observer traveling in most areas of Bulgaria who was familiar with the physical landscape of Muslim villages, towns and cities in the Middle East and elsewhere would have been struck by the changes in the architectural landscape of Bulgaria; he would have been hard-pressed to even guess that Muslims had been living in Bulgaria for more than 600 years.

Traditionally, Muslim villages and Muslim neighborhoods in towns and cities in Bulgaria were organized around and dominated by the mosque. For Muslims the mosque served not only as a place of worship but also as a focus of ceremonies associated with core events in Muslim life – birth, circumcision, marriage, and death – and as an assembly house where the elders of the community gathered to discuss community affairs. The religious leaders were also community leaders who served as teachers, mayors and "doctors". As the only literate members of their communities, they were the source of both civil and religious authority, which in Islamic practice were not considered to be separate domains of power.

After the Second World War that landscape and its attendant activities changed significantly. Mosques and religious schools were closed, neglected, or deliberately destroyed. Government policy was to restore and maintain mosques and other religious buildings from the Ottoman period only if they had architectural and historical value and only in areas that were likely to be visited by foreign dignitaries and/or tourists. The government allowed a small number of mosques to function, but this was essentially for propaganda purposes: the number of functioning mosques and the personnel serving in them was totally inadequate for a population of over one-and-a-half million Muslims in the country. As Baest observes (1985: 22), "the Islamic clergy, already severely weakened since 1948, were further decimated" during and after the winter campaign of 1984-5 against Turkish Muslims. Between 1984 and 1989 there was a conspicuous absence of mosques in the overwhelming majority of Muslim villages in Bulgaria. Those Muslims who wanted to participate in Friday prayers had to travel a considerable distance to find a functioning mosque. Another feature of the traditional Muslim village, the voice of the *muezzin* calling the faithful to prayer from the *minaret* was silenced. The call to prayer had to be said inside the mosque, which defeated the whole purpose of the exercise. The disappearance of mosques from the village scene removed an important focus of community activity and solidarity.

During the so-called "revival process" between 1984 and 1989, many more mosques were closed down or demolished. The traditional Muslim funerary ritual was replaced with a so-called "socialist" funerary ritual. Party officials were sent to Muslim funerals to make sure that the proper "socialist"ritual was carried out and that prayers were said in Bulgarian only. Muslims were not allowed to bury their dead in their own cemeteries. Turks and other Muslims were sent letters ordering them to cover with cement the tombstones of their close relatives with any Turkish or Arabic inscriptions or any Islamic symbols on them (see Appendix A). Orders were issued to store and restaurant managers and clerks not to serve Turkish and other Muslim women wearing traditional clothes (see Appendix B). The Bulgarian authorities began strictly enforcing the ban against circumcision of young Muslim boys. Muslim parents were required to sign documents promising not to circumcise their male children (see Appendix C). Health officials regularly visited Muslim households and schools to make sure that the ban against circumcision was observed. If the health officials discovered that the ban had been violated, both the parents and the person who performed the circumcision were punished. During the entire communist period, for propaganda purposes, a Muslim religious governing body with a Chief Mufti and regional muftis would be maintained. However, these individuals were appointed to their positions not on the basis of their religious training but for their loyalty to the government and its policies.[15] After the official completion of the campaign for the assimilation of Turkish Muslims in early March 1985, the Chief Mufti and most regional muftis and *imams* declared their full support for the government. In light of what we know today, these declarations sound surreal. The Declaration of the Chief Mufti published in the *Otečestven Front* newspaper on 26 March 1985 reads in part (see Appendix D):

> We declare clearly and unambiguously that Moslems in Bulgaria enjoy complete freedom which is guaranteed by the Constitution and the country's laws. They can profess Islam and perform their rites with the same freedom enjoyed by all other religions in this country. All mosques in the country are open and the clergy regularly perform their religious rites and services. There have been no cases of preventing or in any way restricting Moslems from performing religious rites and services. There have been no cases of mosques or other Moslem shrines being desecrated (Sofia Press 1985: 27).

Declarations by district *imams* in support of the muftis soon followed. The following is a passage from the declaration of the *imams* of the district of Silistra supporting the Chief Mufti's declaration and defending the replacement of Muslim names with Bulgarian ones:

> The laws in our country allow every citizen to choose his name and to change it whenever he wants to. [...] We have sufficiently good reason to do this not only because we feel an inseparable part of the Bulgarian people but also because

---

[15] For example, Nedim Gencev, after long service in the Ministry of Internal Affairs, without any religious training whatsoever, was appointed to the position of mufti of the district of Kŭrdžhali. After his appointment he was sent, not to Turkey but to Syria, for six months' study. This limited training was apparently enough to elevate him to the position of Chief Mufti in 1988. The highlights of Gencev's career are found in Topčiev (1992).

Turkey has been trying to use our names as a reason to have claim on us, to speak on our behalf and to arbitrarily determine our national identify. [...] We are part of the Bulgarian nation and have never belonged to the Turkish nation (Sofia Press 1985: 29-30).[16]

A declaration expressing similar sentiments signed by a group of native Turkish intellectuals was published in *Otečestven Front* on 26 July 1985 (Sofia Press 1985: 13-19; Appendix E). All of the individuals who signed these declarations used their Bulgarian names.

The Bulgarian authorities continued to deny the existence of Turkish Muslims in Bulgaria until late 1989 and to insist that Muslims in Bulgaria were the descendants of Bulgarian Orthodox Christians who had been converted to Islam by the sword during Ottoman rule. A reasonable discourse on this issue became possible after the ouster of Živkov from power on 10 November 1989.

On 29 December 1989 the new leadership of the Communist Party announced the reversal of the assimilation policy of the Živkov era and promised that it would work toward the creation of a democratic society in which the civil and religious rights of minority populations in the country would be guaranteed and protected. After the June 1990 multi-party elections, Bulgaria's freely elected parliament voted to end anti-Muslim and anti-Turkish measures and promised to establish the conditions for the free exercise of all religions in the country.[17] The 1991 constitution included a number of provisions to bring this about. Article 13 states, "(1) The practicing of any religion shall be free. (2) The religious institutions shall be separate from the state . . . (4) Religious institutions and communities, and religious beliefs shall not be used for political ends" (Sofia Press Agency, 1991: 6-7). Article 37 guarantees the inviolability of freedom of conscience, freedom of thought, freedom of choice of religion. Moreover, this article promises that the "state shall assist the maintenance of tolerance and respect among believers from different denominations." Article

---

[16] The full texts of these declarations are found in Sofia Press (1985: 27-48). For an elaboration on these themes see Iliev (1989: 1-20), who was the mufti of the district of Smolyan in southeastern Bulgaria at the time.

[17] Article 29 (1) of the 1991 Constitution prohibits forced assimilation. "No one shall be subjected to torture or to cruel, inhuman or degrading treatment, or to forcible assimilation" (Sofia Press Agency 1991: 10).

44(2) prohibits the formation of organizations for the purpose of inciting "racial, national, ethnic or religious enmity or an encroachment on the rights and freedoms of citizens" (Sofia Press Agency 1991: 11-13).

These constitutional guarantees and other developments in Bulgaria since 1989 have led to a revival of Islam in the country. All restrictions on religious rights imposed arbitrarily by the government before 1990 have been removed. The Islamic schools closed during the communist era have reopened and new religious schools have been established. Religious classes are available to young Muslims in their communities. Between the summer of 1990 and the end of 1991 over 80,000 Muslim children learned to recite the Koran. The Muslims, once again, have the right to build new mosques and to repair old ones. By the end of 1991 eight new mosques were built. The Chief Mufti has asked the Directorate of Religions for permission to build an additional forty mosques and a new Islamic center. Hundreds of old mosques have been repaired and renovated. The minarets of old mosques which were demolished during communist rule have been replaced with new ones. While the number of functioning mosques had been reduced to under 300 by 1989, by 1992 there were 920 mosques open for religious services and the number was rising as repair and renovation of old mosques and the building of new ones continued. The restrictions on the importation and distribution of Korans and other religious texts imposed during communist rule were lifted, and they are available once again. In 1990 the Chief Mufti's office sold 10,000 Korans. A project to translate the Koran into Turkish and Bulgarian is under way (Tomova and Bogoev 1992: 7-8). Muslims are freely celebrating important religious holidays, carrying out traditional funeral, marriage, and circumcision rituals without government interference.

However, significant problems remain. One of the most serious is the power struggle for the leadership of the Muslim community which has been going on since 1989 and remains unresolved. Under communism the religious leaders of the community were political appointees who carried out government dictates without regard to the welfare of Muslims in the country. The Chief Mufti Nedim Gencev and most regional muftis and *imams* were supporters of the anti-Muslim policies of the regime. Nevertheless, because Nedim Gencev had powerful supporters within the Bulgarian

Socialist Party (formerly communist), he and his supporters remained in their positions until 1992. In response to protests by Muslims against Gencev's leadership, the Directorate of Religions nullified the March 1986 law on religious organizations and the statutes governing the leadership of the Muslim community in Bulgaria. Nedim Gencev had been appointed Chief Mufti in 1988 on the basis of these statutes. The Directorate of Religions relieved Gencev of his duties (Cafer 1992: 1-2). In September 1992 the Muslim community elected a new Chief Mufti and regional muftis. Between September 1992 and January 1995 the legitimacy of the new leadership was recognized by three successive governments. But Gencev was not going to relinquish his position voluntarily or peacefully. He had a hard-core Muslim following and powerful supporters within the Bulgarian Socialist Party who urged him to reclaim his position. They condoned patently illegal activities of his supporters to that end, such as occupation of the Chief Mufti's office in Sofia and the offices of regional muftis, preventing the legitimately elected religious officials from performing their duties. In 1994 the BSP and other Bulgarian nationalist groups encouraged Gencev to form a political party and run candidates in the December 1994 elections for Parliament in spite of the constitutional ban on religiously based parties. In fact, the BSP had used this same ban in attempts to disenfranchise the Movement for Rights and Freedoms several times. After the BSP victory in the December 1994 elections, the Directorate of Religions reversed its 1992 decision and recognized Nedim Gencev's faction as the legal representatives of Muslims in Bulgaria. This decision clearly violated the constitutional separation of church and state enshrined in Article 13 (2) by lending support to a faction battling for power within the Muslim community. This decision also violated the constitutional prohibition against using religion for political ends as articulated in Article 13 (3). After January 1995, the activities of the legitimately elected Supreme Theological Council in September 1992 were declared illegal. Communiqués issued during the March 1995 National Conference of Muslims in Bulgaria and protests of government interference in Muslim religious affairs sent to the Prime Minister and the President of Parliament were ignored (*Hak ve Özgürlük* 1995: 2). The BSP government encouraged factionalism within the Muslim community by recognizing and supporting one faction against the other. There were two Supreme Muslim Theological Councils, two Chief Muftis, parallel regional muftis and parallel *imams* at the local level. Such actions were clearly meant to fan antagonisms among Muslims, encourage factionalism within the Muslim community and weaken it politically.

Another example of gross government interference in religious affairs of Muslims was the decision of the Directorate of Religions in 1995 to prohibit students from the Islamic High School in Šumen from going to villages during religious holidays to act as *muezzins* and help to officiate in marriage and funeral rituals (Ömer, 1995: 2). Traditionally, this practice was a kind of internship for advanced students to put into practice what they had learned in school, and hence, an integral part of their education. Such government interference in religious affairs creates unnecessary tension between government and citizens.

The leaders of the Muslim community are also concerned about Article 13 (3), which declares that "Eastern Orthodox Christianity shall be considered the traditional religion of the Republic of Bulgaria" (Sofia Press Agency 1991: 7). They fear that this clause "could provide potential legal barriers for the full revival of Muslim life" in Bulgaria (Lewis 1994: 28). The constitutional recognition of the primacy of Orthodox Christianity in Bulgaria is likely to be used as a pretext to establish it as the official religion of the country and to discriminate against Islam and other religions. Discrimination against Muslims is already a fact. For example, the government and the Orthodox church hierarchy have taken steps to curb missionary activity among the Orthodox Christian population. No such steps have been taken against such activity among the Muslim population. Orthodox priests have been extremely active among the Bulgarian-speaking Muslims and Gypsy Muslims since 1989 and their success in converting Muslims to Christianity is widely reported in the mass media. In addition to Orthodox missionaries, representatives of mainstream Protestant denominations, Evangelicals, Catholics, Mormons, Church of Scientology and various cults are competing with one another to "save" Muslim souls. Muslim missionary activity among the Orthodox population, of course, is unthinkable. Christian religious services are regularly broadcast over television but not Muslim religious services. On the occasion of the Ramazan holidays in 1995, the Chief Mufti was allowed to address the faithful over television. His request to include a short greeting in Turkish for the benefit of the older Turkish Muslims in his address was denied. He was allowed to recite only a short passage from the Koran in Arabic.

Another serious problem that faces the Muslim leadership is the low level of religious awareness among Muslims in Bulgaria. Government policies from the end of the Second World War up till 1989, such as the closing of mosques and religious schools, imprisonmnent of religious teachers, confiscation of Korans and other religious texts and prohibition against importation of religious texts from the outside meant a general deterioration of knowledge about important Islamic beliefs and practices. This was especially true for those Muslims who were born during and following the Second World War. There was a significant erosion of knowledge about the content and sources of the Five Pillars of Islam. These conditions had a profound impact on the level of religiosity and religious consciousness of Muslims as revealed in studies carried out during the 1960s and 1970s.

A sociological survey on religious attitudes among the adult population carried out in March 1992 illustrates the current state of Islam in Bulgaria. The results of the survey indicate that since 1989 a recovery of Islamic beliefs and practices has gotten under way. I briefly summarize affirmative responses to several questions by Muslims (see Table 2.6).

Table 2.6. MEASURES OF RELIGIOSITY AMONG MUSLIMS, 1992

Topics	Responses (%)
Deeply religious	30.5
Pray regularly	41.7
Go to mosque regularly	20.0
Read religious literature regularly	17.2
Observe religious fasts regularly	45.1
Religious rituals are the best way to celebrate life-cycle events – naming, marriage, funerals	23.1
Observe restrictions against working on religious holidays	49.5
Are familiar with the entire Koran	22.4
Believe in afterlife	59.0
Believe in miracles	51.1
All students should study religion in public schools	37.6
Celebrate religious holidays regularly	84.4
Religion has a positive influence on family relationships	66.6

Source: Nacionalen Statističeski Institut 1993a: 57-113.

The factors influencing the level of religiosity among Muslims in earlier studies – residence, gender, age, level of education, and occupation – remain important. The survey found that rural Muslims were more religious than urban Muslims; Muslim women were more religious than Muslim men; older Muslims were more religious than younger Muslims; peasants were more religious than blue-collar and white-collar workers, and so on. Tables 2.7 and 2.8 illustrate the influence of these factors on two measures of religiosity: frequency of attendance of Friday prayers at the mosque, and regular performance of daily prayers. Overall, 20 per cent of adult Muslims said they attended Friday prayers at the mosque regularly. However, the percentage for rural Muslims was more than twice as high as urban Muslims, 23.9 to 10.6 per cent. The lower percentage for women is not surprising since traditionally Muslim women in Bulgaria did not attend religious services at the mosque. Mosque attendance increased with age – 42 per cent of Muslims sixty and over attended prayers at the

Table 2.7. MOSQUE ATTENDANCE BY RESIDENCE, GENDER, AGE AND LEVEL OF EDUCATION

Population categories	Frequently	Sometimes	Rarely	No
Total	20.0	16.1	19.3	44.7
Residence				
Town	10.6	14.3	15.6	59.5
Village	23.8	16.8	20.9	38.5
Gender				
Male	27.0	18.8	18.8	35.5
Female	12.9	13.4	20.0	53.8
Age				
18-29 years	1.9	12.7	22.3	63.1
30-39	16.1	13.4	24.1	46.5
40-49	14.5	11.8	13.2	60.5
50-59	25.6	21.3	13.8	39.3
60 and above	42.0	20.0	21.0	17.0
Education				
Elementary	33.1	17.2	16.6	33.1
Middle school	12.1	26.4	21.2	40.3
High school	12.5	12.5	22.3	52.6

Source: Nacionalen Statističeski Institut 1993a: 59.

mosque regularly but only 1.9 per cent of eighteen to twenty-nine-year-olds did. The level of education also influenced mosque attendance. The more educated people were, the less likely they were to attend prayers at the mosque. For example, 33.1 per cent of adult Muslims with elementary education went to mosque regularly but only 12.1 per cent with middle school education and 12.5 per cent with high school education did so. The low level of religiosity among the young and the educated is understandable because these were the groups that were targeted for atheistic education and anti-religious propaganda during communist rule. The study found similar correlations between regular performance of daily prayers and residence, gender, age, and education (see Table 2.8).

Table 2.8. REGULAR PERFORMANCE OF DAILY PRAYERS BY RESIDENCE, GENDER, AGE AND LEVEL OF EDUCATION

Population categories	Yes, regularly	Yes, but not regularly	Only on some occasions	No, never
Total	41.7	18.3	23.6	16.3
Residence				
Town	31.2	15.6	28.4	24.8
Village	46.0	19.4	21.7	13.0
Gender				
Male	39.3	21.3	21.7	17.6
Female	44.2	15.3	25.6	14.9
Age				
18-29 years	16.5	19.4	37.9	26.2
30-39	31.5	21.6	34.2	12.6
40-49	32.9	19.7	25.0	22.4
50-59	53.2	20.2	11.7	14.9
60 and above	73.5	10.8	7.8	7.8
Education				
Elementary	64.8	14.8	8.5	11.9
Middle school	33.9	20.6	27.5	18.0
High school	18.0	21.6	38.7	21.6

Source: Nacionalen Statističeski Institut 1993a: 65.

The 1992 survey results confirmed the greater religiosity among Muslims than among Christians in the country noted in earlier surveys. Another finding of the survey rejects the prevailing opinion among Bulgarians that Muslims are religious fanatics. In fact, responses to questions designed to elicit feelings about the influence of religion on relations between the members of different faiths consistently show that Muslims are less prejudiced toward the members of other faiths than Christians. To the question, "Do you think that belief in God (Allah) makes people behave better toward each other?" 61 per cent of Muslims responded affirmatively, while only 39.1 per cent of Christians thought so. To the question, "According to you, is it possible to have friendly relations between people with different religions?" 83.2 per cent of Muslims answered yes, while 67.2 per cent of Christians thought so. To the question, "According to you, what is the effect of religion on relations among colleagues and friends?" 55 percent of Muslims thought religion had a positive influence on such relations, but only 36.7 per cent of Christians thought so.

The results of the 1992 survey indicate that since 1989 there has been a revival of Islam in Bulgaria. During the 1970s and 1980s it appeared that Islam had lost its vitality and relevance for most Muslims. It appeared that the attempts of the communist regime to eradicate Islamic beliefs and practices, Islamic institutions, and the visible symbols of Muslim presence from the landscape were succeeding. Few people believed that Islam could ever recover from this onslaught. However, the unexpected and dramatic collapse of totalitarian communist regimes in Eastern Europe would create the conditions necessary for the free exercise of religion.

The events following the ouster of Živkov from power in November 1989, such as the replacement of one-party rule with a multi-party system, a new constitution that restored freedom of conscience and religion, the reversal of the assimilation campaign against Muslims and the elimination of repressive laws, led to the revival of religion among all groups in the country.

After 1989 the mosques were full with enthusiastic worshippers week after week. Muslims began to repair old mosques and build new ones. It appeared that a genuine revival of religion was under way. Unfortunately this seeming religious boom did not last long. By 1995 the number of Muslims attending Friday prayers at mosques had declined considerably. As in the past the worshippers were mostly older men. The reasons for this trend are not difficult to find. Religious life demands a discipline for which most Muslims in Bulgaria, especially the young, were ill-prepared. A more important reason is the increasingly divisive factionalism within the

Muslim community, exacerbated by the government support of one faction against the other. In this power struggle most religious leaders have put their personal ambitions ahead of the spiritual needs of Muslims. Instead of presenting themselves as role models to be emulated by rank and file Muslims, they have become symbols of pettiness and greed. Such behavior inevitably leads to lack of confidence in and trust of religious authorities. Lack of trust in religious leaders alienates people from religion, jeopardizing the potential for a genuine revival of Islam in Bulgaria.

Number and geographic distribution of Muslims

From 1946 until the 1992 census, reliable official statistics on the number and distribution of Muslims were not available. Starting with the 1946 census the government dropped the category "religious affiliation" from census forms. Statistics on the religious affiliation of Bulgarian citizens would not be collected again until the 1992 census. During the 1956, 1965 and 1975 censuses, statistics were collected on mother tongue and nationality only. Statistics on ethnic affiliation and nationality collected during the 1975 census were declared a state secret and not published. During the 1985 census no information was collected on the ethnic and linguistic composition of the population. The authorities claimed that such information was no longer needed because by 1985 Bulgaria was a homogeneous single-nation (Bulgarian) state. From 1965 until the 1992 census results were published, scholars interested in ethnic and religious statistics about Muslim groups in Bulgaria had to rely on unofficial estimates. These estimates ranged from a low of 800,000 to 1 million to a high of 1,700,000 (Szajkowski and Niblock 1993: 172-3). The 1992 census restored the category of religious affiliation to census forms. Also, during the 1992 census the Sunni and Shiite Muslims were counted separately. The reasons for this were not purely demographic. During the debates in parliament before the census, some nationalist deputies argued that the Shiites in Bulgaria were a distinct ethnic group with unique religious beliefs and practices. Moreover, they claimed that the Shiites were not Turks but descendants of Bulgarians who had been converted to Islam during the Ottoman period. It was another attempt to divide the Muslim community.

Official Bulgarian statistics on the number of Muslims in Bulgaria between 1881 and 1992 are shown in Table 2.9. As the figures

indicate, between 1881 and 1910 the proportion of Muslim population in Bulgaria was more than halved, from 28.8 per cent in
1881 to 14 per cent in 1910. Since then the proportion of Muslims
has remained between 15 and 13 per cent.

Table 2.9. NUMBER OF MUSLIMS IN BULGARIA, 1881-1992

	Total population	*No. of Muslims*	*% of total*
1881	2,007,919	578,060	28.8
1888	3,154,375	676,215	21.4
1900	3,744,283	643,300	17.2
1905	4,035,575	603,867	15.0
1910	4,337,513	602,078	14.0
1920	4,846,954	690,734	14.2
1926	5,478,740	789,296	14.4
1934	6,077,939	821,298	13.5
1946	7,029,349	934,418	13.3
1956	7,613,709	n.a.	–
1965	8,227,866	n.a.	–
1975	8,727,771	n.a.	–
1985	8,948,649	n.a.	–
1992	8,487,317	1,112,331	13.1

Source: Mitev 1994: 214-15; and Donkov 1994: 37.

The preliminary results of the 1992 census showed that more
than three-quarters of Muslims were Turks. Table 2.10 illustrates
the composition of the Muslim population in Bulgaria by ethnic
affiliation and by mother tongue. Turks accounted for 75.3 per
cent of Muslims by ethnic affiliation, followed by Bulgarians with
13.5 per cent, and Gypsies with 10.5 per cent. Of Muslims, 75.8
per cent identified their mother tongue as Turkish, 15.2 per cent
as Bulgarian, and 8.3 per cent as Romany. The others, 1 per
cent and 0.7 per cent respectively, were mainly Tatars and Albanians. The differences in the figures for ethnic affiliation and
mother tongue for Gypsy Muslims and Bulgarian Muslims (Pomaks)
is due to the fact that some Bulgarian-speaking Muslims identify
their ethnicity as Turkish, while Romany-speaking Gypsies identify
themselves as either Turks or Bulgarians. Turkish Muslims were
concentrated in southeastern and northeastern Bulgaria. Approximately half lived in the districts of Kŭrdžali, Razgrad, Šumen,

Burgas, and Silistra. Pomaks lived mainly in the central and western Rhodopes of southern Bulgaria. The Gypsy Muslims were found throughout the country, although most lived in or near other Muslim communities (see map). The overwhelming majority of Muslims, 1,026,758 or 92.3 per cent, were Sunnis of the Hanafite school while a much smaller number, 85,573 or 7.7 per cent, were Shiites (Mitev 1994: 215).

Table 2.10. ETHNIC GROUP, MOTHER TONGUE
AND MUSLIM AFFILIATION IN 1992

Ethnic group	Muslims	%	Mother tongue	Muslims	%
Turkish	812,067	75.3	Turkish	817,609	75.8
Bulgarian	142,938	13.5	Bulgarian	163,735	15.2
Gypsy	112,923	10.5	Gypsy	89,530	8.3
Other	10,398	1.0	Other	7,452	0.7
Total	1,078,326	100.0	Total	1,078,326	100.0

Source: Nacionalen Statističeski Institut 1993b: 96-7.

In Bulgaria the Shiites are known as Alevi, Aliani, or more generally as Kızılbaş ("red head") after their traditional headgear with twelve red stripes representing the twelve *imams*. The main Kızılbaş communities in Bulgaria are found in northeastern Bulgaria, in Gerlovo and around Stara Zagora of east-central Bulgaria, and in southeastern Bulgaria south of the town of Haskovo. The Kızılbaş are divided into several sects, each with its own leader (*Dedes*) and minor differences in belief and practice (De Jong 1993: 204-5).[18]

The origins of this population are disputed. Limited historical evidence and elements in their beliefs and rituals point to their Safavid origins (Savory 1980). Fragmentary historical evidence and the folk traditions among the Kızılbaş themselves suggest that they are a synthetic population containing Iranian, Kurdish, Turkish, and Bulgarian elements. Whatever their origins, today they are linguistically assimilated into the Turkish community. They speak Turkish and identify themselves as Turks. They may have begun to settle in Bulgaria as early as the thirteenth century. However, most of the Kızılbaş settled in Bulgaria in large numbers,

[18] A detailed discussion of Kızılbaş beliefs and rituals is found in Georgieva (1991).

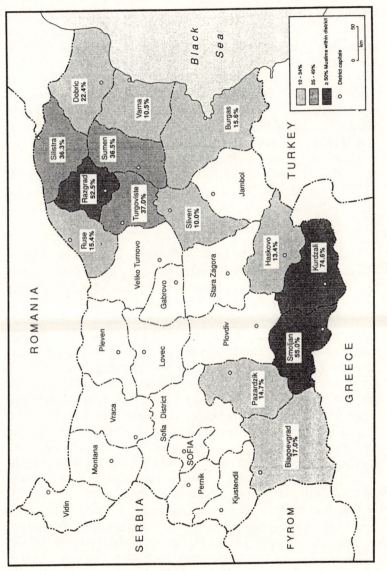

Muslims in Bulgaria

either voluntarily or deported there from Anatolia by the Ottomans, between the fifteenth and seventeenth centuries (De Jong 1993: 206-9). Since the Kızılbaş were considered "heterodox", even heretical, by the majority Sunnis, they have been subject to periodic persecutions. In the face of such persecution, they have adopted the strategy of concealment in an attempt to maintain their true identity, "outwardly professing to be orthodox Sunnis to their Turkish or Bulgarian neighbors, or alternately claiming to be Bektashis, depending on who is addressing them" (Norris 1993: 98). Besides concealment, village and confessional endogamy have helped them maintain their religious traditions.

Traditionally the Kızılbaş were associated with various Sufi brotherhoods active in the Balkans during the Ottoman period (Norris 1993:82-137). The most important of these was the Bektashi order of dervishes (See Birge 1937). Because this order was closely associated with the Janissary corps (Hasluck 1929: 483-596), the Bektashis were protected from persecution by the Sunni Ottoman state until 1826, when the Janissary corps was disbanded by Sultan Mahmud II. After the disbanding many Bektashi lodges were closed down or destroyed, Bektashi properties were confiscated, and persecution of members of the order increased.

After the establishment of independent Balkan states during the nineteenth century the activities of most Sufi brotherhoods were curtailed. Outside Albania and Bosnia, and among Albanian Muslims in Kosovo and Macedonia, few dervish orders remained active (See Popovic 1986b). In Bulgaria some Sufi orders survived into the late 1930s (See Kowalski 1937). Under the communist regime in Bulgaria, the relationship between the leaders of various Sufi orders and their counterparts outside the country was severed. An important aspect of the government's goal to create a homogeneous Bulgarian state was the elimination of architectural reminders of Muslim presence from the Bulgarian landscape. Along with hundreds of mosques, most dervish convents were closed and fell into ruin. During the 1970s and 1980s the government reinforced its anti-Islamic propaganda and atheistic education by outright ban of most Islamic rituals, whether Sunni or Shiite. According to De Jong (1986a: 308), in 1982 the meetings of the last remaining Sufi orders in northeastern Bulgaria, the Nakşibendi and Kadiri *tarikats*, were prohibited by the local authorities. After that date De Jong could not find any informants willing to acknowledge the existence of any active orders in northeastern Bulgaria, or who even acknowledged their existence in the past.

After the collapse of totalitarianism in 1989 there was a general revival of Islam in the country. Some Sufi convents, especially the Demir Baba *tekke* near the town of Isperih north of Razgrad, have become the focus of Muslim solidarity. The reestablishment of contacts between the leaders of the few surviving orders in Bulgaria and their brethren in Turkey should rejuvenate these orders. During the last two decades Sufi brotherhoods have become extremely important in Turkish political life. The Nakşibendi, its numerous offshoots, and the Kadiri orders were crucial in the recent electoral success of the Islamic Welfare Party in Turkey. These orders have expanded their activities outside Turkey, establishing hundreds of prestigious high schools in the Turkic republics of the former Soviet Union and in the Balkans (Ayata 1996: 48-51). Since the Nakşibendi and the Kadiri orders continued to function in Bulgaria till the early 1980s, it is these orders that are benefiting from the activities of their counterparts in Turkey. To what extent other orders that used to exist in Bulgaria will be revived is uncertain. However, given the constitutional restrictions against the formation of religiously or ethnically-based political organizations in Bulgaria today the politicization of Islam in Bulgaria to the extent that has occurred in Turkey and elsewhere is unlikely. Moreover, since the religious leadership of the Muslim community in Bulgaria is largely Sunni, the members of Kızılbaş and other "heterodox" groups would be reluctant to perform their rituals and to profess their beliefs openly. They are likely to continue to use their traditional strategies of concealment and confessional endogamy to maintain their identity and their unique traditions.

3

MAJOR MUSLIM MINORITIES
IN BULGARIA

The three major Muslim minorities in Bulgaria are Turks, Gypsy Muslims, and Pomaks. Other Muslims consist of small groups of Albanians, descendants of those who settled along the commercially and militarily important route between the Black Sea port of Varna and Dubrovnik on the Adriatic during the Ottoman period, and Tatars, descendants of Crimean Tatars settled in northeastern Bulgaria during the mid-nineteenth century. Their numerical strength is estimated at between 5,000 and 10,000. Although both groups have assimilated into the Turkish Muslim community to some degree, they have also managed to maintain their separate ethnic identities. The few Muslim Circassians who remained in Bulgaria after 1878 have become thoroughly assimilated into the Turkish community.

Turks

The earliest recorded settlement of Turks from Anatolia in the Balkans dates from the middle of the thirteenth century. Sultan Kaykavus, who had been defeated by Kilij Arsian IV in his attempt to establish himself in the western Anatolian marches, sought refuge in Byzantium in 1261. He was joined by a fairly numerous group of Turcoman nomads on Byzantine territory. Kaykavus and his followers asked Emperor Michael VIII Paleologus for land to settle on. They were granted permission to settle in Dobrudža, "then a no-man's-land between the Golden Horde, Bulgaria and the Byzantine Empire . . . These Muslim Turks from Anatolia, mostly nomads, formed there 'two or three towns and 30-40 *oba*, clans'" (Inalcik 1965: 610). The new settlers came, for a time, under the protection of the Muslim Khans of the Golden Horde. After the death of Nogay and the accession to the Khanate by

Tukal Bogha, a pagan, these Muslim Turks came under strong Christian missionary pressure and many returned to Anatolia between 1307 and 1311. Those who remained in Dobrudža converted to Christianity. These Christianized Turks played an important role in the subsequent history of the region. The followers of Kaykavus who remained behind in Dobrudža were one of the groups that contributed to the formation of the Gagauz, Turkish-speaking Christians most of whom today live in the Republic of Moldova. Small groups of Gagauz are also found in Ukraine, Romania, Bulgaria, Yugoslavia, Greece and the Central Asian Republics.[1]

However, as discussed in Chapter 2, the more widespread settlement of Turks from Asia Minor and Anatolia dates to the middle of the fourteenth century. Such activity continued throughout the Ottoman period, reaching a peak during the mid-nineteenth century when large numbers of Tatars from Crimea and Circassians from the Caucasus were settled in Bulgarian lands. The Tatars were settled mostly in Dobrudža and in towns along the northern Black Sea coast (Pinson 1972a, 1974). The Circassians were settled throughout present-day Bulgaria (Pinson 1972b). The Ottoman administration went to considerable expense to settle these refugees, even founding a new town, Mecidije, to settle the Tatars (Karpat 1984-5).

Although the settlement of Turks from Anatolia and other parts of the Empire continued throughout the Ottoman period, a demographic balance between Christians and Muslims was achieved within a century and a half of the Ottoman conquest of Bulgaria, where the urban areas became largely Muslim and the hinterlands populated by Christians. This demographic equilibrium began to be reversed only toward the end of the nineteenth century, during and after the Russo-Turkish War of 1877-8.

[1] The origins of the Gagauz are disputed. Over the years, they have been regarded as the descendants of Greek, Bulgarian, Albanian, and Wallachian Christians who had maintained their religion but were Turkified during the Ottoman period (See Gradešliev 1993). A more popular traditional view supports the Anatolian Turkish origins of the Gagauz. The researches of Kowalski in Dobrudža (1933, 1938) established a close connection between the Turkish spoken by the Gagauz and Anatolian Turkish. Wittek's (1952, 1953) informative articles lent support to this hypothesis. Other authors who support this view include Zajaczkowski (1965, 1974), Inalcik (1965), and Karpat (1976). However, more recent analysis of historical and linguistic evidence indicates that the Gagauz are a synthetic population, formed by the melding of Peçenegs, Uz, Cumans and Anatolian Turks (Güngör and Argunşah 1991, 1993).

During and following the war large numbers of Turks and other Muslims (almost all of the Circassians and most of the Tatars), especially from among the urban population, left with the retreating Ottoman armies toward Thrace, Istanbul and Anatolia. This was especially true for the western and central parts of the Danubian Province because the area was directly in the path of war. The rural areas of the eastern region of this province, being remote from the war zone, did not experience a general exodus of the Turkish population. But a steady stream of Turkish and Muslim emigrants continued to leave for Turkey after 1878, significantly eroding the Turkish presence in Bulgaria.

The Russo-Turkish War of 1877-8 and its aftermath led to major demographic restructuring of the ethnic and religious make-up of Bulgarian towns. As a result of massive Turkish/Muslim emigration during and following the war there was a precipitous decline in the proportion of Turks in most towns and a corresponding increase in the proportion of Bulgarians. Substantial numbers also left during and following the Balkan wars and the First World War in accordance with the compulsory exchange of population agreements between Greece, Bulgaria, and Turkey, the warring parties. After the Second World War the emigration of Turks from Bulgaria to Turkey proceeded under various bilateral agreements between the two countries. After the expiration of the latest bilateral agreement in 1978, such emigration virtually ceased. The latest wave of Turkish emigration from Bulgaria began with the mass exodus in 1989 and has continued, although at a slower pace, ever since. Reliable statistics on Turkish emigration, especially for the period from 1878 until the end of the First World War, are hard to come by. Estimating the number of Turks who died during the Russo-Turkish War (in battle, of starvation, and exposure), and the number of those who emigrated during and immediately following the war is even more difficult. One source (Ipek 1994: 40-1) estimates that 500,000 Turks and other Muslims died during the war, and more than 1 million emigrated from Bulgaria and other areas of the Balkans immediately following the war. Table 3.1 presents the most reliable statistics available on emigration of Turks from Bulgaria from 1878 to 1992. The Balkan wars and the First World War precipitated another wave of Turkish emigration. Turkish sources estimate that 440,000 Turks emigrated from Bulgaria during the Balkan wars. Taking Turkish emigration during the Balkan wars and the First World War into account, a total of 1.5 million Turkish emigrants from Bulgaria between 1878 and the present is a reasonable estimate. Turkish estimates are much higher. Özbir's (1986: 31-32) summary of reliable Turkish sources for the period 1879-1978 puts the number of Turkish emigrants from Bulgaria at more than 1.6 million.

Table 3.1. EMIGRATION OF TURKS
FROM BULGARIA, 1878-1992[2]

1878-1912	350,000
1923-33	101,507
1934-9	97,181
1940-9	21,353
1950-1	154,198
1952-68	24
1969-78	114,356
1979-88	0
1989-92	321,800
Total	1,160,614

Although the estimates of the number of Turkish emigrants for the first three decades following the Russo-Turkish war are unreliable, the magnitude of emigration is indicated by the extent of the decline of Turkish population in Bulgarian towns during those three decades. Crampton's (1990: 44-77) analysis of the statistics from the twenty largest towns in Bulgaria between 1880/4 and 1910 shows that "The total percentile decline . . . was between a third and a half in five towns. [. . .] In ten settlements the Turkish percentile was between half and three quarters. [. . .] The percentile fall was over three-quarters in Tatar Pazardjik (76.81), Samokov (88.52), Chirpan (90.56), Kiustendil (95.36), and Kavaklii, where the tiny Turkish community disappeared completely" (Crampton 1990: 57).

As a result of these migrations the percentage of Turks in

[2] The estimate for the period 1878-1912 is from Xristov (1989: 51); Vasileva (1992: 346) cites Höpken (1987: 252) as the source of this estimate, but I could not find this information in the article cited under her references. The figures for the 1923-51 period are from Şimşir (1986a: 6); the figures for the period 1952-92 are from Donkov (1994: 39).

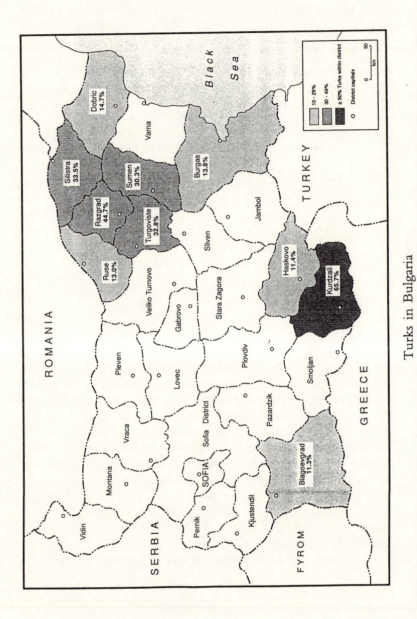

Turks in Bulgaria

Bulgaria was reduced from more than one-third of the population immediately after the Russo-Turkish War to less than 15 per cent (14.2 per cent) in 1900. It fell under 10 per cent in 1934 and continued to fall fractionally during the subsequent decades but started to climb again during the late 1960s and 1970s (see Table 12). According to the results of the 1992 census, 822,253 Bulgarian citizens (or 9.7 per cent) identified their ethnic affiliation as Turks. In the district of Kŭrdžali in southeastern Bulgaria they were in the majority, with 65.7 per cent of the district population. In the district of Razgrad in northeastern Bulgaria Turks made up 47.4 per cent of the district population. Other districts with significant Turkish populations included Silistra (33.5 per cent), Tŭrgovište (32.8 per cent), Šumen (30.3 per cent), Dobrič (14.7 per cent), Burgas (13.8 per cent), Ruse (13.0 per cent), Haskovo (11.4 per cent), and Blagoevgrad (11.3 per cent).[3] The map opposite shows the districts where Turks make up 10 per cent or more of the population.

Table 3.2. NUMBER OF TURKS IN BULGARIA, 1900-92

	Total population	*No. of Turks*	*% of total*
1900	3,744,283	531,240	14.2
1905	4,035,575	488,010	12.1
1910	4,337,513	465,641	10.8
1920	4,846,954	520,339	10.7
1926	5,478,740	577,552	10.5
1934	6,077,939	591,193	9.7
1946	7,029,349	675,500	9.6
1956	7,613,709	656,025	8.6
1965	8,227,046	780,928	9.5
1975	8,727,771	n.a.	–
1985	8,948,649	n.a.	–
1992	8,487,317	822,253	9.7

Source: Donkov 1994: 37-8.

[3] After the completion of the census the results from the district of Blagoevgrad were a source of contentious debate in Parliament. The Bulgarian nationalists in Parliament insisted that many Bulgarian Muslims in the district had been coerced by the Movement for Rights and Freedoms to declare themselves Turks. Although evidence for such coercion was lacking, the Parliament nevertheless declared invalid the figure of 39,550 Bulgarians who had designated their ethnic affiliation as Turks.

The 1992 census results show that more than two-thirds of Turks (68.5 per cent) lived in villages and less than one-third (31.5 percent) lived in towns. Bulgarians, on the other hand, were overwhelmingly urban. Close to three-quarters, 71.5 per cent, lived in towns and only 28.5 per cent lived in villages (Nacionalen Statističeski Institut 1993b: 92).

The slight increase in the number of Turks and other minorities during the 1960s and 1970s apparently alarmed the party leaders in Bulgaria enough to initiate an assimilation campaign against Turkish and other minority populations in the country. Recently secret documents from the archives of the Central Committee of the Bulgarian Communist Party have come to light indicating government plans to reduce the Turkish population in Bulgaria by 10 to 15 per cent every ten to fifteen years through the twin processes of migration and assimilation. The first episode of forced migration occurred during 1949-50 when more than 150,000 Turks were forced to leave Bulgaria for Turkey. This episode provoked an international outcry and for a brief period Bulgaria reversed its policy of forced migration and assimilation. Instead, the Communist Party leadership experimented with socialist internationalism marked by a relative tolerance of ethnic diversity in the country. In 1951 the government recognized the Turkish-speaking population as a national minority. During the 1950s the official government policy was to encourage the maintenance of Turkish identity as separate from Bulgarian identity through specific programs such as Turkish-language schools, Turkish teacher-training institutes, Turkish-language press, and state-supported regional Turkish theaters and folk groups as well as the encouragement of amateur folk groups in Turkish villages.

However, with hindsight it is clear that these programs were not established because the Bulgarian government sincerely believed in cultural pluralism. On the contrary, they were initiated for pragmatic, political reasons in order to placate a very restive Turkish population whose sensibilities had been badly shaken by the actions of the government towards them between 1946 and 1951. These actions not only eliminated the semi-autonomous status the Turkish-speaking community had enjoyed in Bulgarian up to that time, but also saw the inauguration of a period of active government interference in the life of the community. Such interference began in 1946 when all private Turkish schools were placed under government supervision. In 1949 the religious affairs of the Muslim community came under government regulation. In late 1949 the government began its initial collectivization drive in the fertile plains of Dobrudža, where most of the land was owned by Turkish farmers. These and other government actions were met with fierce and determined resistance on the part of Turks and other Muslims; there was considerable agitation to be allowed to emigrate to Turkey. In early 1950 the Bulgarian government suddenly began to deport large numbers of Turks, especially from northeastern Bulgaria. The lands of the Turkish farmers were confiscated outright and Turks were herded *en masse* to the border stations, many with only the clothes on their backs. In 1949 only 1,525 Turks had emigrated from Bulgaria to Turkey. During the first nine months of 1950 alone 28,250 left Bulgaria. Then, in September of the same year Bulgaria informed Turkey that 250,000 additional Turks were "willing to emigrate" and that the transfer of this number must be completed by 10 November 1950 (*The World Today* 1951: 33). This enormous transfer of population at such short notice and in such a short period of time was in clear contravention of the procedures for orderly migration established by the Ankara Agreement of 1925.[4] By the end of 1951, approximately 155,000 Bulgarian Turks had crossed into Turkey. Unable to absorb such a large influx of immigrants within such a short time, Turkey closed its border (Kostanick 1957). These experiences generated widespread dissatisfaction among the Turks. The more liberal attitude of the Bulgarian government toward Turks after 1951 must be understood within this context.

Even during the period of apparent. liberality in the 1950s, the underlying motive of the government remained the assimilation of Turks into the dominant Slavic majority. Since the Turkish population was largely monolingual at that time, it was felt that the Turkish language was the most effective propaganda vehicle through which the government could accomplish its goals. A

[4] This agreement had a number of provisions to safeguard the life and property of prospective emigrants. Among these the agreement required "that all emigrants shall have the right to take with them all their moveable property and savings, as well as to dispose of all their immovable property" without any interference (*The World Today*, 1951: 31). Even after agreeing to abide by the provisions of the Ankara Agreement in the fall of 1950, Bulgaria continued to ignore them, Consequently, Turkey closed the border in December 1951. Between the end of 1951 and 1969, when a new agreement on emigration went into effect, emigration of Turks from Bulgaria to Turkey virtually ceased.

wide-ranging attack on Islam among Turks dates from this period. This campaign included closing of Koranic schools, prohibition of religious classes in public schools, arrest and imprisonment of religious teachers, propaganda among the young not to attend services at mosques, and propaganda against a number of customs and cultural practices among Turks, such as wearing of traditional dress by the women, celebration of religious holidays, fasting during the month of Ramazan, circumcision of boys, traditional burial practices, arranged marriages, and religious marriage ceremonies.[5]

Nevertheless, emphasis on the development of Turkish language and culture ("national in form, socialist in content") were welcomed by many members of the Turkish-speaking community. As long as programs supporting Turkish-language schools, press, and theaters continued to function, many Turks became supporters of the regime. It was only after the elimination or drastic curtailment of many of these programs starting in the early 1960s that Turkish restiveness and demands for emigration returned once again.

By the mid-1950s it became clear that the policy of socialist internationalism was not working. The encouragement and support of ethnic Turkish institutions, instead of weakening parochial identities and replacing them with an overall socialist identity, as had been hoped, were having the opposite effect. Not only was the Turkish identity becoming stronger, but as they came under strong assimilatory pressures non-Turkish Muslims – Bulgarian-speaking Muslims (Pomaks), Gypsy Muslims, Tatars and others – were increasingly identifying themselves as Turks. This "Turkification" process was seen as a mortal danger to the viability and integrity of the Bulgarian nation and state.

The April 1956 Plenum of the Party recommended important correctives to the previous government policies toward minorities. Soon after the April 1956 Plenum and during subsequent plenums decisions were made to assimilate Turkish and other minorities in the country into the mainstream Bulgarian culture. The word assimilation was never used. Instead "ethnic unification", "integration of the Bulgarian Gypsies, Turks and others into the socialist way of life", "raising the class, party, patriotic and international consciousness of the people", "asserting a socialist lifestyle and culture, a set of socialist rituals", and so on became the operative

---

[5] Mizov (1965) treats Islam as nothing more than a compilation of superstitions and prejudices and advocates a determined fight to eradicate it in Bulgaria.

phrases. Apparently these decisions were made by a small group of Politburo members and in great secrecy.

It is difficult to ascertain exactly how and when the decision to force Turks to assimilate was made. According to the well-known Bulgarian historian, diplomat, and politician Nikolai Todorov, discussions of the topic started in the late 1960s. Toward the end of the 1960s, the then foreign minister, Ivan Bašev, proposed the development of a comprehensive strategy to deal with the "Turkish problem" in Bulgaria. During the middle 1970s a special committee was established within the Central Committee of the BCP to study the issue and make recommendations to the Politburo. Nikolai Todorov was a member of the original committee but left it soon after its establishment. Apparently the committee made various recommendations to the Politburo which were found unacceptable and sent back to the committee for further work. One recommendation suggested the use of several approaches to integrate the Turkish population into Bulgarian society. These included programs to raise the cultural level of this population; to disseminate socialist values among Turks; to develop programs to overcome religious obstacles to their integration, and to take steps to gain their trust and confidence. These recommendations were accepted by the Politburo but were not implemented. It seems that some of its members, including Živkov, felt that stronger measures were needed to assimilate the Turks into mainstream Bulgarian culture, including replacement of Turkish names with Bulgarian ones. This new approach was presented to a meeting of influential party members by Georgi Atanasov. He reminded the participants in the meeting that the Constitution recognized the right of every citizen to change his/her name. In the same meeting Atanasov suggested that the low cultural and educational levels among Turks and the use of the Turkish language could create serious obstacles to change of names. Serious opposition was a real possibility. Any opposition to the name-change campaign, in Atanasov's words, "will be eliminated by fire and sword" (Acaroğlu 1992: 17-22).[6] That is what exactly happened during

[6] This article is a translation of a report prepared by Nikolai Todorov for presentation to the Cental Committee on 11 November 1989, one day after the ouster of Živkov from power. Because the report was extremely critical of the assimilation campaign and named prominent party leaders as major players in it, he was not allowed to present it to the Central Committee or to publish it in Bulgaria. The report was made available to Radio Free Europe and broadcast on 25 December 1989.

the winter months of 1984 and 1985 when close to one million Turks were forced to replace their Turkish-Muslim names at gun point. For several years afterwards the triumphant words "Finally we found a solution to a very difficult problem" were frequently mentioned in the news media. At the same time no one was willing to take credit for this triumph, although some credited the party leader Živkov as the creator of a new Bulgarian nation.

Even after 1989, the responsibility for the "revival process" has not been established. In a sociological survey carried out among party workers in ethnically mixed areas after the ouster of Živkov in November 1989, 13.1 per cent of the respondents believed that it was a Politburo decision; 6.3 per cent believed the decision was made by the Central Committee; and 4.2 per cent thought that it was Živkov who made the decision. More than two-thirds of the respondents, 69 per cent, had no idea of who made the decision and how it was made. More than 90 per cent also doubted the existence of any documents that would shed light on these issues (Petkov and Fotev 1989: 210-11).

Given the enormity of the problem, the name-changing campaign among the Turks must have involved careful planning, close coordination with trusted regional party leaders and police officials, and massive deployment of police and armed forces. The campaign was carried out in two stages. During the first stage, which lasted from late December 1984 until 14 January 1985, all Turks living in the Rhodopes region of southeastern Bulgaria were forced to assume Bulgarian names. Also during this stage, Turks who were born in the Rhodopes region but had moved to other parts of the country were also forced to change their names. The campaign was carried out in great secrecy. According to Kertikov, "[O]nly the first secretaries of district committees and some other responsible party, state and public figures *were officially informed* [by the Ministry of the Interior] *for the first time* of the 'results of the substitution of Turkish-Arab names with Bulgarian ones' at a meeting with a part of the Politburo members on 18 January 1985" after the campaign was well under way (Kertikov 1991: 84). Four days earlier, on 14 January 1985, "over 310,000 persons had already had their names changed, including 214,000 in Kurdjali, 41,000 in Haskovo, 22,000 in Plovdiv, 5,000 in Pazardjik, 3,500 in Silistra 11,000 in Stara Zagora, 9,000 in Bourgas and 3,000 in Blagoevgrad districts" (Kertikov, 1991: 84).

The impression was created among the Turks of northeastern Bulgaria that they were the only "true" Turks in Bulgaria; that the Turks of southeastern Bulgaria were really the descendants of "Islamized Bulgarians". Immediately after the completion of the first stage of the campaign there were sad episodes of Turks from the northeast who had married Turks from the Rhodopes divorcing or leaving their spouses because they did not want to live with "Bulgarians". But in February 1985 the Turks living in the rest of Bulgaria were also forced to change their names. The entire Central Committee was officially informed about the campaign in a closed session during the February 1985 Plenum of the Central Committee, after the campaign was over.

Specific methods used during the name-changing campaign varied according to whether Turks lived in ethnically homogeneous villages or ethnically mixed villages or urban areas. Radenkov, in a comprehensive description of the treatment of the Turkish minority during and immediately after the 1984-5 campaign, provides details about the specific methods used in villages and urban areas.[7] Since this is a rare eyewitness account of the specific methods used during the campaign, I quote extensively from it. According to Radenkov's account (in *East European Reporter* 1989: 27):

> The village was surrounded by the militia and/or special internal troops or regular army troops using armored personnel carriers, trucks or even light tanks. The village thus isolated, the mayor, the Communist Party Secretary and a few officials were then summoned and asked to sign a declaration that the village(rs) be given Bulgarian names . . . They were handed lists of Bulgarian names and then usually allowed twenty-four hours to consider. Most of these men agreed to cooperate and were then held up as models for the rest of the village . . . Those who refused to comply, however, were taken by the militia from their homes . . . Eventually they signed. Those who still refused were often held in a cellar for several days, abused, threatened and beaten. If they still persisted, then imprisonment ensued.

In some instances, "officials with new identity cards . . . visited

---

[7] This study was smuggled out of Bulgaria and made available to the *East European Reporter*, which published excerpts from it.

every household and the inhabitants were forced, in some cases allegedly at gun-point, to accept the new cards and to sign 'voluntary' forms requesting their new names. In other instances the inhabitants of ethnic Turkish villages were assembled in the main square of the village, where they were then obliged to accept the new cards" (Amnesty International 1986: 9).

Similar methods were used in villages with ethnically mixed populations, but in urban areas with predominantly Bulgarian populations, show of massive force would have been impractical. In these areas "the name-changing operation and the issuing of new identity cards were carried out at the work-place, and in some instances ethnic Turks were given a period of days to accept the new cards or else lose their jobs" (Amnesty International 1986: 9). In urban areas, the authorities also used a provision in the law to call up all Turkish males up for reserve duty. Radenkov's account continues:

> The Turks were called up individually and placed in well-guarded military camps somewhere in the country. Once there, they had no communication with their families, as their destinations were a military secret, and care was taken that each individual did not come into contact with any Turks; they were surrounded by Bulgarians. They were then summoned by their commanding officer and informed that the Ministry of Defense had issued an order whereby all Turks in the army had to assume Bulgarian names. Each Turk was warned that should he refuse, he would be court-martialled for disobeying an order from his superiors. Furthermore, he was reminded that his family now was alone, and since they would have to go through the same procedure, they might be in need of his help. He was then locked in a guarded room, as if under arrest, and given a few hours to consider a list of Bulgarian names from which he would be able to choose. At this point, the majority of the men agreed to sign a declaration stating that they wished of their own free will to adopt the Bulgarian name selected. If a man refused to sign, he was threatened, abused, kept in custody and in some cases beaten. If he persisted, he was not court-marshaled (since in all likelihood, no ministerial order actually existed), but was escorted to a labor camp and detained there until he eventually signed the declaration. With

few exceptions, even the most stubborn gave in after two or three months and were then released.

Meanwhile, local party officials, accompanied by police, would visit the families of the men and tell them that their sons/husbands/fathers had changed their names, as required by army regulations. The family members of the men were urged to follow suit. Their refusal, they were told, would create serious difficulties, not only for their loved ones in the army, but for themselves as well. Many, especially women, refused to change their names at this point. They wanted to wait until they heard from their menfolk in the army. However, they quickly found that life without new passports with Bulgarian names would be difficult, if not impossible.

> Then, however, when collecting their salaries women were asked to produce their passports; if the name in the passport was still Turkish, then no money was issued "by special orders from above" (no written order was ever shown). If a woman then ran to the bank to withdraw some money, she was refused on the same grounds. If she or her children needed medical help, they were refused treatment or admission to the hospital [. . .] It was also possible, of course, that she might come across a passport check in the street or on a bus, and her passport would be stamped "not valid". From that point on, she might be detained "for identification", fined, arrested and finally even sentenced for "violation of the passport regulations." The militia thus turned her into a criminal and she was punished accordingly. This combination of threats and economic and administrative sanctions . . . was effective; the mothers signed both for themselves and on behalf of their children. . .

After the completion of the name-change campaign an all-out assault was launched on everything Turkish or Muslim. Villages would be surrounded by large police and armed forces and the militia would then

> . . . . go from house to house and anything that resembled Turkish garment they would seize . . . tear up, and trample into the mud. Ancient folk costumes that had been passed down from mother to daughter for generations were taken from old wooden chests and thrown onto a heap outside. To this pile would be added all books found in Turkish, whether

copies of the Koran, kept as heirlooms, or atheist communist propaganda. The raid was always timed so that all the able-bodied men or women in the village would be away working in the nearby town or in the fields, leaving just grandparents and children.

After the new names had been adopted, using the old Turkish names was forbidden. If anyone was caught doing so, they would be harassed, fined and sometimes even fired from their jobs. The state in fact even went one step further and decided to eliminate all traces of the old names totally. In order to give the new names more credibility, old men were forced to change the names of their forefathers to correspond with the names they had chosen for themselves. Not even tombstones were spared: the old name had to be removed, which often meant breaking the stone. Furthermore, all case histories of Turkish patients were removed from hospitals and destroyed for fear someone might use them to prove that in fact a few Turks did exist in Bulgaria . . .

The name-changing campaign among Turks was met with violent resistance, with predictable results. Scores of Turks who resisted the campaign were killed, hundreds, if not thousands, were arrested and sent to hard labor camps, and scores were banished to different parts of Bulgaria far from their home communities. It was alleged that scores of Turks were beaten, tortured, and committed suicide. There were also reports of rapes, stripping of Turkish women in public in order to force their menfolk into submission, public beatings, and the like. Turks were forced to sign documents declaring that they had no relatives in Turkey and that they did not want to emigrate to Turkey. Even more than ten years after the campaign, a full accounting of the number of Turks killed, arrested and imprisoned or sent to internal exile is not available. Many of the civil and police authorities who abused their powers during the campaign have not been brought to justice. Worse still, many of these people remain in their jobs to this day.

Soon after the conclusion of the campaign the Turks were forbidden to speak Turkish in public conveyances and public places. Those who disobeyed were subject to harassment and fines (see Appendix F). Signs saying "It is forbidden to speak in a non-Bulgarian language in this shop" and "Communication between Bulgarian citizens should be carried out in Bulgarian" were prominently displayed in shops and restaurants in areas where Turks lived. Although the wording of these signs appears ambiguous their meaning was clear to everyone. Radios and tape recorders were confiscated so that Turks could not listen to news programs from Radio Istanbul, Radio Free Europe, Voice of America and similar independent sources. Turkish areas of Bulgaria were declared off-limits to foreigners. No criticism of these draconian measures, public or private, was tolerated. The letters written by Turks to their relatives in Turkey were routinely read. Those Turks who had complained to their relatives about their plight were accused of slander against the state and sentenced to long prison terms (see Appendix G).

As a response to continuing international pressure the Bulgarian authorities finally admitted that Turks were replacing their Turkish names with Bulgarian ones, but insisted that they were doing so voluntarily and on their own initiative. The Bulgarian government launched a propaganda blitz, both for foreign and domestic consumption, in an attempt to repudiate the charges leveled against it in the international press. Seven members of the Central Committee Secretariat were sent to the districts of Blagoevgrad, Kŭrdžali, Haskovo, Burgas, Ruse, Silistra, Veliko Tŭrnovo, and Razgrad, which had large Turkish and Muslim concentrations, to brief local party officials on the party line.

The criticism and concerns expressed in the international press were ignored. The request by the government of Turkey for a high-level meeting to arrive at a comprehensive migration agreement was rejected on the grounds that there were no Turks in Bulgaria. The request for a Turkish parliamentary delegation to visit affected areas was rejected on the grounds that what was happening in Bulgaria was entirely an internal matter. Even the suggestion of such a visit was interpreted as meddling in the internal affairs of Bulgaria. The charge of persecution of Muslims and forcing them to change their names was false, Bulgarian officials said, because freedom of religion and freedom from deprivation of nationality were protected by the Constitution (*Sofia News* 1985a: 9).

The reasons behind the assimilation campaign

What may have been the reasons behind the forced assimilation campaign against Turks and other Muslims? Several reasons have been suggested, some more plausible than others. First, for the last twenty years or more there had been serious concerns among Bulgarian demographers about population trends in the country. They had projected that by the 1990s the Bulgarian population would experience a zero or negative population growth. Government policies to stimulate the birth rate, such as generous paid maternity leaves, job security at the end of maternity leaves, and other material benefits to families who chose to have additional children, had not worked among Bulgarians. Turkish and other Muslim families took advantage of these benefits to a greater degree than Bulgarian families. The reason for this difference is not hard to find: most Muslims lived in rural areas, where additional children were seen as economic assets in the agricultural economy, while in urban areas, where most Bulgarians lived, additional children were an economic liability. If the trend of a declining Bulgarian population and an increasing Muslim population is seen against the backdrop of a projected increase in the demand for labor in the future, the concern of demographers is understandable. If the Muslim population was growing at twice the rate as the Bulgarian one, as demographers said it was, then, in the future the country would have to rely on Muslims, a suspect population, for its labor needs. Higher growth rate among Turks was especially worrisome.

On the one hand, Turkish citizens of Bulgaria were in a position to supply the future labor needs of Bulgaria. As Baest (1985: 26) observes:

> A labor reserve of 1.2 to 1.5 million Bulgarian Muslims, two-thirds of whom are Turks lacking appropriate education and "consciousness", can only be completely integrated when potential sources of conflict – e.g., national consciousness, religion, language, and education – are eliminated.

On the other hand, a substantial rise in the number of Turks in Bulgaria, it was feared, could lead to demands for some sort of autonomy on their part in the future if they were not assimilated quickly. Bulgarian officials heightened this fear by spreading panicky rumors that by the year 2000 Turks and Gypsies would make up the majority of the population in Bulgaria. This projection was wildly inaccurarte. Baest (1985: 26) continues:

Even allowing for a slight decline in the Bulgarian growth rate – for which there is some evidence – the proportions could alter only slightly. In fifteen years time a population of 83% Bulgarians would confront 15% Turks and Romani [Gypsies], instead of 85% to 12.5% – hardly a dramatic shift.

A serious problem with most official statistics in Bulgaria from the communist period is that they are unreliable or suspect. The authorities often manipulated statistics for political purposes. Even a cursory glance at the figures in Table 3.3 reveals them as suspect. Figures indicate no appreciable decline in fertility among Bulgarians between 1956 and 1974 (from 17 per thousand to 16.5 per thousand), while they indicate a significant decline in fertility among Turks (from 40.4 to 24.5) and Gypsies (from 36.5 to 18.3) during the same period. These figures are probably close to the truth. The figures on mortality for the three groups are problematic, however. They indicate that while the mortality rate had actually increased among Bulgarians, there had been a precipitous decline in mortality among Turks (from 15.5 to 6.8) and Gypsies (from 10.7 to 5.3). A comparison of mortality figures for Bulgarians and Gypsies is especially instructive. The fertility figures for the two groups are virtually the same.

Table 3.3. BIRTHS, DEATHS AND NATURAL INCREASE BY ETHNIC GROUP (per 1,000 population)

	Bulgarians			Turks			Gypsies		
	Births	Deaths	Natural increase	Births	Deaths	Natural increase	Births	Deaths	Natural increase
1956	17.0	8.7	8.3	40.4	15.5	25.2	36.5	10.7	25.8
1965	13.8	8.3	5.5	29.0	7.3	21.7	18.5	4.2	14.3
1966	13.5	8.4	5.1	26.7	7.6	19.1	24.1	5.4	18.7
1967	13.6	9.1	4.5	26.3	8.0	18.3	23.2	6.3	16.9
1968	15.4	8.8	6.6	28.9	7.0	21.9	25.7	5.4	20.3
1969	15.7	9.7	6.0	27.3	7.8	19.5	24.5	6.2	18.3
1970	15.1	9.3	5.8	26.4	7.0	19.4	23.0	5.4	17.6
1971	14.8	10.3	4.8	25.2	7.5	17.7	18.3	5.6	12.7
1972	14.4	10.2	4.2	23.2	7.3	15.9	18.2	5.7	12.5
1973	15.5	9.9	5.6	23.2	6.7	16.5	18.5	5.1	13.4
1974	16.5	10.3	6.5	24.5	6.8	17.7	18.3	5.3	13.0

Source: Donkov 1994: 43.

The higher natural increase among Gypsies is accounted for

almost entirely by their much lower mortality. Since most Gypsies lived in rural areas or urban ghettos where access to health care was poor, and most Bulgarians lived in urban areas with better access to health care, the significant differences in mortality between the two groups cannot be true. Moreover, the alarmist pronouncements of Bulgarian demographers that Gypsy families averaged more than twice as many children as Bulgarian families are not supported by the statistics. The same can be said about differences in mortality rates between Bulgarians and Turks. Nevertheless, such dubious statistics were often used by party officials to justify assimilation campaigns against Turks and other Muslims.

More recent statistics indicate that there is not a significant difference between the birth rate among Bulgarians and other ethnic groups in the country. According to Donkov (1994: 45), in 1992 the number of births per thousand for the country as a whole was 10.5. In districts with Turkish, Gypsy, and Pomak concentrations the number of births was higher, ranging from 14.7 in Kŭrdžali to 10.7 in Haskovo (Sliven 13.2; Razgrad 13.1; Tŭrgovište 12.6; Šumen 12.6; Silistra 11.7; Pazardžik 11.6; and Smoljan 11.0), nowhere near high enough to justify frequent warnings during recent decades of an impending demographic catastrophe for the Bulgarian nation. Dire warnings that the "demographic invasion of minorities" would make the Bulgarians a minority within their own country were politically motivated and nothing more than fear mongering. If Bulgarian demographers had analysed demographic trends in Bulgaria within a broader European context, they would have realized that trends in Bulgaria were neither unique nor catastrophic. Declines in fertility rates, in one form or another, even in greater strength, have been a pattern in many European countries for a century or more. This trend has been closely associated with the spread of industrialization or the rate of economic development, because as people switched from an agricultural to an industrial economy, they increasingly viewed children as an economic liability and began to have fewer of them. Demographers have called this phenomenon the third and final stage of the demographic transition, or the second demographic transition. Since Bulgarians started migrating from rural to urban areas earlier than other groups and joined the industrial economy in large numbers, they completed the demographic transition earlier. During recent decades, Turks too, especially men, have joined the industrial economy in large numbers. One consequence of this switch from agriculture to industry has been a decline in fertility. Within such a broader context the demographic trends in Bulgaria fit into the normal pattern of historical development.

Bulgarian perceptions about Turkey's intentions concerning a sizable Turkish minority in Bulgaria in the future may have been another reason behind the assimilation campaign. The Bulgarian authorities may have felt that the presence of Turks in Bulgaria, whatever their number, would color the relations between the two countries. As economic conditions in Turkey improved, Turkey might have asked for a comprehensive emigration agreement under which Bulgaria stood to lose close to 1 million people. That would have been a serious labor drain that Bulgaria could ill afford or tolerate. Moreover, the presence of a population of non-Bulgarian origin experiencing higher natural growth than the ethnic Bulgarian population would have seriously retarded the avowed goal of the government to create a homogeneous one-nation state. This may have been an important motivating factor behind the campaign (see Lewis 1995; Brisby 1985).

Third, the planned census for December 1985 may have been another factor in the decision of the Bulgarian authorities to "complete" the Bulgarization of Turks during the winter of 1984-5. Yugoslav commentators, looking back to what happened in the 1965 census, when most Macedonians were counted as Bulgarians, and the teaching of the Macedonian language was abolished by decree, called this procedure "administrative genocide". After the 1965 census, the last census which provided official information on Turks in Bulgaria, the Bulgarian authorities consistently under-reported the number of Turks in the country. The 1975 census results on the Turkish-speaking population may have considerably alarmed these same authorities and may have convinced them to undertake the drastic steps that they did. This information was declared a state secret and never published. Through forcible name changes among Turks prior to the 1985 census, the authorities may have hoped to reduce the number of Turks in Bulgaria by administrative fiat.

A fourth reason why the Bulgarian authorities decided to act when they did was the unsubstantiated fear of the influence of Turkish and/or Muslim propaganda among the Turks in Bulgaria during recent years. The influence of fundamentalism has increased significantly in Turkey during the 1980s and 1990s, with large amounts of air time devoted to religious programs on Turkish radio and television as a result. There was an increasing concern about these developments in the Bulgarian news media during the late 1970s and early 1980s.[8] Turks in Bulgaria were listening to Turkish radio programs frequently, some exclusively; some even watched Turkish television programs by modifying their television sets in order to be able to receive programs from Turkey. Turks in Bulgaria were also listening to the Turkish-language broadcasts of the BBC, Voice of Germany and Voice of America. Jamming activities against such broadcasts were not as successful as the Bulgarian authorities would have liked. To counteract religious broadcasts from Turkey and elsewhere, Bulgaria increased its own anti-Islamic propaganda output, which portrayed Islam as the handmaiden of Turkish bourgeois nationalism and religious fanaticism. The religion of Islam was seen as the major obstacle to the integration of Turks and other Muslims into Bulgarian society (see Iljazov 1981; Džambazov 1981). The Bulgarianization of the Turks was supposed to undercut the influence of Islam in the country.

Even if the demographic and other concerns of the Bulgarian authorities were legitimate, it is not clear how they thought mere replacement of names could obliterate the religious and ethnic consciousness of a population of at least 1 million Turks, perhaps 1.5 million Muslims altogether. Although the ancestral ethnicity of some Turks may have been obscure, an overwhelming majority of them spoke Turkish, identified themselves as Turks, and professed the Islamic faith. Scholars of ethnicity have noted that membership in an ethnic group is a matter of self ascription and ascription by others. Turks in Bulgaria identified themselves as Turks and were so identified by those around them. No ideological statements, no replacement of names could change that fact. On the contrary, the assault on Turkish identity in Bulgaria had the opposite effect: it strengthened the resolve of Turks to cling to their ethnic and religious identities even more tenaciously. That resolve was main-

---

[8] Džambazov (1981), for example, speculates about the hidden motives behind the renewed emphasis on religious education in Turkey during the last decade, and sees such developments as a danger to the integration of Turks into Bulgarian society.

tained throughout the 1980s and eventually led to public demonstrations against government policies beginning in May 1989. These demonstrations began on 18 May in northeastern Bulgaria and spread quickly to other Turkish areas. The uncompromising and brutal response of the authorities to these demonstrations only increased the determination of Turks to intensify their struggle. These demonstrations prompted the government to try to solve its "Turkish problem" once and for all. Scores of native Turkish intellectuals, leaders and potential leaders of Turks, were expelled from the country. A week after the start of demonstrations the government announced on national television that those "Bulgarians who had been converted to Islam" who wished to visit Turkey would be issued passports on demand. The response to this announcement was unanticipated and overwhelming. The passport offices were besieged by hundreds of thousands of Turks immediately after the announcement. Passports were issued rapidly and the Turks were told to put their affairs in order quickly and leave, and so began the biggest mass exodus in post-Second World War European history. The government euphemistically called the mass exodus "the grand excursion of 1989". Between June and August, when Turkey closed its border with Bulgaria to emigrants without proper visas, over 350,000 Turks left the country.[9] The mass exodus of Turks from Bulgaria over such a short period of time caused severe economic and social dislocations in the country which contributed to the downfall of the Živkov regime on 10 November 1989. Eventually, especially after the ouster of Živkov from power, over 150,000 Turks returned to Bulgaria, but more than 200,000 chose to remain in Turkey permanently (Vasileva 1992: 348).

The efforts of the government to eradicate the Turkish social, cultural, and religious heritage between 1984 and 1989 in its attempt to create a single-nation state not only failed but heightened the already existing differences between Bulgarians, Turks, Gypsies, and Pomaks. The feelings of exclusivity and separateness which had existed between these groups prior to 1984 were strengthened. These feelings have not only carried into the post-communist

[9] Vasileva (1992: 348), using information from newspapers, polls, and information provided by municipal authorities, estimates that 369,839 Turks left Bulgaria in 1989; for the expulsion of Turks from Bulgaria, see also Helsinki Watch (1989) and Poulton (1993: 153–61).

period, but have become more pronounced than ever. Ilchev and Perry (1993: 36-7) note that the mutual perceptions of Bulgarians and Turks largely depend on whether or not they are personally acquainted.

> In most areas of the country contacts between ethnic Bulgarians and ethnic Turks have traditionally been limited. In fact, many Bulgarians spend their entire lives without becoming personally acquainted with a Turk or a Pomak, and vice versa. Among those ethnic Bulgarians who have friends in the ethnic Turkish community, the PER researchers discovered that the general perception of Turks as a group differed significantly from that of ethnic Turks as individuals. In general, the Bulgarian perception of the generic "Turk," formed by memory, education, and the media as well as by oral tradition, is negative. Turks, for their part, tend to see Bulgarians as distant or even hostile. On the other hand, individuals from one group often respond positively to individuals from the other. The highest degree of intolerance is found in northeastern and southeastern Bulgaria, where there are mixed populations in which ethnic Turks are in the majority, particularly in the countryside. The probable cause of this intolerance is fear on the part of ethnic Bulgarians that they will become economically disadvantaged as a result of being a local minority or that they will ultimately be forced to abandon their homes and property because increasing Islamization and Turkification of the region will make non-Muslims unwelcome. But even in these areas, ethnic Bulgarian negativism is usually displayed toward the amorphous group "the Turks," not toward individual Turks.

> Preliminary findings indicate that Turks make the same sort of distinctions concerning the group versus the individual as do ethnic Bulgarians. They tend to have positive views of Bulgarian Christian neighbors but mixed feelings about ethnic Bulgarians as a people.

The negative portrayal of Turks as the traditional enemy, as devious, duplicitous, rapacious, cruel, and barbaric has been perpetuated in Bulgaria through literature, schoolbooks, works of art, folklore, and other means. Generations of students, including Turkish students, have been exposed to this negative image of Turks as a group. As Ilchev and Perry observe, "No attempt was made until very recently to balance the unfavorable and often inaccurate historical image of Turks . . . with the contributions of Turks to Bulgaria's history, society, culture, and economy." Apparently, Bulgaria is still not ready for such a reappraisal. A recent textbook with a more positive portrayal of Turks, approved by the Ministry of Education, was met by loud protests from Bulgarian teachers and intellectuals (Ilchev and Perry 1993: 37).

The ethnic Turks have reacted to all the ordeals inflicted upon them – the assimilation campaign under communist rule and its tragic aftermath in 1989, and the recent nationalist propaganda – with extreme forbearance. Unlike various ethnic groups in other East European countries, such as former Yugoslavia and the republics of the former Soviet Union, the Movement for Rights and Freedoms (MRF), the so-called Turkish party, has not called for independence, not even autonomy in areas where Turks and other Muslims are concentrated. They have only called for the recognition of their rights as Turks and as Muslims and for a chance to participate in the political, social and economic life of the country on an equal footing with all other citizens.

Pomaks[10]

Because of the inconsistent and conflicting government policies toward Pomaks and the controversies about their status since independence from Ottoman rule in 1878, few reliable statistics exist on this population. During the initial decades after independence, they were identified as Turks based on their religious affiliation. They were encouraged either to emigrate to Turkey or to assimilate by converting to Orthodox Christianity. For most of the twentieth century, Pomaks have been characterized as Bulgarian Muslims, descendants of Bulgarians who had been forced to convert to Islam during the Ottoman period. However, the Bulgarian origins of Pomaks did not gain wide currency for several decades. Čičovski, writing in 1934 accused the Bulgarian authorities of not being able "to make a difference between Turks and Bulgarian

---

[10] Although the word Pomak has some negative connotations, the alternative designations are not much better. "Bulgarian-speaking Muslims" is unwieldy, while "Bulgarian Muslims" or "Bulgarian Mohammedans" are confusing. There is no consensus among Bulgarian Muslims themselves. Depending on the specific situation, they identify themselves as Bulgarians, Turks, Muslims or Pomaks. Moreover, Bulgarians, Turks and other groups generally refer to them as Pomaks.

Mohammedans. We regard them as Turks because of the religion and often hate them. We persecute them. In their willingness to buy their property for nothing, crafty speculators make every effort to fan our hatred towards them, to discredit them so as to achieve their emigration" (quoted in Mancev 1992: 37).

From 1878 until the end of the First World War no reliable statistics were available on the number of Pomaks in Bulgaria. The 1920 census listed 88,339 Muslims who identified their ethnicity as Bulgarian. In 1926 102,351 Muslims identified their ethnic affiliation as Bulgarian and in 1934 134,125 Muslims identified their mother tongue as Bulgarian (Shoup 1981: 136). Most of these were Pomaks who lived in the Rhodope region. Table 3.4 shows the ethnic and religious composition of the Rhodope population in 1939. Pomaks were in the majority in Devin, Zlatograd, and Smoljan districts. Overall, they accounted for 25.6 per cent of the Rhodope population.

Table 3.4. ETHNIC AND RELIGIOUS COMPOSITION OF THE RHODOPE POPULATION, 1939

District	Bulgarians		Turks	Others	Total
	Christians	*Muslims*	*Turks*	*Others*	*Total*
Ardino	2,426	15,234	27,831	47	45,538
Asenovgrad	77,908	5,493	3,851	2,245	89,497
Devin	6,146	13,000	2,431	193	21,770
Zlatograd	1,052	14,635	6,534	91	22,312
Krumovgrad	2,683	4,667	32,764	610	40,724
Goce Delčev	35,780	15,043	2,540	1,190	54,553
Peštera	42,135	9,057	3,340	3,436	57,968
Razlog	26,075	8,256	37	982	35,352
Smoljan	15,946	17,197	10	432	33,585
Totals	210,151	102,584	79,338	9,226	401,299

Source: Monov 1972: 11.

In the several censuses carried out in Bulgaria after the Second World War Pomaks were counted as Bulgarians. The estimates of the number of Pomaks in Bulgaria during the post-Second World War period ranged from 134,460 in 1956 (based on Mizov 1965: 196) to about 170,000 in 1972 (Monov 1972: 11) and 286,971 in 1989 (Konstantinov, Alhaug and Igla 1991: 104). The latter figure was provided to the authors by the Ministry of Internal Affairs and local authorities. During the 1992 census the category "religious affiliation" was restored to census forms. According to the preliminary results of the 1992 census, 163,735 Bulgarians by mother tongue and 142,938 by ethnic affiliation identified their religious affiliation as Muslim.

Today the Pomaks live in compact communities in the Rhodope mountains in southern Bulgaria from the Mesta River valley in the west to the Haskovo-Kŭrdžali line in the east. A small number of Pomaks also live in several villages around Loveč on the northern slopes of the Balkan mountains. Some of these are families of Pomak activists: the inhabitants of the village of Hadžijska, for example, were resettled there from the Rhodopes between 1948 and 1952 as a punishment for resisting government efforts to assimilate them. Although these families were given permission to return to their native villages in 1954, some chose to remain in their new communities. Compact Pomak settlements are also found in the adjoining regions of northern Greece and the Republic of Macedonia.

Depending on the ideology of political leaders, the Pomaks have been allowed to maintain their religious identity unhindered (even, at times, encouraged to practice their religion), while at other times considerable pressure has been applied to make them assimilate into mainstream Bulgarian culture by replacing their Muslim names with Bulgarian ones and by renouncing their faith. The changing attitudes of various Bulgarian governments towards the Pomaks is illustrated by a number of name-changing campaigns carried out during the twentieth century. They were forced to replace their Turkish/Muslim names with conventional Bulgarian names four times this century, in 1912, 1942, 1962, and 1971-4, and allowed to reclaim their original names four times, in 1913, 1945, 1964 (partial restoration), and 1990 (Konstantinov, Alhaug and Igla 1991: 24). The name-changing campaigns of 1912 and 1942 were also marked by intense missionary pressure upon Pomaks to convert to Orthodox Christianity, and thousands were converted.

Because of the controversy about their origin, Bulgaria, Greece, and Turkey have all claimed Pomaks as their own. Scholars in each country have presented "history" to serve their own national myths about the origin of this population. Over the years various theories have been offered about their origin, each theory supported by evidence of dubious value. To some Balkan historians they are the descendants of ancient Thracian tribes who, over the centuries, "were Hellenized, Latinized (Romanized), Slavicized, Christianized, and were converted to Islam" (Seypel 1989: 42). Greek historians point to some Greek words preserved in the language spoken by Pomaks that have been lost to modern Greek to make the case for the Hellenic origins of this population, while conveniently forgetting that today the Pomaks speak a dialect of Bulgarian and that the language also contains many Turkish words. Both Bulgarians and Greeks have also pointed to the physical appearance of Pomaks – predominance of fair skin and blue eyes – as proof of their Bulgarian or Greek origin. They have even resorted to DNA analysis of blood collected from Pomaks to prove the "racial purity" of this population. There was a scandal in Bulgaria in 1994 over a project by a group of doctors at the Stara Zagora hospital to collect blood from Pomaks and send it to a laboratory in Skopje, Macedonia, for analysis to prove their Bulgarian origins.

Bulgarian scholars have used mainly linguistic evidence in support of their contention that Pomaks are of Bulgarian origin: that they speak a Bulgarian dialect which contains numerous archaic Bulgarian constructions, conveniently forgetting that the language spoken by Pomaks also includes many Greek and Turkish words as well as linguistic patterns unique to it. They also have pointed to "Christian" and "pre-Christian" features in Pomak culture. Silverman (1989: 614) notes that,

> Pomaks, especially women, have continued to enact Christian and pre-Christian rites such as keeping holy water and crosses, venerating Christian shrines and priests and making offerings to saints and pagan deities. Pomaks share with Bulgarian Christians many institutions such as fictive kinship (god-parenthood) and such customs as exchange of red eggs on Easter, the tapping of cornel branches on New year's Day, the divining of young girls' fortunes on St John's Day and the decoration of the house on St. George's day . . . Pomak life-cycle celebrations, such as weddings, conform to Christian practice . . .

Consequently the "Pomaks not only are Bulgarians, but have also preserved their ancient Bulgarian culture in a 'purer' form and substance than their Christian brethren" (Seypel 1989: 42). They are Muslim today only because they were forced to convert to Islam by the Ottomans during the seventeenth century. However, does the existence of "Christian" elements indicate the origins of the Pomaks or something else? Alternative explanations have rarely been explored. The Pomaks have lived in a largely Bulgarian Christian milieu for centuries. Where members of different religious traditions live in close proximity to one another, mutual borrowings of elements from each tradition are quite common, while the core belief systems are maintained intact.

Turkish scholars, on the other hand, have dispensed with linguistic and cultural arguments and have emphasized the Islamic religion of the Pomaks as proof of their Turkish origin. They are Muslim, therefore they must be Turks. They have also attempted

.... to find relationships between Pomaks and Turkish tribes – Perchenegs, Avars, Kumans – who trickled into Europe before the conquest of the Balkans by the Ottomans. For example, Memişoglu (1991) calls them "Pomak Turks" and traces their origins to the Cumans who settled in the Rhodopes during the eleventh century. Moreover, he asserts that the Cumans were converted to Islam prior to the Ottoman conquest of the Balkans, presumably by Muslims from North Africa and the Middle East who made sporadic contacts with Balkan populations from the end of seventh century on. When the Ottoman Turks moved into the Rhodopes during the fourteenth century the Cumans were already Muslims and aided the Ottomans in conquering the area. Christian Bulgarians called the Cumans *'pomagač'* (helper or collaborator). This name was later shortened to "Pomak". Thus, Pomaks and Turks are not only related by religion, but Pomaks are also "pure-blooded" Turks, representing the oldest Turkish population in Europe (Seypel 1989: 43).

The word "Pomak" itself has been subject to heated debate as scholars in Bulgaria, Greece, and Turkey have put their spin on it to support their own particular myths about the origin of this population (Seypel 1989: 47-8). The ideas of the Pomaks themselves about their origin and history have been generally ignored in these debates. They have had to react to externally imposed notions about their identity, notions that have changed according to the whims of different governments in power over the years. A brief review of their experience in Bulgaria during this century will illustrate the point.

After the Second World War the Bulgarian origins of Pomaks gained official support. Now they were considered Bulgarians, "flesh of the flesh and blood of the blood" of the Bulgarian nation. After 1948 repeated attempts were made "to induce Pomaks to change their names, renounce their faith and become integrated into the socialist Bulgarian state" (Poulton 1993: 111). Some Pomaks who resisted the initial campaign (1948-52) were resettled to other areas of Bulgaria, far away from their natal communities.

As Pomaks came under increasing assimilatory pressure, many among them began to identify themselves as Turks in an attempt to preserve their Muslim identity and integrity. This "Turkification" process was seen by the government as a mortal danger to its goal of establishing a single-nation state. After the April 1956 Plenum of the Communist Party steps were taken to counteract this alarming trend among Pomaks. In April 1962 the Politburo approved "Measures against the Turkish Self-identification of Gypsies, Tatars and Bulgarians professing the Mohammedan Religion" (see Appendix H). The Politburo decision identified numerous factors to explain this trend, including Islam, Turkish/Arabic names, Turkish reactionary propaganda, religious fanaticism, resettlement of Pomak families from the Rhodopes to Turkish areas in the late 1940s and early 1950s, intermarriage between Pomaks and Turks and bringing up children born to such unions as Turks, homogenous Muslim units in the armed forces, and so on. Similar explanations were given for the Turkification of Tatars and Gypsy Muslims.

The Politburo recommended specific measures to counteract and reverse this trend. It also called for "a systematic ideological and political struggle against the Turkish religious and chauvinistic propaganda and its pan-Turkish and pan-Islamic aims and aspirations" (Helsinki Watch 1991: 71). The specific recommendations included developing detailed instructions for people working in registry offices "that religion and personal names are not criteria for nationality. It must also be made clear that intermarriage does not lead to change of nationality of the spouses. The children of the intermarried couples can be registered as Bulgarians completely voluntarily and with the explicit agreement of the parents" (Helsinki Watch 1991: 71). Citizens of non-Bulgarian descent must be informed that they can change their names and register themselves and their families as Bulgarians by a simplified procedure that does not require court permission or a written application. More specifically:

> The people's councils must not allow Bulgarian Muslims and Gypsies to move to villages or towns with compact Turkish populations.
>
> The Ministry of Education and Culture and the regional people's councils must take measures so that the Turkish language is not taught to the children of Gypsies, Tatars, and Bulgarian Muslims. These children must be taught in Bulgarian. The appointment of Turkish teachers at schools where the children of Gypsies, Tatars, and Bulgarian Muslims predominate must be avoided. The children of Bulgarian Muslims and Gypsies must not be allowed to live in hostels or study in the same groups with Turkish children whenever this is possible (Helsinki Watch 1991: 72).

Muslim clergymen should be fully informed about this decision and communicate it clearly to Bulgarian and Gypsy Muslims and Tatars. Moreover, they should comply fully with all socialist legislation and refrain from carrying out reactionary propaganda in favor of Turkish affiliation of non-Turkish Muslims. Turkish clergymen should not be appointed to villages with compact Pomak, Gypsy Muslim and Tatar populations (Helsinki Watch 1991: 72-3). The decision cautioned the governmental bodies responsible for its implementation against the use of violence or other forms of force. Instead, it recommended a systematic propaganda campaign of persuasion to convince the members of the target populations of the rightness of the decision. The Politburo also recommended that,

> The Bulgarian Academy of Sciences must send complex expeditions of historians, ethnographers, philologists, etc. for the comprehensive study of the national origins and the nationality of the population in the respective regions of the country; the expeditions should establish especially the ethnic origins and the national peculiarities of Turks, Tatars, Gypsies who live in Bulgaria. The study of the historic past of the Bulgarian Muslims in the Rhodopes, the Lovech region and other parts

of the country must continue in order to make further discoveries about the historical truth about the results of the assimilation policies of the Turkish oppressors, about the mass and individual conversions to Islam.

A special section must be set up at the Institute for the History of Bulgaria at the Bulgarian Academy of Sciences for the study of the historic past of the Bulgarian Muslims (Helsinki Watch 1991: 73).

Soon afterward, part of the Pomak population were forced to replace their Muslim names with Bulgarian ones and pressured to give up their Muslim beliefs and practices. Resistance to the assimilation campaign was brutally put down. On 12 May 1964 the Politburo issued a directive, entitled "Work among the Bulgarian Mohammedan Population in the Blagoevgrad District and Its Abuses", strongly condemning the overzealousness of local party officials in carrying out the name-changing campaign, and the Muslim names of the Pomaks were partially restored. However, several years later, on 17 July 1970 the Politburo again reconfirmed the necessity of "changing Turkish-Arab names and dress" of the Bulgarian Muslim population (Kertikov 1991: 83-4). This directive was carried out between 1971 and 1973 when all Pomaks were forced to adopt Bulgarian names. The official explanation was that "the Bulgarian Mohammedan (the prescribed reference to the Pomak) was given the opportunity to regain his/her original Bulgarian identity. The Mohammedan was expected to embrace that chance with gratitude and henceforth proceed in life as a member of the Bulgarian community" (Konstantinov, Alhaug and Igla 1992; 24-5). Resistance to the campaign was fierce. Scores were killed and hundreds were arrested and sentenced to long years of hard labor.

Violence flared up again in 1989. In response to Živkov's announcement on national television on 28 May 1989 that "all Muslims who wish to go to Turkey either to visit or to remain and live there" could do so, hundreds of Pomaks in western and central Rhodopes filed applications for passports to emigrate to Turkey. While Turks were issued such passports by the tens of thousands, applications by Pomaks were denied. Local party officials explained that Živkov's announcement did not cover the Muslims living in the Sofia and Plovdiv provinces because they were "another category of people", presumably meaning Bulgarians. Local party officials categorically stated that they would not allow anyone to emigrate to Turkey and threatened anyone who persisted in their demands with arrest and imprisonment and even death. Widespread strikes, demonstrations, and riots followed, and were brutally put down. Sofia and Plovdiv provinces were sealed off from the rest of Bulgaria until the authorities could gain control of the situation (Ashley 1989: 19-23).

The change of names among Pomaks during 1971-4 required a person to acquire numerous documents with his/her new name: a new passport, a new birth certificate, new property deeds, new savings account documents, new court certificates, and so on, all reflecting the person's new status. Pomaks living in a particular town or village were required to attend public ceremonies to receive their new passports with their Bulgarian names. In Rudozem (a predominantly Pomak town in southeastern Bulgaria) the person whose name had been "restored" would be asked to walk "up to a ceremonial rostrum set up in the town square, where the applicant had to hand in his/her 'old' passport and receive a 'new' one. Naturally, many Pomaks, especially of the older generation, did not find the strength to pass through this public ordeal" (Konstantinov, Alhaug and Igla 1991: 26). Those who initially refused to go through this humiliating procedure found themselves in administrative limbo. Without documents showing their new status, they could not receive their salaries or pensions; they had no access to their bank accounts; they could not apply for a change of residence; they could be fired from their jobs and could not apply for new jobs; and people without new passports (everyone in Bulgaria was required to carry an internal passport on his/her person at all times), could be fined or imprisoned. Refusing to receive a new passport with a Bulgarian name "therefore was equivalent to administrative suicide. On the other hand, the change to the 'new' passport meant a change of one's entire administrative history. One was indeed administratively reborn" (Konstantinov, Alhaug and Igla 1991: 26). Gradually most of those who had initially refused to get a passport and other documents with their Bulgarian names were obliged to do so. Those who refused were arrested and imprisoned.

The name-changing campaign was accompanied by a series of prohibitions against Islamic rituals and practices. From 1970 until the end of 1989 it was difficult to be a Muslim in Pomak villages.

Lewis (1994: 26-7) describes the experience of Pomaks in Lutovo, a Pomak village in the Rhodope mountains:

> The mosque was closed, residents were forced to adopt Christian names, and overnight the village – originally called Lutovo – was re-dubbed Sveta Petka, after the medieval patron saint of the Bulgarian nation.
>
> For almost two decades, circumcision was forbidden in Sveta Petka, as was the celebration of Muslim holidays. Soldiers and militiamen patrolled the streets to ensure that prohibitions were enforced, and in neighboring villages protesters were shot. Women were forbidden to wear their traditional dress of loose-fitting pantaloons under skirts or embroidered aprons; those refusing to abandon traditional attire were ejected from rural buses. Many chose to walk 10 or 20 kilometers to and from work or school each day rather than compromise Muslim codes of modest dress.

As Seypel (1989: 43) puts it, "Several historic 'interruptions' have driven the Pomaks into a state of confusion in respect to their identity. The question put to them: 'Who are you?', forces them to all kinds of reactions, to taking this or that position, to optioning in this or that way, to either resistance or opportunism, depending on the assumed purpose of the question or the questioner". As a result, it is almost "impossible to penetrate into Pomak identity and its way of thinking. They themselves, the Pomaks, are indeed quite sensible as to their own psychic insecurities and their social belonging or disbelonging. [. . .] When they are asked as to their identity, Pomaks practically always tend to hesitate. Some people prefer to utter the word 'Pomak' only in a subdued manner, just like the word 'Gypsy' or 'Jew' elsewhere" (Konstantinov, Alhaug and Igla 1991: 46). Recent studies of Pomaks in Bulgaria indicate that in contrast to Bulgarians, whose answers to questions about their identity are unambiguous and straightforward, Pomak answers to similar questions indicate a two-level identity structure as indicated in Table 3.5. Which one of these levels will be activated at any given time depends on contexts. Konstantinov, Alhaug and Igla (1991: 46) note:

> In a formal, out-group context – such as an official discussion of identity problems at a meeting, when reading and discussing what the papers write about the issue, or in conversation with

Bulgarians – the religious level seems to be activated. Consequently Pomaks find it difficult to believe that they are Bulgarians, since that will mean that they are non-Mohammedans. An 'ethnic' interpretation of the identity issue is only possible therefore in an in-group context of discussion, but even then, it has to be borne in mind, a popular description such as 'impure Turk' does not automatically lead to identifying with the Bulgarian majority.

Table 3.5. TWO-LEVEL IDENTITY STRUCTURE AMONG POMAKS

	Pomak	*Turks*	*Bulgarian*
First (Islamic) level	Pomak = Muslim	Turk = Muslim	Bulgarian = non-Muslim
Second (ethnic) level	Pomak = not-pure Turk	Turk	Bulgarian

Source: Konstantinov, Alhaug and Igla 1991: 27.

Pomak notions about their identity are also influenced by the identity of their neighbors. According to Tomova, of the President's Office of Minority Affairs, "In the Western Rhodopes, where Bulgarian Muslims live among Bulgarian Christians, they refer to themselves as Turks; in the Eastern Rhodopes, where they are surrounded by ethnic Turks, they stress their identity as Bulgarians" (quoted in Lewis 1994: 27). When a Pomak who does not speak Turkish but claims to be a Turk is pressed to explain, he may assert that Pomaks have lost their original Turkish language but have preserved their faith; or that what is important is not the language a Muslim speaks but that he is a Muslim and there are no differences among Muslims. "Caught in traditional nationalistic conflicts between Bulgarians and Turks (for the Pomaks who live in Bulgaria, and between Bulgarians, Greeks and Turks for those who live in Greece), the Pomaks find it difficult to say who they are in any consistent terms beyond the label 'Pomak' " (Konstantinov, Alhaug and Igla 1991: 26). As Lewis (1994: 27) observes:

Despite the strength of their beliefs, Bulgarian Muslims are caught between two worlds – that of the Bulgarian Christians to whom they are related linguistically and that of their ethnic-Turkish fellow Muslims. To complicate matters further, the arrival in the Rhodopes of Muslim teachers from Turkey,

North Africa, and the Middle East gnaws away at local customs, even while strengthening the religious identification of Bulgarian-speaking Muslims.

Pomaks have their own version of their history, which is at odds with the official version and has been generally ignored. According to Konstantinov, Alhaug and Igla (1991: 28), this parochial version of Pomak history, based partly on myth, and partly on historic truth, goes something like this:

> The Pomaks lived for many centuries in the Rhodopes and Southern Thrace. When the Bulgarians overran those regions in 1912 (the Balkan War) their Bulgarian priests made us give up our language [Turkish] and names, but we did not give up our religion. The Bulgarians have been trying to do that ever since, but with no success.

For a while it appeared that with the end of totalitarianism in Bulgaria the Pomaks, along with other minorities, would be allowed to freely construct their own identities according to their own wishes. On 29 December 1989 the forced assimilation campaign of the communist regime was reversed. In 1990 the parliament passed a Law on Names guaranteeing the right of citizens to freely chose their names and provided legal mechanisms for the restoration of Muslim names which had been replaced by Bulgarian names (Sofia Press 1990). Article 13 (1) of the constitution approved by parliament in 1991 guaranteed freedom of conscience and religion (Sofia Press 1991: 6); Article 29 (1) declared that "No one shall be subjected to torture or to cruel, inhuman and degrading treatment, or to forcible assimilation" (Sofia Press Agency 1991: 10); and Article 54 (1) recognized the right of every citizen "to develop his own culture in accordance with his ethnic self-identification, which shall be recognized and guaranteed by law" (Sofia Press Agency 1991: 15). Unfortunately, during the last six years all of these constitutional and legislative guarantees have been ignored and the situation of the Pomaks has actually worsened. While during communist rule they had to contend only with arbitrary police coercion, today they have to respond to assaults upon their identity from a variety of sources. The parliament, the Directorate of Religious Affairs, political parties, nationalist organizations, Muslim and Christian missionaries, various cults, Turks and Bulgarians are all trying to impose their own notions of who the Pomaks are. None of these groups is willing to accept Pomak definitions of their own identity. To give only one example: during the 1992 census some 35,000 Pomaks in Blagoevgrad district identified their ethnic affiliation as Turks. In 1993 the parliament nullified these results, insisting that they were Bulgarians.

Some Pomaks, in an attempt to support an identity separate from Bulgarians and Turks, have resurrected several myths about their ancient origins. One such myth is that they are the descendants of ancient Thracians who converted to Islam during the seventh and eighth centuries as a protection against Bulgarian attempts to Slavicize them and Byzantine attempts to Christianize them. A more recent myth is that they are descendants of Arabs sent by Prophet Muhammad to the Balkans during the seventh century to spread the true faith. In each case they are claiming an ancestry that predates the history of Bulgarians and Turks on the Balkan Peninsula. Neither myth has gained a large following and both are met with ridicule by Bulgarians and Turks alike. The conflicting demands made upon them by outside forces and the unwillingness of others to take their claims seriously have led to increasing confusion, frustration and alienation among this population.

Gypsies

Demographic information about Gypsies in Bulgaria is incomplete and unreliable. The authorities have frequently manipulated demographic data about Gypsies by undercounting them, assimilating them, or even denying their existence. During communism, for example, official statistics about Gypsies were not published. After 1970 even mentioning the word "Gypsy" in the official press was taboo. Since no credible argument could be made about the Bulgarian origin of Gypsies, as far as government officials were concerned, Gypsies ceased to exist as a people. High walls were constructed around Gypsy ghettos in major towns to shield them from the view of foreigners. Nevertheless, after 1989 it was revealed that the Ministry of Internal Affairs and its local organs continued to collect demographic information about Gypsies for its own use. Ministry of Internal Affairs figures for 1975 listed 373,200 Gypsies. Apparently this figure was inadequate for the needs of the Ministry, which instructed representatives of its local organs to broaden the category "Gypsy", to include not only those who identified themselves as Gypsies, but also those who were identified by their neighbors as Gypsy as well as those who could be identified as Gypsy by "lifestyle", "cultural peculiarities", and so on. The use of these new criteria led to a substantial increase in the number of Gypsies in Bulgaria. According to the Ministry of Internal Affairs sources, in 1989 there were 576,927 Gypsies in Bulgaria, making up 6.4 per cent of the population. The authorities also noted that over 50 per cent of Gypsies preferred to identify themselves as Turks. The same sources put the number of Gypsies at 553,466 in 1992, just before the December census (Marushiakova and Popov 1993: 92-4). Yet, the 1992 census counted only 313,396 Gypsies in Bulgaria, which is considered unreliable (Table 3.6). Because Gypsies have been targets of repeated assimilation campaigns, there is a tendency for many Muslim Gypsies to identify themselves as Turks and many Christian Gypsies as Bulgarians. Marushiakova and Popov (1993: 95) consider 800,000 to be a more reliable estimate than either the census figures or those provided by the Ministry of Internal Affairs prior to the 1992 census.

Table 3.6. GYPSIES IN BULGARIA BY ETHNIC
AFFILIATION, 1900-92

	Total population	No. of Gypsies	% of total
1900	3,733,283	89,549	2.4
1905	4,035,575	99,004	2.4
1910	4,337,513	122,296	2.8
1920	4,846,954	98,451	2.0
1926	5,478,740	134,844	2.5
1934	6,077,939	149,385	2.5
1946	7,029,349	170,011	2.4
1956	7,613,709	197,865	2.6
1965	8,227,866	148,874	1.8
1975	8,727,771	n.a.	–
1985	8,948,649	n.a.	–
1992	8,487,317	313,396	3.7

Source: Donkov 1994: 37.

Information on the religious composition of the Gypsy population is even less complete and reliable because no such information

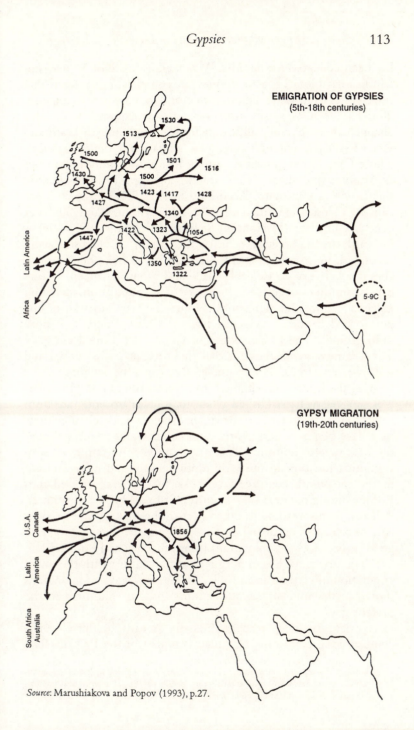

EMIGRATION OF GYPSIES
(5th-18th centuries)

GYPSY MIGRATION
(19th-20th centuries)

Source: Marushiakova and Popov (1993), p.27.

has been collected for decades. A general estimate of 50 per cent Muslim has often been mentioned. A complicating factor is that the Gypsies have used religious affiliation as a strategy of adaptation. This has been especially true for nomadic Gypsies, who have changed their religious affiliation from Christianity to Islam and vice versa depending on the religious affiliation of their neighbors. Those Gypsies living near or among Muslims identify themselves as Muslims and those living near or among Christians identify themselves as Christians. According to the 1992 census 39.2 per cent of Gypsies identified themselves as Muslims and 60.4 per cent as Christians (Nacionalen Statističeski Institut 1993b: 96).

Until the eighteenth century the origins of Gypsies were shrouded in mystery. Wild speculations about their origins abounded. Every conceivable place and group has been, at one time or another, suggested as the source of this population, including Atlantis![11] Since the eighteenth century the accumulation of linguistic and historical evidence has put Gypsy studies on more solid ground. The Indian origin of Gypsies has gained currency and it is now generally clear that they originated in central and northwestern India. For example, Romany, the language most Gypsies speak, has close affinities to Sanskrit and Hindi. However, it is not yet well established when they began to emigrate from India. Linguistic and historical evidence suggest that such migrations may have begun as early as the fifth century and continued over the next several centuries. There is mention of their presence on Byzantine territory in the early ninth century and in Byzantium in the mid-tenth century. From Asia Minor they crossed into Europe during the next two centuries, first settling in the southern Balkans, then spreading to other areas of the Balkans and beyond. The two maps reproduced on page 113 visually illustrate the two great waves of Gypsy migrations (Marushiakova and Popov 1993: 27). The first wave began during the fifth century with the initial emigration of Gypsies from India. The second wave of migrations started in the mid-nineteenth century and has continued to the present day.

Gypsies may have reached Bulgaria as early as the eleventh century, long before the Ottoman conquest of the Balkans. The

---

[11] A thorough discussion of the sources and literature on the origins and historical migrations of Gypsies is found in Marushiakova and Popov (1993: 19-38). This work also includes a very useful and comprehensive bibliography (pp. 219-33).

mention of Gypsy villages in western Bulgaria in a 1378 land grant indicates that Gypsies had been established in Bulgaria for quite a while (Malcolm 1994: 114). By the end of the fourteenth century they were found throughout the Balkans.

Evidence suggests that some Gypsies may have converted to Islam soon after the Ottoman conquest of the Balkans. According to Malcolm (1994: 15), "a law issued in 1530 by Süleyman the Magnificent for the *eyalet* of Rumelia (which included Bosnia at the time) distinguished sharply between Muslim and non-Muslim Gypsies. The former had to pay a tax of twenty-two aspers per household, the latter twenty-five; and Muslim Gypsies were forbidden to lodge with non-Muslim ones."

Compared to the treatment they received in Christian Europe, the Gypsies were relatively well treated by the Ottoman administration during the early period of Ottoman rule. Nevertheless, their social and economic position in Ottoman society was not much different than elsewhere – they were at the bottom. Even though they had the same basic legal rights as other Christians and Muslims in the Empire, they were targets of discrimination, Malcolm (1994: 115-16) notes:

> City administrations preferred to leave them living outside the city boundary, instead of assigning them a *mahala* of their own, unless they could persuade them to settle down as craftsmen. One record from Bulgaria in 1610 shows that the *cizye* or the poll-tax was set at 250 aspers for non-Muslim Gypsies and 180 for Muslim ones; despite the discount, this looks as if it must have been a form of discrimination, since Muslims generally were not to pay the *cizye* at all.

By the seventeenth century the situation of Gypsies had deteriorated and Ottoman attitudes toward them seem to have hardened. "A campaign was started in which Gypsies were accused of being prostitutes and pimps, and their taxes were heavily increased" (Malcolm 1994: 116). Ever since then the Gypsies have remained the outcast and outsider ethnic group in Bulgaria and elsewhere, at the bottom of the economic and social hierarchy and despised by Muslim and Christian alike. They have been subject to centuries of open social and economic discrimination.

Despite such discrimination, many non-Gypsies in Bulgaria have come to depend on Gypsies for a variety of services. Traditionally, the Gypsies were fortune tellers, musicians and entertainers, horse dealers and animal traders, bear keepers, blacksmiths, coppersmiths and tinsmiths, wood workers, sieve makers, comb makers, basket weavers, shoemakers, and seasonal agricultural workers (Silverman 1986: 52-4). Many of these occupations remain important to the present day.

To the average Bulgarian, the Roma constitute a homogeneous group; but there are in reality perhaps sixty or more subgroups of Roma with different outlooks and political programs. Recent research on the Gypsies of Bulgaria has led to the emergence of a much more detailed picture of the Roma than before. It is possible to categorize Gypsies broadly in accordance with three, sometimes overlapping, criteria: religion, life-style, and language. According to Ilchev and Perry (1993: 38),

> The largest category of Roma consists of the so-called *Jerlii*, who are descendants of the first Romany settlers in the Balkans. They are subdivided into the *Horohane* Roma (Muslims) and the *Gajikane* [or Dasikane] Roma (generally Christians). The second most numerous group is the *Kardarashi*, descendants of nomads who were forced to settle in the 1950s as a result of government policy [to instill in them the socialist work ethic and to assimilate them into the Bulgarian Slavic community]. They, too, are generally Christian. *Kardarashi* Roma typically live in a closed, conservative society, tightly controlled by leaders who resolve all disputes internally and without help from the state authorities. Associated with illegal activities, they have a comparatively high standard of living and see themselves as superior to the other groups of Roma. They are Christians and do not support the predominantly Turkish Movement for Rights and Freedoms (MRF), fearing that it will eventually make the Roma part of the Turkish ethnos. As a partial defense against such assimilation, Romany, the language of Gypsies, is now being taught in some primary schools.

In addition to these broad divisions, in order to understand the complexity of Roma identity, one needs to take into account such factors as endogamy, dialect, profession, traditions, taboos, and in some cases old Indian caste divisions (See Troxel 1992). Marushiakova and Popov (1993: 97-9, 109-27 and 1995: 12-20) identify ten categories of self-identity that Gypsies use to distinguish themselves from one another. These include ethnonyms that indicate whether the group is settled or nomadic, religious identity, the origin of the group, attachment to certain places, regions, towns and villages, specific professions, property status, pejorative names, kinship relations, and ethnonyms from unknown origin or meaning. Further divisions within each category complicate the matter even more. For example, three types of Turkish Gypsies are distinguished: Muslim Gypsies who speak Romany, Muslim Gypsies who speak Turkish, and Christian Gypsies who speak Romany but identify themselves as Turks indicating an historical memory of being Muslims in the past (Marushiakova and Popov 1993: 96-7).

Briefly, under communism, the government supported the development of Gypsy culture, but every decade between 1950 and 1990 they came under assimilatory pressure. A decree issued by the Council of Ministers in December 1958 called for the settlement of nomadic Gypsies. In 1959 regional and local representatives of the party were ordered to implement the decree by settling and integrating nomadic Gypsies into the Bulgarian work force. According to the decree, "In the People's Republic of Bulgaria there are not and there cannot be conditions for unemployment, begging, and traveling. Every citizen can earn his living by honest work." Therefore, the main task of regional and local party officials was "the location and employment of those Gypsies who are not engaged in socially beneficial labor [i.e., nomadic], in the factories, the cooperative farms, the cooperatives of craftsmen, the State Owned Agricultural Farms, etc." (Helsinki Watch 1991: 9-10).[12] The decree also identified tendencies among some Gypsies to identify themselves as Turks and to send their children to Turkish schools as wrong, but did not recommend specific measures to reverse this trend. This issue was addressed by a separate decision of the Politburo in April 1962. The Politburo decision noted that,

> A considerable part of the Gypsies, the Tatars, and the Bulgarian Muslims still tend to affiliate with the Turks under various forms, a tendency which is especially helped by the Muslim religion and the Turkish and Arabic names. Stimulated by the Turkish reactionary propaganda and religious fanaticism, and

---

[12] A full text of this decree is found in Helsinki Watch (1991: 61-7).

helped by the incorrect activities of a number of bodies of the people's government, more than 130,000 Gypsies and tens of thousands of Tatars and Bulgarian Muslims in many parts of the country have registered themselves as Turks (Helsinki Watch 1991: 69-70).

As discussed earlier with reference to Pomaks, the Politburo recommended a systematic campaign of education among Gypsies about the personal status laws of the country and to persuade them that all Bulgarian citizens regardless of ethnic, religious, and marital status could register themselves as Bulgarians. The Politburo recommended a series of concrete steps to reverse the trend toward Turkish identity among Gypsies as well as Tatars (see Appendix H). Soon after the announcement of this decree, over 100,000 Gypsies who had previously registered as Turks were forced to replace their Muslim names with Bulgarian ones. The same fate would befall the rest of the Gypsies with Muslim names. They, along with all of the Turks, would be forced to assume Bulgarian names during the 1984-5 winter assimilation campaign. Only after the ouster of Živkov from power in 1989, and the end of one-party rule in 1990, were Gypsies, Turks, Pomaks, and Tatars allowed to reclaim their original names. However, the recognition of the personal and civic rights of Gypsies after 1989 has not led to any improvement in the status of Gypsies in Bulgaria.

Profound economic crisis and rapid social change in Bulgaria since 1989 have led to increased prejudice, discrimination, and intolerance toward this most vulnerable minority. They have been made convenient scapegoats for the country's ills. Tomova (1992a: 20-1) mentions numerous examples of pogroms against Gypsies. For example, in the mostly Gypsy neighborhood of Stolipinovo of the city of Plovdiv, Bulgarian residents organized a "civil disobedience" protest in 1990, demanding housing in a non-Gypsy residential area, during which Gypsy houses were set on fire and scores of Gypsies were beaten. In the village of Podem sixteen Gypsy houses were burned down, several Gypsies were wounded in clashes with Bulgarians, and an elderly Gypsy woman was beaten to death. "Disputes between Bulgarians and Gypsies often flare up in villages as ex-owners claim their land back. Ex-owners and local authorities frequently resent Gypsies who have worked the land for years and apply for lots from the commons. This heightens the latter's aggressiveness which in turn is invoked by

Bulgarians demanding the local Gypsy community be resettled elsewhere."

Police violence against Gypsies has continued during the last several years. On 29 June 1992 police surrounded a Gypsy neighborhood in Pazardžik, "violently attacked members of the Gypsy community and conducted abusive house searches, damaged Gypsies' property and confiscated money and property" (Helsinki Watch 199:1). The findings of an investigation into police misconduct undertaken by the Ministry of Internal Affairs at the request of President Želev were never made public nor were any police officers disciplined. Helsinki Watch (1994) mentions several instances of police and mob violence against Gypsy neighborhoods and individual Gypsies in several other towns and villages between 1992 and 1994.

Under the transition from communism to post-communism the Gypsies have become even more marginalized than in the past, despised by almost everybody regardless whether they are Christians and Muslims. With a disheartening consistency, both groups reject, despise and resent Gypsies. A 1992 survey on inter-ethnic relations showed that Bulgarians, Turks, and Pomaks had similar and negative stereotype of Gypsies (see Table 3.7). Almost all the attributes associated with Gypsies are negative. Even the attributes such as, "carefree" and "musical/artistic" can be interpreted negatively as not involving socially beneficial labor.

Other findings of the survey also indicate the extreme prejudice against Gypsies on the part of non-Gypsies. For instance, 90.2 per cent of Bulgarians, 86.9 per cent of Turks, and 92.3 per cent of Bulgarian Muslims thought that Gypsies were criminal by nature; 72.2 per cent of Bulgarian Muslims felt that Gypsies should live in separate communities and not mix with them; 85.2 per cent of Bulgarians, 74.6 per cent of Turks, and 88.3 per cent of Bulgarian Muslims felt Gypsies alone were responsible for their plight; 64.1 per cent of Bulgarians, 57.9 per cent of Turks, and 70 percent of Bulgarian Muslims thought the government was spending too much money on the education of Gypsy children. They felt that this was a waste of money because, to them, Gypsy children were not educable (Kŭnev 1992a: 48). Eighty-nine per cent of Bulgarians, 87.8 per cent of Turks and 78 per cent of Bulgarian Muslims would not marry a Gypsy; 62.7 per cent of Bulgarians, 49 per cent of Turks, and 60.2 per cent of Bulgarian Muslims could not live in the same urban neighborhood with Gypsies; 48.2 per cent of Bulgarians, 31.5 per cent of Turks, and 35.9 per cent of Bulgarian Muslims would not live in the same village with Gypsies; 64.1 per cent of Bulgarians, 47.7 per cent of Turks, and 60.2 per cent of Bulgarian Muslims would not have Gypsies as friends; and, if they had a choice, 48.2 per cent of Bulgarians, 20.7 per cent of Turks, and 21.5 per cent of Bulgarian Muslims would not live in the same country with Gypsies (Kŭnev 1992b:55).

Table 3.7. BULGARIAN, TURKISH AND POMAK
STEREOTYPES OF GYPSIES

Bulgarians	%	Turks	%	Pomaks	%
Thieves	99	Thieves	99	Thieves	90
Carefree	94	Lazy	88	Musical/artistic	84
Lazy	93	Carefree	87	Lazy	84
Undisciplined	86	Undisciplined	79	Undisciplined	82
Musical/artistic	84	Musical/artistic	77	Carefree	78
Treacherous	65	Ungrateful	67	Profligate	63
Clannish	65	Profligate	60	Ungrateful	58
Profligate	63	Cruel	60	Treacherous	52
Ungrateful	62	Treacherous	52	Cruel	50
Cruel	60	Poor	50	Poor	41

Source: Tomova 1992b: 37.

The process of democratization in Bulgaria since 1989 created the conditions for formal participation of the Gypsies in the political process, but their participation as a community remains nominal. There are several reasons for this. First, the Bulgarian constitution prohibits the formation of political parties exclusively on ethnic or religious bases. So far no Gypsy party has been allowed to register. Second, the patterns of traditional clan-based leadership among Gypsies make unity difficult, if not impossible. As Ilchev and Perry (1993: 39) observe, political programs among the Gypsies "are often determined by the aspirations of individuals; thus, there is no cohesion at the political level, and it is not clear who represents whom. In fact, sometimes Roma leaders do not seem to represent anyone but themselves and their closest kin . . ." The linguistic, religious, ethnic, occupational, and residential diversity within the Gypsy community leads to fragmentation in political leadership and internal rivalries, which in turn make agreement on common political goals and methods for collective action difficult (see Marushiakova 1995). The lack of educated and politically experienced Gypsies also works against the possibility of forming effective organizations. Because of the general negative stereotypes of Gypsies among Christians and Muslims alike, the existing political parties are reluctant to recruit Gypsies to leadership positions.

4

THE EDUCATION OF TURKISH
SPEAKERS IN BULGARIA[1]

This chapter explores the educational experience of Turkish speakers in Bulgaria within two broad historical periods: the patterns of education that were inherited by Bulgaria from the Ottoman period which persisted relatively intact until the end of the Second World War, and the conflicting trends in the education of Turkish speakers from the end of the war to the present.

Education of Turkish speakers from 1878 till the Second World War

Bulgaria inherited a pluralistic educational system from the Ottoman Empire. From the beginning of the Ottoman state, certain groups within the state were permitted to retain their independence as separate ethno-religious communities under certain conditions. According to Sugar (1977: 3, 5),

> Any monotheist who accepted the political supremacy of Islam and was willing to live in a Muslim state under stipulated conditions became a *zimmi*, a protected person. [...] This protection extended beyond the religious freedom. [...] It involved a sort of self-government that under the Ottomans became institutionalized as the *millet* system, which was basically a minority home rule policy based on religious affiliation.

Sugar (1977: 46; see also pp. 47-9, 252-79) goes on to note that each *millet* had its own leader (*milletbaşı*) chosen by the Sultan and given "full ecclesiastical powers and jurisdiction". He also "acquired legal powers in those areas, such as marriage, divorce,

---

[1] The first half of this chapter was published under the same title in *Ethnic Groups*, (vol. 5, no. 3, 1983: 129-50). Included here with permission.

and inheritance that were regulated by canon law". As long as these *millets* fulfilled their political obligations to the state, they were free, within limits, to organize their cultural, religious, and educational institutions in accordance with their own needs and desires.[2]

In the Ottoman Empire there was no empire-wide system of education supported by taxes and administered by the state; there was no state recognized system of school districts or state established system of supervision of educational institutions. Each *millet* had the responsibility for the education of its members.

The principle of ethno-religious autonomy in the organization and support of educational institutions, especially for Turks and other non-Bulgarian minorities, survived relatively intact in Bulgaria until after the Second World War. The minority status of Turks and their cultural and religious rights were written into the provisions of numerous international treaties and bilateral agreements between Bulgaria and Turkey going back to the Berlin Peace Treaty of 1878. These rights were reaffirmed in all subsequent bilateral agreements between Bulgaria and Turkey. For example, according to Article 54 of the Neuilly Peace Treaty of 1919, national minorities in Bulgaria have "an equal right to establish, manage and control at their own expense . . . schools and other educational establishments, with the right to use their own language" in these schools (Şimşir 1986b: 4). Later on these guarantees were incorporated into the legal system of Bulgaria.

After 1878 various Bulgarian governments made attempts to introduce reforms into the educational system inherited from the Ottoman period. These reforms were aimed primarily at providing education for all school-age children, and making the teaching of the Bulgarian language compulsory in all non-Bulgarian schools. For example, Article 78 of the 1879 constitution made primary education compulsory for all school-age children. It also made the study of Bulgarian mandatory in non-Bulgarian schools. These provisions of the constitution were reaffirmed in subsequent educa-

---

[2] Beginning in the eighteenth century, the Ottoman Empire entered a period of serious decline. Taking advantage of this, many foreign powers sought to use the *millet* system to their advantage by demanding that its privileges be granted to them. By 1914, the number of the *millets* had increased to 17. During the nineteenth century, the *millet* system was also used by revolutionaries among the non-Muslim subjects of the Empire to further their nationalist aims and to gain their independence from the Ottoman state (see Lord Kinross 1977: 320ff, 527-93).

tion laws passed by Parliament. The education law of 1885 in-augurated a national system of public primary education supported and administered by the state. Although these schools were open to all children regardless of ethnic or religious affiliation, the overwhelming majority of students in public primary schools were Bulgarian. This law also recognized the legitimacy of the existing private schools. These schools were established by non-Bulgarian communities at their own expense but under the supervision of the Ministry of Education. Article 192 of the Bulgarian Education Law of 1891 obligated the Bulgarian government to provide financial aid to private Turkish schools. However, such aid was minuscule compared with that provided to public schools. According to Şimşir (1988: 23), during the 1894-5 school year 51 per cent of the budgets of public (Bulgarian) schools were funded by the government. During the same school year government financial aid to Turkish schools amounted to only 4 per cent of their budgets. The lack of adequately trained Turkish teachers, their low salaries and the general lack of resources contributed to a poor quality of education in these schools (Şimşir 1988: 13-30). Since a very small percentage of school-age children were able to attend school, the Turkish population in Bulgaria remained largely illiterate. For example, in 1905 the literacy rate for Turks of all ages was only 4 per cent. This compared with a literacy rate of 32.3 per cent for Armenians. Only the Gypsies were worse off than the Turks, with a literacy rate of 2.3 per cent (Mishkova 1994:86).

An important study by Negencov and Vanev (1959) of education in southeastern Bulgaria covering the period 1879-85, illustrates the ethno-religious organization of schooling in the region (see Table 4.1). Each ethno-religious community continued to provide education to its members, structure its own curricula, publish its own books, newspapers and journals, and provide appropriate cultural and religious activities for its members.[3] Almost every Turkish village in Bulgaria had a primary school (*ilk okul*). Towns with significant Turkish minorities had several such schools. Turkish high schools (*rüştiyes*) were located in towns.

In addition to Turkish primary schools, there were secondary and higher institutions or *medreses,* where students were taught

---

[3] A good description of educational and religious organizations among the Turks of the Dobruca region is found in Ülküsal (1966: 105-70).

the Arabic language and the Islamic religion exclusively. The graduates from these schools were prepared to minister to the spiritual needs of Turks and other Muslim minorities in the country (Ülküsal 1966: 105-21).

Table 4.1. ELEMENTARY SCHOOL STUDENTS IN EASTERN RUMELIA BY ETHNO-RELIGIOUS COMMUNITY, 1880-3

	1880-1		1881-2		1882-3	
Nationality	No. of schools	No. of students	No. of schools	No. of students	No. of schools	No. of students
Bulgarian	866	49,268	852	53,004	866	51,288
Turkish	771	26,390	770	29,000	763	27,113
Greek	58	3,925	59	4,088	48	3,471
Jewish	13	818	13	780	14	918
Armenian	4	190	5	233	5	201
Totals	1,712	80,591	1,699	86,905	1,696	82,991

Source: Negencov and Vanev 1959: 128-9.

The new compulsory education law introduced in 1879 had little impact on traditional patterns of school attendance. Negencov and Vanev (1959: 129) show that these traditional private schools provided a very limited education to a limited segment of the population. Most of the students were male (70 per cent among Bulgarian students, almost exclusively male among Turkish students) and it appears that in spite of compulsory education laws 35 to 50 per cent of school-age children did not attend schools during the period under study. For example, in 1883 only 64 per cent of Bulgarian children attended school; the percentage was even lower among Greek and Turkish children. Moreover, many children did not complete a year of school. Of those who did, many failed to graduate from elementary school, and of those who graduated from elementary school, very few continued their education any further.

The instability of post-independence governments, lack of resources, poor communication with rural areas where most of the Turks lived, the maintenance of the principle of communal autonomy with regard to school organization, and other reasons all contributed to the maintenance of poor educational conditions in the country.

No significant improvements in education were made in Bulgaria between the two world wars, the various governments being faced with serious problems that impeded their attempts to improve the educational system in the country. These problems included the lack of adequately trained teachers, shortage of funds, mass illiteracy, and the reluctance of parents to dispense with the valuable labor of their children. The education that was available was of very poor quality. Stavrianos (1958: 606) summarizes the quality of education in the Balkan countries between the two world wars in the following terms:

> The nature of teaching in the lower schools left much to be desired. The teachers were poorly trained and the classrooms were overcrowded because of the lack of funds with which to provide more schools. As a result, the pupils rarely received more than a grounding in the 'three Rs,' together with a healthy dose of nationalistic indoctrination. They were taught to look back to their respective periods of glory and greatness during the medieval ages and to regard the neighboring peoples as inferior in culture, morals, and military prowess.

The inconsistent policies of post-independence governments toward private Turkish schools exacerbated the educational problems of the Turkish minority. Immediately after independence the Bulgarian authorities closed down many private Turkish schools in northern Bulgaria. This was followed by a period of relative tolerance, even encouragement, of Turkish education. During the last decade of the nineteenth and the first two decades of the twentieth centuries, the educational situation of the Turkish community in Bulgaria improved considerably and the future of Turkish-language education in the country seemed very bright. The schools which were closed following the Russo-Turkish War of 1877-8 were reopened and new schools were built. By the early 1920s the number of Turkish schools of all types had reached 1,712 (Omarčevski 1922: 604). Unfortunately, the tolerant attitude of the Bulgarian authorities did not last long. After the assassination of the Agrarian Premier Stambolijski in 1923 the situation of the Turkish minority began to deteriorate. Under a series of anti-Turkish and anti-Muslim regimes, many private Turkish schools, especially in rural areas, were closed, so that by 1936 only 545 private Turkish schools remained in Bulgaria. Conditions continued to deteriorate through the Second World War, reducing the number of private schools by 75 per cent to 367 by the start of the 1943-4 school year (Şimşir 1988:105-25; Table 4.2).

Table 4.2. PRIVATE TURKISH SCHOOLS IN BULGARIA, 1921-44

School year	Primary schools	High schools	Total
1921-2	1,673	39	1,712
1928-9	922	27	949
1936-7	585	20	605
1937-8	572	20	592
1938-9	508	21	529
1939-40	483	20	503
1940-1	448	19	467
1941-2	440	20	460
1942-3	398	20	418
1943-4	344	23	367

Source: Jusein Memişev 1977: 126 and Şimşir 1988: 112.

The closing down of many private Turkish schools in rural areas where most of the Turks lived meant that the remaining schools could accommodate less than 40 per cent of school-age children (Şimşir 1988:170-1). As indicated by the figures in Table 4.3, over an eight-year period the primary school student population declined by 36.2 per cent while the number of teachers in these schools declined by 43.2 per cent. The number of students and teachers in secondary schools showed little change during the same period since these schools were located in towns and were not targeted by government authorities.

Table 4.3. STUDENTS AND TEACHERS IN PRIVATE TURKISH PRIMARY AND SECONDARY SCHOOLS IN BULGARIA, 1936-44

School year	Students			Teachers		
	Primary	Secondary	Total	Primary	Secondary	Total
1936-7	51,457	1,878	53,345	1,372	66	1,438
1937-8	49,089	2,130	51,219	1,325	60	1,385
1938-9	44,674	2,298	46,972	1,139	69	1,208
1939-40	41,189	2,264	43,453	1,102	62	1,164
1940-1	39,132	2,115	41,247	1,041	59	1,100
1941-2	39,846	2,128	41,974	1,040	68	1,108
1942-3	39,643	1,888	41,531	909	64	973
1943-4	32,808	2,509	34,317	779	72	851

Source: Şimşir 1988: 126

Nevertheless, the remaining schools were still under the control of the Turkish community, which continued to provide education to its members, structure the curricula of its schools, publish its own books, newspapers, and journals, and provide appropriate cultural and religious activities for its members. Major changes in these traditional patterns of education were put into effect only after the Communist Party consolidated its power in Bulgaria after the Second World War. Even then, some of the major reforms drawn up by the new government penetrated into remote rural villages very slowly.

Education of Turkish speakers in the People's Republic, 1945-1989

The education of Turkish speakers in the People's Republic of Bulgaria can be roughly divided into three periods: the first, marked by substantial freedom in educational and cultural matters, lasted until the 1958-9 school year; the second, characterized by drastic limitations of this freedom, began with the consolidation of Turkish schools with Bulgarian schools after the 1958-9 school year and culminated in the elimination of all Turkish language instruction by the early 1970s. During the third period, which began in the 1970s, and increasingly in the 1980s, the Bulgarian government attempted to repress Turkish identity entirely. Between early 1985 and late 1989 the government claimed that there were no Turks in Bulgaria; Bulgaria was a homogeneous one-nation (Bulgarian) state. Since there were no Turks in Bulgaria, there could be no discussions about Turkish language and culture.

The post-war reorganization of the educational system was completed by the end of 1947. The concept of compulsory education originally introduced in 1879 was reaffirmed and a socialist orientation was adopted for the entire system. Over the years, a number of other reforms were introduced into the educational system, the major thrust of which was to develop a closer relationship between schools, research institutes, and the various units engaged in agricultural and industrial production (see Georgeoff 1978). A momentous change in the education of Turkish speakers occurred in 1946. According to the provisions of the Education Law approved by the Bulgarian National Assembly during that year, all Turkish schools and school properties were nationalized.

As a result, the Turkish community in Bulgaria, for the first time, lost control of its educational institutions. Article 154 of "The Appendix to the Bulgarian National Education Law", adopted by the National Assembly in September 1946, dealt specifically with the education of non-Bulgarian children. It reads in part:

> For the purpose of meeting the educational needs of the minority people in Bulgaria and to ensure education in their own language, the State and the Municipalities may open minority schools of any grade according to the needs observed. The material expenses of these schools are met by the Municipalities while the salaries of teachers and administrative staff are paid by the State (Şimşir 1986b: 7–8).

Article 155 (2) of the same law gave the Council of Ministers, upon the recommendation of the Minister of Education, the right to decide "which minorities in Bulgaria will benefit from minority rights and receive education in their mother tongues in their schools" (Şimşir 1986b: 9). The education of students of non-Bulgarian origin was given constitutional protection. Article 79 of the Bulgarian Constitution adopted by Parliament on 4 December 1947 reads: "*National minorities have a right to be educated in their vernacular and to develop their national cultures* while the study of Bulgarian is compulsory" (Triska 1968: 163; emphasis added). Article 79 also affirmed the responsibility of the state to provide quality education to all of its citizens.

The language of instruction in nationalized schools remained Turkish. A uniform nationwide curriculum was imposed on these schools and the compulsory study of Bulgarian was implemented. The curriculum was expanded and classes in religion were gradually eliminated. Before their nationalization in 1946, education in private Turkish schools was heavily weighted toward religion; schools were normally attached to mosques and clerics served as teachers. For example, during the 1905-6 school year the curriculum in elementary schools in the Razgrad region of northeastern Bulgaria consisted mostly of classes in religion and Turkish language. Only fourth graders were required to study Bulgarian, for three hours a week. In addition, the weekly schedule included classes in calligraphy, mathematics, and singing (Şimşir 1988:29). In contrast, the expanded curriculum of nationalized Turkish elementary schools (1947-8) included in addition to Turkish, Bulgarian, and mathematics, classes in geometry, applied science, geography, history, natural history, biology, music, gymnastics, drawing and handicrafts. The study of the Koran was reduced to two hours a week (Şimşir 1988:155-6). After 1952 religious classes were eliminated from the school curriculum. Religious instruction literally went underground for a while – being confined to the basements of schools after school hours – and later disappeared altogether.

In addition to the implementation and enforcement of compulsory education for all school-age children and the study of Bulgarian as a compulsory subject, a number of far-reaching reforms were introduced into the educational system. The goal of education was to be the development of an atheistic-scientific world view among students through the use of Marxist-Leninist principles. A comprehensive examination system was devised through which students graduating from middle schools could be channeled into technical schools, teacher-training institutes, or higher educational institutions. Education was seen as the principal instrument for the socialist reconstruction of the country and the creation of the socialist man as envisioned by the Communist Party.

The implementation and strict enforcement of compulsory education for all school-age children necessitated the building and staffing of additional Turkish-language schools. Old schools were renovated, many mosques were turned into secular schools, and new schools were built. As a result, the number of Turkish schools, students, and teachers increased dramatically in Bulgaria during the early years of the post-war period. A comparison of the number of Turkish-language schools, students and teachers during the 1943-4 and 1949-50 school years shows marked improvement in all three categories. As Table 4.4 illustrates, the number of teachers in Turkish-language schools more than tripled while the number of students enrolled in them almost tripled. There was almost a sixfold increase in the number of middle schools. The foundation of a nationwide system of kindergartens was laid down, including twenty in Turkish areas. The educational needs of older Turkish speakers, who were overwhelmingly illiterate, began to be addressed with the establishment of adult night literary classes. By the mid 1950s there were more than 1,000 Turkish elementary and middle schools, seven Turkish coeducational high schools, one girls' high school in Ruse, and three Turkish teacher-training institutes.

Table 4.4. TURKISH SCHOOLS, STUDENTS AND TEACHERS
IN BULGARIA, 1943-4 AND 1949-50 SCHOOL YEARS

Type of school	1943-4			1949-50		
	Schools	Pupils	Teachers	Schools	Pupils	Teachers
Kindergartens	–	–	–	20	755	22
Primary schools	397	35,253	802	1,018	89,917	2,454
Middle schools	27	2,082	69	157	13,692	511
High schools	–	–	–	1	618	21
Teacher-training institutes	–	–	–	1	284	20
Night schools	–	–	–	2	110	9
Totals	424	37,335	871	1,199	105,376	3,037

Source: Şimşir 1988: 155.

As a result of these developments the number of Turkish students enrolled in Turkish-language schools increased steadily, reaching 150,000 by the mid-1950s. While during the 1941-2 school year less than half of Turkish school-age children were enrolled in schools (36,541 out of 78,600), many of whom dropped out before the end of the school year, by the 1952-3 school year attendance among Turkish school-age children was close to 100 per cent (Markov 1971:70, 72). Over a few short years literacy rates among Turks showed a significant improvement. The compulsory study of Bulgarian also led to a marked increase in bilingualism among young Turks.

Turkish-language broadcasts over Radio Sofia, publication of Turkish-language newspapers and journals and state encouragement and support of Turkish fine arts created the impression that a renaissance of Turkish culture was under way. After the establishment of a Turkish branch at the Narodna Prosveta Publishing House, the number of publications in Turkish in Bulgaria steadily increased. Many of these works were translations into Turkish from other languages. However, among them we also find literary works, mostly poetry, by native Turkish poets and writers. During the 1950s and 1960s such works were published in significant numbers. The two decades between 1950 and 1970 in Bulgaria are known as the *Lale Devri* (Tulip Period)[4] when native Turkish literature in Bulgaria reached its creative heights. Significant developments took place in the fields of poetry and short story writing. Noteworthy accomplishments were achieved in the fields of cultural and political humor, folk tales, literary criticism, folk theater, and plays. Many plays by native Turkish playwrights were performed by members of government-supported professional Turkish theaters to enthusiastic audiences. The decade of the 1960s saw the publication of annual anthologies of poetry and short stories, and works by individual native Turkish writers were also published (see Hafiz 1987; Şimşir 1988:223-39; Cavuş 1988).[5] Through these developments, the Bulgarian government, for a time, gained the loyalty and goodwill of the Turkish minority.

Even though Turkish parents disagreed with some aspects of educational policies in the nationalized Turkish schools, especially the atheistic orientation and the requirement that all school-age girls attend school, the retention of Turkish as the language of instruction mollified many of them. Indeed, many members of the Turkish-speaking community interpreted these developments as a genuine concern on the part of the government to lift the cultural and education level of Turkish speakers by encouraging the development of Turkish language, literature, and the arts. Morale was high and Turks generally developed a positive attitude toward the government.

Unfortunately, this seeming renaissance of Turkish language and culture was short-lived. After the 1958-9 school year, the Bulgarian government embarked upon a forced assimilationist policy toward the Turkish-speaking minority, as well as toward other minorities in Bulgaria, such as Pomaks, Gypsies, and Macedonians. This new policy led to the merger of Turkish schools with Bulgarian ones. Although the government mandated

---

[4] Named after a period in early eighteenth-century Ottoman history (1703-30) under the reign of Sultan Ahmet III and his Grand Vizier and son-in-law Ibrahim Paşa, when Ottoman accomplishment in all fields of arts and sciences reached their creative heights.

[5] Çavuş's work is especially valuable because it includes an historical essay on Turkish literature in Bulgaria from the fifteenth century to 1985 as well as informative biographies of major native Turkish writers of the twentieth century in Bulgaria, including information about their fate during and after the forced assimilation campaign. Two pamphlets by Şimşir (1986b, 1986c) provide valuable short histories of the Turkish press and Turkish education in Bulgaria. Large sections of his *The Turks of Bulgaria* (1988) are devoted to the education of Turkish speakers in Bulgaria.

the teaching of the Turkish language in all schools with ten or more Turkish students, this requirement was largely ignored. The teaching of Turkish was phased out entirely after 1972. Turkish students attending Bulgarian schools were prohibited from speaking Turkish among themselves in classrooms, school corridors, and school playgrounds. After 1984 the prohibition against speaking Turkish in public would be extended to all Turks in Bulgaria.

It is ironic that during a time when the Bulgarian government was actively engaged in dismantling Turkish-language educational institutions as well as other Turkish cultural institutions in the country, Bulgarian officials continued to reiterate the government's commitment to the maintenance and development of these same institutions. For example, General Secretary of the Communist Party Todor Živkov (1964b:1–2) in his congratulatory message to *Yeni Hayat*, the Turkish-language monthly, on its tenth anniversary in 1964, said:

All possible opportunities have been created for the Turkish population to develop their culture and language freely. . . The children of the Turkish population must learn their [mother] tongue and perfect it. To this end, it is necessary that the teaching [of the Turkish language] be improved in schools. Now and in the future the Turkish population will speak their mother tongue; they will develop their progressive traditions in this language; they will write their contemporary literary works [in Turkish] . . . they will sing their wonderfully beautiful song [in Turkish] . . . Many more books must be published in this country in Turkish, including the best works of progressive writers in Turkey.

The process of merging of Turkish schools with Bulgarian schools coincided with government efforts to impoverish the written Turkish of native Turkish writers by requiring them to substitute Bulgarian and Russian words in place of Turkish ones. For this purpose an extensive list (over 10,000) of Turkish words and their Bulgarian/Russian equivalents was drawn up as a guide to editors and writers (see Appendix I).

Special style editors were appointed to the editorial offices of Turkish periodicals and the Turkish branch of the Narodna Prosveta Publishing House, to make sure that all submissions adhered to the new requirements. These style editors were not specialists in linguistics or on language use. Their only qualification was their loyalty and defense of government policies. Those Turkish writers who continued to use the "forbidden" Turkish words in their writings were heavily censored and reprimanded. Often, works submitted in the unapproved style, regardless of merit, were not published (Çavuş 1988:67).

After 1969 the government took the decisive step to eliminate Turkish literature, both works translated into Turkish from other languages and original works, altogether. Toward the end of that year the Politburo of the Central Committee of the Bulgarian Communist Party published its "secret" decisions on the topic "About Ideological Work among Turks". The Central Committee recommended that these directives be put into effect as quickly as possible. Çavuş (1988:68-69) summarizes the main points of this ideological work:

(1) The main goal of communism being the ethnic unification of all groups into a single whole, it is necessary that members of a nation-state share a single language, literature, art, culture and customs.

(2) Native Turkish literature in Bulgaria, by confining itself only to questions about the Turkish minority, being influenced by bourgeois Turkish literature from Turkey, incites Turkish nationalism among Turks in Bulgaria, and is, therefore, contrary to the communist ideology.

(3) Native Turkish poets and writers, by concentrating on topics of the past in their writings, step outside the bounds of socialist literature [which is supposed to be future oriented]. By so doing they betray the laws of the state and bring harm to Marxism-Leninism.

(4) The literary works of native Turkish poets and writers, being written only in Turkish, keep alive Turkish identity and nullify the force of socialist Bulgarian literature among Turkish speakers. This is contrary to internationalism and ethnic unification.

(5) Under the influence of bourgeois Turkish writers [from Turkey], native Turkish writers are trying to purify the Turkish language by freeing it from foreign elements [Bulgarian]. The goal of this is to de-emphasize the use the Bulgarian language among the members of the Turkish minority.

(6) Native Turkish literature is unable to instill communist

consciousness among Turks, is unable to counteract the harm of Islam among them, and is unable to animate the life of communist man.

A series of actions to undermine and eliminate the foundations of native Turkish literature in Bulgaria followed. Native Turkish writers were told to write only in Bulgarian, to communicate to their readers messages that praised socialism, and to sever all of their relations with Turkey and Turkish literature. Everything was done to intimidate native Turkish writers and to force them to toe the party line. Native Turkish intellectuals who objected to these policies were arrested and imprisoned.

With the implementation and enforcement of the directives of the Central Committee of the Party, a native Turkish literature that had survived and even flourished in one form or another for generations was eliminated. Reminiscent of Nazi Germany, all works in Turkish, including works by Soviet and Western writers translated into Turkish and published in Bulgaria, were taken off library and bookstore shelves, confiscated from the personal libraries of individuals and destroyed. Possession of Turkish books became a crime (Şimşir 1986c: 1988: 239-45).

The government also withdrew its support of other Turkish educational and cultural institutions. The Turkish teacher-training institutes were closed down. The Department of Turkish Philology at Sofia University became the Department of Arabic Philology. The activities of the Turkish branch of the Narodna Prosveta Publishing House were terminated. Regional Turkish theaters were disbanded. Amateur Turkish folk groups in villages and towns were not allowed to stage Turkish performances. The few remaining Turkish-language newspapers, which by the 1970s had become anti-Turkish and anti-Islamic propaganda pieces, began to appear in bilingual editions, and after 1984 they appeared in Bulgarian only.

After March 1985, with the official completion of the forced assimilation campaign against Turks, speaking Turkish in public places became a subversive act punishable by a stiff fine. Signs saying "It is forbidden to speak in a non-Bulgarian language in this shop!" and "Communication between Bulgarian citizens should be carried out in Bulgarian!" were prominently displayed in shops and restaurants in areas where Turks lived. Although the wording of these signs appears ambiguous, it was clear to everyone who their targets were. This campaign against Turkish speakers would continue until the ouster of Živkov from power in a parliamentary coup on 10 November 1989.

Official explanations for the merger of Turkish schools with Bulgarian schools after 1959 stressed that Turkish-language state schools were never meant to be permanent institutions. They were established to remedy specific problems among Turkish speakers in Bulgaria. Since the Turkish-speaking population was largely monolingual in Turkish at the time the post-Second World War educational reforms began to be implemented, Turkish-language instruction along with the compulsory study of Bulgarian was seen as the best way to increase literacy and bilingualism rates among Turkish speakers. Turkish-language instruction would also serve as a propaganda vehicle to develop an atheistic world view among Turks, to fight Islamic beliefs and practices, and to disseminate socialist values. Ultimately, the Bulgarian authorities hoped to weaken separate ethnic and religious consciousness among Turkish speakers, thus furthering their assimilation into Bulgarian society (Amnesty International 1986: 27-8). According to Beitullov (1975), by the mid-1950s the goal of universal literacy among the younger generation of Turks had been achieved. The introduction and implementation of compulsory study of Bulgarian in Turkish-language schools had led to high rates of bilingualism among the young. They were ready to participate fully and equally in Bulgarian society. Turkish-language schools had achieved the progressive function for which they were established. The continuation of Turkish-language schools beyond that point would have encouraged the development of particularism, regionalism, and nationalism, retarding the integration of Turkish speakers into Bulgarian society. From 1960 on, increasing pressure was applied to make Bulgarian the sole language of instruction in the country, culminating in requiring Bulgarian as the sole language of communication among Bulgarian citizens in early 1985. The expectation was that the exclusive use of Bulgarian by Turks in public would extend to its use in private so that over time the use of Turkish as the primary medium of communication among Turks would diminish and ultimately disappear. This turned out to be a very naive expectation. It has been shown that when the public use of a language is officially banned (e.g., Catalan in Franco's Spain), the banned language becomes a secret weapon to its speakers, "a readily available expression of defiance and complicity, a bond felt in the tongue" (Reid 1994: 55). As Madjarov (1993: 10) observes, of all the prohibitions,

> . . . . the Turkish population reacted most acutely to the ban on the use of Turkish language . . . [because] the ban on Turkish touched the most emotional and delicate point –honor, dignity, the right to speak one's mother tongue, the most important element in ethnic consciousness.

Turks who decided to emigrate to Turkey during the mass exodus of 1989 gave the ban against speaking Turkish in public as one of the main reasons for their decision to leave. Moreover, the effect of the ban was the opposite of what was intended:

> In spite of the illusory disappearance of the Turkish language from public spaces, unlike the previous situation, when the Turkish young preferred to use Bulgarian even in the home, the Turkish language following the prohibition became the only medium of communication inside the ethnic community (Madjarov 1993: 10).

The prohibition acted as a powerful ethnic consolidating force, strengthening cultural, religious, and familial bonds. The prohibition also turned the Turkish community inward. Contacts between Turks and Bulgarians shrank.

The forced assimilation campaign led to the birth of a Turkish underground resistance movement in early 1985. The leaders of this movement encouraged Turks to abandon their passive assimilation to Bulgarian society since the end of the Second World War and reaffirm once again the symbols of their ethnic identity. Even though the top leaders of the resistance movement were betrayed to the police, arrested and imprisoned in June 1986, they were able to plan and direct the activities of the movement from prison and were able to organize mass demonstrations against government policies in May 1989 before the opening of the Paris Conference on human rights. These demonstrations by Turks led to Živkov's "final solution" of the Turkish problem by opening the borders and expelling over 350,000 Turks by the time Turkey closed the border on 22 August 1989. These events hastened his ouster from power several months later.

After the ouster of Živkov from power in a parliamentary coup on 10 November 1989, the new leaders of the Communist Party quickly repudiated the excesses of his regime and promised to work toward a more democratic society. On 29 December 1989, the government reversed the forced assimilation policy of the previous regime. Calling it a grave political error, the government declared that henceforth the cultural and civil rights of all citizens would be guaranteed and protected. More specifically, Turkish and other Muslims would be allowed to reclaim their Turkish-Muslim names; they would be allowed to practice their religion without any government interference; Turks would be free to speak Turkish and Turkish-language instruction would be reintroduced in municipal schools in ethnically mixed areas. The government's promise to restore the rights of Turkish and other Muslims produced an immediate nationalist backlash leading to widespread demonstrations in early January 1990.

Developments since 1989

Bowing to nationalist pressure the ostensibly reform-minded communist government was in no hurry to implement the promised reforms. The Ministry of Education promised to work on the matter and come up with a concrete plan to reintroduce Turkish-language classes in municipal schools soon.

However, it quickly became clear that the Ministry of Education did not have a plan, nor was it interested in developing one. The Movement for Rights and Freedoms (MRF) representatives took it upon themselves to develop their own proposals, and submitted them to the Ministry of Education for implementation. The 1990-1 school year was designated as a year of preparation for the full implementation of these proposals. The Ministry of Education ignored them.

Schools opened in September 1990 without any Turkish-language instruction. During subsequent months the Ministry of Education engaged in a series of delaying tactics with the purpose of postponing the implementation of any kind of Turkish education. Claiming that the Ministry needed more time to study the issue, it proposed that implementation of teaching Turkish be delayed until the second semester of the 1990-1 school year. The Grand National Assembly imposed a moratorium on Turkish classes until 15 November 1991 ostensibly to give educational specialists enough time to study the issue and to come up with concrete proposals.

In the meantime, the Ministry of Education advanced a number of impractical, unreasonable, and unrealistic proposals. According to Ministry officials, these proposals were based on a thorough study of the issue by educational specialists. It was proposed, *inter alia*, (1) that Turkish be taught in selected schools for two hours on an experimental basis only; (2) that, according to specialists, the most convenient grade to start teaching Turkish was the third grade; (3) that Turkish instruction be offered as an optional subject, and only if the parents submit a written and signed petition to school officials requesting such instruction for their children; (4) that only teachers with certificates from Turkish pedagogical and educational institutes in Bulgaria and from the Department of Turkish Philology of the University of Sofia be eligible for appointment as Turkish teachers; and (5) that it was the responsibility of municipal schools to recruit, train, and pay the salaries of Turkish teachers as well as to secure appropriate textbooks and other resources necessary to implement Turkish-language instruction. The government was not to provide any financial or other resources for the implementation of Turkish-language instruction. The Ministry also suggested that the Turkish community could establish its own private schools under government control if it assumed full financial responsibility for running such schools (Tatarlı 1993: 5). If most of these requirements were met, then, the Ministry suggested, teaching of Turkish could began in October 1991, one month after the beginning of the 1991–2 school year.

During the spring of 1991 the leaders of the MRF and officials of the Ministry of Education held wide-ranging discussions on Turkish-language education and reached an agreement on the outlines of a plan for implementations of Turkish-language classes in schools in ethnically mixed areas. The agreement called for offering Turkish classes as a required subject for all Turkish students from second through the eighth grade; the government would pay the salaries of Turkish teachers; and the government would sponsor workshops for Turkish teachers for three months during summers. However, the implementation of this agreement was delayed even after the adoption of a new constitution by Parliament on 12 July 1991, which recognized the right of citizens of non-Bulgarian origin to study their mother tongue. Article 36 (2) of the constitution reads: "*Citizens whose mother tongue is not Bulgarian shall have the right to study and use their own language* alongside the compulsory study of the Bulgarian language" (Sofia Press Agency 1991: 11; emphasis added). Article 53 of the constitution recognized the right of citizens and organizations to establish private schools at their own expense and Article 54 (1) spoke of the right of everyone "to avail himself of the national and universal cultural values and to develop his own culture in accordance with his ethnic self-identification" (Sofia Press Agency 1991: 15).

The bad faith of the government was confirmed on 1 October 1991. Just before the parliament dissolved itself for the October 13 elections, the BSP and its supporters in parliament pushed through a law prohibiting the teaching of minority languages in the country's schools. The Turks were told that if they wanted to provide their children instruction in their mother tongue they could establish private schools at their own expense but under government control as provided in Article 53 of the constitution. The passage of this law led to widespread boycott of schools by Turkish parents and students who vowed to continue the boycott until the government presented a plan to reintroduce Turkish-language instruction in municipal schools in ethnically mixed areas that was acceptable to the Turkish community. The resolution of this problem had to await the outcome of the 13 October 1991 elections.

The anti-communist coalition, the UDF, scored a narrow victory over the BSP. The only other party that was able to elect deputies to parliament was the MRF, the so-called Turkish party. The UDF was able to form a government with the unofficial support of the MRF. With the BSP out of power and the MRF in the government as the unofficial partner of UDF, the way was finally clear for the restoration of Turkish-language classes in municipal schools in ethnically mixed districts. The Ministry of Education finally announced its plan to reintroduce Turkish-language classes in December 1991. The Ministry's plan diverged significantly from the agreement reached in the Spring of 1991. The directive of the Ministry to local school authorities called for offering Turkish classes as an optional subject for four hours a week and not as a required subject as in the original agreement. Moreover, Turkish students could not automatically enroll in these classes. The parents of Turkish students were required to petition school authorities to assign their children to such classes on a yearly basis. The Ministry also instructed school authorities that the salaries of Turkish teachers be paid by municipalities and not by the government.

The Ministry also reneged on its promise to sponsor workshops for Turkish teachers over a three month period during the summer. Instead it set aside only five days in early October for this purpose, after the start of the school year. The Ministry promised to assume full financial responsibility for the implementation of the plan, including the provision of textbooks and other instructional resources as well as the recruitment and training of qualified teachers. This plan fell short of the expectations of the Turkish community, but the government's position on its concerns seemed flexible and open to future negotiation. A promising start was made. After a hiatus of more than twenty years, Turkish students would once again be provided instruction in their mother tongue.

The reintroduction of Turkish-language classes in municipal schools faced serious difficulties. One problem was the lack of an adequate number of qualified Turkish teachers. The problem was exacerbated by the exodus of hundreds of Turkish teachers to Turkey in 1989 during the so-called "grand excursion" Many had also left before 1989 following the elimination of Turkish-language instruction in Bulgaria. Most of the current teachers came out of retirement to teach. They had not taught Turkish for over twenty years. Others had only high school diplomas. They would need considerable help to retrain and upgrade their pedagogical and methodological skills. Five days set aside for training and workshops for potential Turkish teachers by the Ministry of Education were inadequate for the task. However, promising steps were taken to train new teachers. The Department of Turkish Philology was restored at the University of Sofia and a new department of Turkish Philology was established at Šumen University. The first group of Turkish students was sent to universities in Turkey for training (Piroğlu 1993: 1, 3).

Another serious problem that faced Turkish teachers was the lack of textbooks in Turkish. During the so-called "revival period" between 1984 and 1989, all Turkish textbooks published in Bulgaria during the 1950s and 1960s had been collected and destroyed. A Turkish writers' collective made up of prominent native Turkish intellectuals in Bulgaria worked closely with the Turkish Ministry of Education and evaluated a set of Turkish textbooks to be used in Bulgaria from first through the fifth grade. The collective recommended these textbooks for approval to the Bulgarian Ministry of Education in 1992. The Ministry approved the proposal. An adequate number of textbooks to meet the needs of all Turkish students in Bulgaria was secured and a distribution system was set up. By the beginning of the 1992-3 school year the Turkish textbooks problem was essentially solved.

There were other issues of immediate concern to Turkish students, parents, and teachers as well (See Bakoğlu 1993: 1, 5; Beytulla 1993: 1, 7; Çete 1993: 5; Mutlu 1993: 3, 5; and Tunalı 1993: 5). Turkish teachers have petitioned the Ministry of Education, the parliament, and the MRF parliamentary group on numerous occasions to make the Turkish language a required subject for all Turkish students but without success at the time of writing. In most schools in ethnically mixed areas Turkish-language classes continue to be offered as optional subjects before or after normal school hours. This practice inconveniences teachers, parents, and students, especially in rural areas. To cite one example, during the planting and harvesting seasons the labor of young children is indispensable to their families. Consequently, while attendance in Turkish-language classes is high in winter, when there is little to do, in spring and fall attendance declines sharply as parents require their children to come home after normal school hours. In addition, they have demanded that full-time Turkish teachers be given permanent appointments and be eligible for the same benefits as their Bulgarian counterparts, again without success so far.

Many of these problems are created by the fact that the Ministry of Education does not have a team to coordinate the implementation of its own directives. This task has been left entirely to local school authorities, many of whom had been supporters of the forced assimilation campaign of the Živkov regime. For nationalistic reasons, some school superintendents, principals, and teachers deliberately stonewall, delay, and frustrate the full implementation of limited Turkish-language instruction available to Turkish students. In some schools Turkish-language instruction is limited to two to three hours a week instead of four or not provided to first graders at all. In some schools several classes are intentionally grouped together, which makes instruction difficult. Some local practices are intended to delay the start of Turkish-language classes several weeks after the beginning of the school year. These include not providing an adequate number of Turkish textbooks and dictionaries to schools, delaying the distribution of Turkish textbooks and the appointment of Turkish teachers, requiring the parents to present a signed petition requesting Turkish-language instruction for their children every year instead of only once when the child enrolls for the first grade, and so on. A more insidious practice on the part of some nationalist school officials is to persuade Turkish parents to sign petitions against allowing their children to enroll in Turkish-language classes, telling them that Turkish classes are not required or that studying Turkish hinders their children's progress in other classes. Other Turkish parents, for their own personal reasons, do not want their children to enroll in Turkish classes. All of these practices result in lower enrollments in Turkish classes than expected. For example, at the start of the 1993-4 school year 92,000 Turkish children between the ages of seven and fifteen were attending municipal schools. Of these only 75,000 were enrolled in Turkish-language classes. Some 17,000 for some reason or other were not attending such classes (Mutlu 1993: 3,5). Another negative consequence of having Turkish classes as optional rather than required subject is that Turkish students have to make a choice between taking Turkish or some other foreign language such as English, French, or Russian. Those who enroll in Turkish classes are deprived of studying other languages.

In the December 1994 elections, which were won by the BSP, one of the strong supporters of Živkov's forced assimilation policy, Ilčo Dimitrov, was elected to parliament. The BSP's insensitivity to Turkish concerns was demonstrated by the appointment of Dimitrov to head the Ministry of Education. Since becoming Minister, Dimitrov has stated categorically that under his watch the status quo will be scrupulously maintained. He has appointed loyal BSP supporters as superintendents of schools in Turkish areas and has instructed them to make sure that Turkish classes remain optional and offered before or after normal school hours (Bakoğlu 1995: 5). He has restricted the training available to Turkish teachers. For example, in 1995 he denied permission for Turkish teachers to go to Turkey for additional training even though the government of Turkey was willing to assume financial responsibility for such training. As long as the BSP remains in power, and it has been in power for most of the post-communist period, attempts by Turkish parents to make Turkish-language classes compulsory for all Turkish children will be frustrated.

5

BULGARIAN TURKISH: THE LINGUISTIC EFFECTS OF NATIONALITY POLICY[1]

Changing policies toward ethnic minorities in Bulgaria have led to dramatic changes in the sociolinguistic status of Turkish and Bulgarian in ethnically Turkish areas of the country. The major trends over the last several generations have been a shift toward more frequent and fluent use of Bulgarian by more members of the community and the emergence of significant lexical and grammatical interference from Bulgarian in the native Turkish dialect. However, the more recent policy shifts have led to a resurgence of literacy in Turkish. The aim of this chapter is to describe the sociolinguistic status of the Turkish community in Bulgaria, concentrating on one particular village but with some more general remarks and a brief look at how the situation has changed and is changing.

As discussed earlier, most of the Turks now living in Bulgaria are descendants of colonists who were settled there during the Ottoman period. Despite the centuries separating them from their Anatolian and Asia Minor origins, these Turks have not become assimilated into the surrounding Bulgarian culture but have preserved their own language and culture – slightly different from that of modern Turkey but nonetheless distinctly Turkish. Until recently this cultural separateness was encouraged by the fact that many Turks had very little contact with Bulgarians: they tended to be concentrated in certain parts of the country, for instance in the eastern Rhodopes of southeastern Bulgaria and the Dobrudža region of northeastern Bulgaria. Turks living in remote mountain villages of the Rhodopes had very little contact with Bulgarians.

---

[1] The first half of this chapter is based on an article written jointly with Catherine Rudin, which appeared under the same title in *Anthropological Linguistics* (vol. 32. nos 1-2, 1990: 148-62). Included here with permission.

Men who traveled to the city for trade or other purposes often learned some Bulgarian, but women and children had no use for any language other than Turkish, and most were totally monolingual.

Long-established patterns of education also encouraged community isolation. During the Ottoman period the organization and management of educational and other cultural institutions was left up to each ethno-religious group to handle as it saw fit. Turkish villages and Turkish neighborhoods in towns and cities had Turkish schools, so even those members of the community who had some schooling did not necessarily know Bulgarian. As Grannes (1990) notes, prior to Bulgarian independence from Ottoman rule in 1878, Turkish was the high status language in the country. Consequently, the influence of Turkish on Bulgarian was considerable. Bulgarians living in or near Turkish communities learned Turkish while the Turks remained largely monolingual. Prominent Bulgarian writers used many Turkish words, both literary and colloquial, in their writings.

The extent of bilingualism among Bulgarians during the Ottoman period varied considerably depending on residence, gender, occupation and other factors. According to Todorova (1992: 20-5), the majority of Bulgarians had some knowledge of Turkish and used many Turkisms in their speech (subordinate bilinguals). A significant portion of Bulgarians, mainly merchants and artisans, "had to acquire some fluency in Greek and/or Turkish, for professional reasons" (incipient bilinguals), while a minority of Bulgarians were fluent speakers of Turkish. This category, "apart from cases like intermarriage or mixed ethnic cohabitation, would include mostly the educated class" (co-ordinate bilinguals) (Todorova 1992: 24-5). Turkish was used extensively in certain domains. As Todorova (1992: 23) notes:

> The terminology, covering administrative and commercial life in urban centers, was entirely Turkish (in fact, mostly Arabic and Persian loan-words, entering with Ottoman Turkish). So was the artisan terminology. Turkisms were extremely widespread in the denomination of the flora and fauna, clothing, food etc.

Many Bulgarian merchants, artisans, and craftsmen took their family names from their occupations. Many of these Turkish-derived family names continue to be used today (see Eren 1986).

After Bulgarian independence, the direction of interference was reversed. Bulgarian became the high status language and Bulgarians no longer had a strong incentive to learn Turkish. Moreover, a movement was launched to "purify" the Bulgarian literary language, as well as the vernacular and dialects, of Turkisms and to replace them with Bulgarian and/or Russian equivalents (see Moškov 1985). This movement was relatively successful concerning the literary language but less so in the vernacular and dialects. On the other hand, Turkish speakers felt a need to learn Bulgarian, and Bulgarian words slowly started to enter Turkish literary and colloquial language.

As discussed in Chapter 4, the patterns of education established in Bulgaria during the Ottoman period persisted until after the Second Word War, when all this changed dramatically as a result of the implementation and enforcement of the educational policies of the new communist government. All Muslim religious schools were closed. Turkish schools which had been private and community run for hundreds of years were nationalized. During the 1950s and increasingly thereafter, the policy of compulsory education for all children, including the Bulgarian language as a required subject, began to be strictly enforced. This meant that all young people – even girls – had at least some acquaintance with Bulgarian. Educational policy in Bulgaria with regard to Turks has gone through a series of twists and turns, sometimes even encouraging literacy in Turkish as well as Bulgarian, but the general trend has been greater and greater emphasis on Bulgarian as the language of the schools.

Between 1959 and 1970 all Turkish-language schools were merged with Bulgarian schools. By the early 1970s Turkish-language instruction in Bulgarian schools was effectively eliminated. Consequently, those Turkish speakers who began their educational careers in the early 1970's or later did not know how to read and write in their language. By January 1985 the entire question of Turkish-language instruction became moot since the Bulgarian government officially declared that there were no longer any Turks in Bulgaria. Between the end of 1984 and November 1989 the government took additional steps against the use of the Turkish language. Orders were issued to responsible authorities to implement and enforce decrees against the speaking of Turkish in public places and against the use of Turkish names in places of work.

Changes in the government's language and educational policies since the Second World War have had a significant impact on the language of the Turkish minority. The institution and implementation of compulsory education after the war and the compulsory study of Bulgarian in Turkish schools during the 1950s raised the previously very low rate of literacy and bilingualism among the Turkish-speaking population. Another major change for most Turks was the degree of contact with Bulgarians and Bulgarian language in everyday life. During the period of collectivization in the Rhodope region in the early 1960s, many Turks left their homes in the mountains for an easier life in the already established collective farms in the fertile plains; whole villages sometimes moved *en masse* to new locations where a trip to the nearest fair-sized town meant a few minutes' train or bus ride, rather than a long day's hike. Others left for cities in search of factory jobs. Even for those who stayed behind, radio, television, and improved transportation and communication networks increased contacts with Bulgarians to some extent. All of these changes led to increased use of Bulgarian by Turkish speakers. On the other hand, the forced assimilation campaign of 1984-9 increased the social isolation between Turks and Bulgarians, partially reversing the trend of recent decades.

The village with which we (Eminov and Rudin) are most familiar is Polyanovo, near the city of Aitos, in the Burgas region of east-central Bulgaria.[2] During the early 1980s, the village was inhabited almost entirely by Turks, the majority of whom had migrated there from the village of Avramovo in the eastern Rhodopes during the 1960s, at the time of collectivization. Out of approximately ninety households in the village, all but ten were Turkish.[3] The only Bulgarians in the village were older couples, widows and widowers and one middle-aged couple; there

[2] The linguistic data for this section of the chapter derive from observations in the village of Polyanovo and Aitos during several visits in the late 1970s and early 1980s and from letters written by Turkish-speaking relatives to the author. The sociolinguistic situation described here refers mostly to that period. Additional data were collected in 1990. The linguistic data for the second half of this chapter is from Tahsin (1991).

[3] Some seventy households emigrated to Turkey during the general exodus between June and August 1989. All but three households returned to the village after 1989.

were no Bulgarian children or young people. Two Gypsy families lived just outside the village, and played a marginal role in village life. The local collective was worked and administered entirely by Turks, with the exception of one Bulgarian woman who sold bread and weighed the harvested crops.

Polyanovo was thus an overwhelmingly Turkish environment, and Turkish was by far the majority language. Nevertheless, Bulgarian influence was present in the village. Beside the few Bulgarians who actually lived in the village, there were native Bulgarian kindergarten teachers who came in daily to supervise the young children, and during the summer young people from the nearby Pioneer work camp came in to drink and hang around the village bar and general store in the evenings. In addition, many adult male residents of the village had jobs outside, which brought them into daily contact with Bulgarians, and almost everyone went to the nearby towns and cities at least once in a while. The cities of Karnobat, Aitos, and Burgas were easily reached by train, bus or car from the village; easily enough to make going to the city for an afternoon of shopping or a movie perfectly reasonable. Besides, a number of villagers had relatives living in Aitos who visited them quite frequently. Every household had a television set and young people and children spent many hours watching television. Most significantly, all school age children attended schools where instruction was entirely in Bulgarian, and Turkish students were required to speak with one another in Bulgarian while at school.

As a result, nearly all the residents of Polyanovo were bilingual to some degree. We define a bilingual as "a person who is able to produce grammatical sentences in more than one language" (Lehiste 1988: 1). This definition is broad enough to include a range from persons who are effectively monolingual but can produce a limited number of grammatical sentences in a second language to those who show equal facility in more than one language and who can switch with ease between languages. It is also understood that not all bilinguals produce equally grammatical sentences. Most frequently deviate from the norms of either language, which may interfere with the production of grammatical sentences in the other at a number of levels – phonetics, phonology, morphology, syntax, semantics and lexis. Moreover, bilinguals differ in the degree of interference at a given level.

Our data indicate that the changes in educational policy and amount of contact with Bulgarian over the previous half-century had resulted in quite different linguistic repertoires for Turks of different ages and genders by the early 1980s. Older women were effectively monolingual, although even they exhibited some lexical influence from Bulgarian in their Turkish, as we shall see.[4] Most men born before about 1935, who had completed their education before Bulgarian language study became compulsory in the 1950s, spoke Bulgarian very badly. Middle-aged people – those born between approximately 1935 and the late 1940s – were usually quite fluent in Bulgarian, but at a clearly non-native level, and made many grammatical errors. This was the group that had Bulgarian as a required subject in school, but did not learn it as young children. Women of this middle-aged group were generally somewhat less fluent than their male contemporaries, partly because very few girls went beyond primary school in the past, and partly because most women worked on collective farms near the village and had less contact with Bulgarians than the men did.

The younger generation – those born after about 1950 – were for the most part fully fluent in Bulgarian; many spoke it essentially like natives and some were actually more comfortable in Bulgarian than in Turkish. In this age group the sex difference evident in older and middle-aged speakers disappeared; even though girls still tended to leave school early, this group had learned the language when young and had continuous opportunity to use it, unlike the preceding generation. The youngest children did not know Bulgarian, but as soon as they entered kindergarten they quickly acquired it. Even in heavily Turkish settings like Polyanovo the kindergarten teachers were Bulgarians, and they required the children to speak Bulgarian even among themselves.

In addition to differences in which languages were used, the residents of Polyanovo differed in the extent and type of influence of the two languages on each other. We turn now to some specific linguistic examples. All examples were taken from informal conversations and letters: they were spontaneously produced and typical of normal speech within the ethnic Turkish community. Sentence 1, with its apparently random gender marking, was

---

[4] While there are a number of studies on the influence of Turkish on Bulgarian, as far as we are aware, little or nothing has been done on the influence of Bulgarian on Turkish. For a good summary of the influence of Turkish on Bulgarian see Grannes (1990).

written by a man born in 1944; a representative of the middle-aged, fluent-but-not-native-like group of Bulgarian speakers.

(1) *Minalato*   *ljato*   *i*   *tozi*   *ljato*   *rabotim*
    last(f)-the(n) summer(n) and this(m) summer(n) we-work
    krastavici
    cucumbers
    "Last summer and this summer we work (growing) cucumbers."

In this sentence the neuter noun *ljato* "summer" is modified by one feminine and one masculine adjective and a neuter article. The stereotypical view of Turkish speech among Bulgarians is that they can never get their gender agreement right, and in fact this type of error was frequent among older and middle-aged speakers, probably reflecting the lack of grammatical gender in Turkish. Such errors were, however, not found in the speech of younger Turks.

Sentences 2 and 3 are two more examples of grammatical errors in the Bulgarian of middle-aged speakers. In 2 an impersonal construction is mistakenly treated as personal: the correct construction would be *mene me njama e v kŭšti*, literally "me there wasn't at home" Sentence 3 shows incorrect use of a definite article with another determiner.

(2) *Az pŭk   njamah   v kŭšti.*
    I   though I-wasn't at home
    "But I wasn't at home."

(3) *I   tie   kratkite   redove te piša   ot   Ajtos.*
    and these short-the lines you I-write from Aitos
    "I write these short lines to you from Aitos."

Such examples could be multiplied *ad infinitum*, but the point should be clear: middle-aged Turks made typical second-language-learner errors. Younger Turks in general did not make such errors.

One example of Turkish influence that affected even young speakers was reduplication with *m* to mean "and stuff" in both Turkish and Bulgarian. Several examples are given below: 4a is entirely Turkish, 4b entirely Bulgarian, and 4c contains reduplication of a Bulgarian word, *svetno*, in an otherwise Turkish sentence. This type of reduplication is also used by some Bulgarians, but is considered a Turkicism (Grannes 1978).

(4a) *Korekoma   gittim   pantul mantul aldım.*
Corecom-to I-went pants   I-got
"I went to Corecom (and) got some pants and stuff."

(4b) *Jufka mufka variš   naj-napred v tendžereto . . .*
noodle   you-boil first   in pot-the
"First you boil the noodles and stuff in the pot . . ."

(4c) *Svetno msvetno hepsi oluyor.*
colored   all   it-does
"Colored and everything, it makes all kinds (of pictures)."

It is not surprising, certainly, that the native Turkish of these speakers influenced their non-native Bulgarian. More interesting was the degree to which Bulgarian influence was evident in the Turkish, not only of younger, bilingual speakers, but to a certain extent also of older people and even monolinguals. All of the Polyanovo Turks used Bulgarian loan words frequently. Many of these were lexical borrowings of the most expected sort, that is, words for culture-linked items or concepts which have been taken over from the surrounding Bulgarian society: government bureaucracy with its alphabet soup, education, jobs, and technology acquired in post-Ottoman times, like cars and refrigerators. These were words which even monolingual speakers used; they had fully entered the everyday vocabulary of the Turkish community and were used just like ordinary Turkish words, with appropriate grammatical endings and normal Turkish syntax. Some examples in context are given in 5; a few more words of this type are shown in 6 (Bulgarian lexical items are italicized in these and subsequent examples).

(5a) *Ispit*lerimi   başarıyle   kazanmamı   dilediler.
exams-my-ACC success-with passing-my-ACC they-wished
"They wished me success in passing my *exams*."

(5b) O *TKZC*de   *glaven agronom*   oldu.
he collective farm-in head agronomist became
"He became *a chief agronomist* in the *collective farm*."

(5c) Bu *butilka*yı al *hladilnik*e koy.
this bottle-ACC take refrigerator-in put
"Take this *bottle* (and) put it in the *refrigerator*."

(5d) Benim *rŭčna spiračka*   hiç   tutmıyor.
     my   hand brake   not-at-all holds-NEG
     "My *hand brake* doesn't hold at all."

(6) magaziner(ka)   "storekeeper"(f) tetradka "notebook"
    drugarka   "teacher"   himikalka "pen"
    (ballpoint)
    radiostancija   "radiostation"   lenta   "tape, lane"
    deveti septemvri "Sept. 9"   MVR   "police"
    pŭrvi maj   "May 1"   globa   "fine"
    djado mraz   "SantaClaus"   častno   "privately owned"
    detska gradina   "kindergarten"   otpusk   "vacation"

Somewhat less expectedly, many Bulgarian words were used
for which a perfectly good Turkish equivalent existed, and which
had nothing to do with modern technology or Bulgarian society.
These included common nouns, adjectives, and adverbs, as shown
in 7.

(7a) Babamın   *bratovúcedi*nin   güveysi.
     father-my-POSS cousin-his-POSS son-in-law-his
     "He is my father's *cousin*'s son-in-law."

(7b) *Brat*   daha burda   ya.
     brother still here-at emphatic
     "(Your) *brother* is still here."

(7c) Babam   bir *diva   patka* vurmuş.
     father-my a   wild duck killed
     "My father has killed a *wild duck*."

(7d) Baya *moderno* bir şey   o.
     quite modern a thing it
     "It's quite a modern thing."

(7e) Arabada bir *şum*   çıktı.
     car-in a   noise arose
     "A *noise* started up in the car."

(7f) Vinagi aşağılıyor   *zapadı*.
     always he-puts-down   west-the
     "He's *always* putting down *the west*."

Interestingly, borrowings also included conjunctions and other minor categories. In fact, one of the most frequent Bulgarian words in our Turkish data is *obače* "however".

(8a) Resim var   *pak* sesi   yok.
picture there-is but voice-its there-isn't
"There's a picture, *but* there isn't any sound."

(8b) Recep *obače*   beygirleri hiç düşünmemiş.
Recep however horses-ACC at-all he-thought
"Recep *however* didn't think about the horses at all."

(8c) Bana bakma   *če*   evde   yok.
me   look-NEG because house-in he-isn't
"Don't look at me *because* he's not at home."

(8d) Benim mastikayı   *daže* oturmuşsun içmeye.
my   mastika-ACC even you-sat   to-drink
"You've *even* sat down to drink my mastika."

(8e) *Už*   adamı   aramaya gelmiş.
as-if man-ACC to-seek   she-came
"*It seems* she came to look for the man."

There were even a few candidates for possible transference of bound grammatical morphemes from Bulgarian into Turkish. The Bulgarian *-čo* diminutive suffix had become quite common alongside the native Turkish diminutive *-çik/-cik*, and some young people seemed to use the feminine *-ka* suffix fairly productively in Turkish too.

(9a) Adem*čo*   nasıldır?
Adem-DIM   how-is
"How is little Adem?"

(9b) Şarkıyı   söyleyen Apti ağabeyin   baldız*ka*sı.
song-ACC singing Apti older-brother-POSS sister-in-law-his
"The one singing the song is your brother Apti's sister-in-law."

One particularly interesting pattern of Bulgarian loan word usage was the construction exemplified in 10. Here a Bulgarian verb, nearly always a third person singular present tense form (indicated with "3s" in the examples below) was combined with a form of the Turkish *yapmak* "to do" with appropriate person/number/tense features. Verbs, unlike nouns and other parts of speech, were not assimilated directly into the Turkish morphological system. Rather, a semantically empty Turkish verb root was employed as a carrier for the obligatory grammatical suffixes.

(10a) Ben öyle *obeštava* yaptım.
      I   thus   promise-3s I-did
      "I *promised* (to do) that."

(10b) Akşam sabah *pǔtuva* yapacak.
      evening morning travel-3s she-will-do
      "She will *travel* evening and morning."

(10c) Ben *izpolzva* yapıyorum.
      I   use-3s I-am-doing
      "I am *using* (it)."

(10d) Nerede *otklonjava* yaptık?
      where   turn-off-3s we-did
      "Where did we *turn off?*"

(10e) Onu *prehvǔrlja* yapcaz,   onun yerine   seni alcaz.
      him transfer-1s we-will-do his   place-in you we-will-take
      "We will *transfer him*, we'll take you in his place."

(10f) Ama *osvoboždava* yapmıyorlar   daha.
      but   liberate-3s   they-don't-do   yet
      "But they aren't *releasing* (workers) yet."

All of the above patterns of fitting a Bulgarian lexical item into a basically Turkish sentence contrasted with intrasentential code switching – changing the apparent matrix language in the middle of a sentence – which was comparatively rare in our data. One example is shown in 11.

(11) Sende *voenna*   *knižka*   varmı *imaş pravo za upravlenie na kola.*
     you-at military booklet is-if you-have right to driving of car
     "If you have *a military ID, you are allowed to drive a car.*"

Code switching in the larger sense of choosing the language of each conversation to fit the situation and participants obviously was common; we do not attempt to provide examples of it here. Such situation-based code-switching may have contributed to the actual loss of some Turkish vocabulary and its replacement with Bulgarian words, particularly among the very young, in semantic spheres that would tend to be associated with school or work. Our fifteen-year-old nephew did not know the Turkish names for the months and days of the week, for instance. His thirty-five-year-old parents normally used the Bulgarian forms, but if asked they could sometimes (not always) come up with the Turkish word as well (*eylül* for *septemvri* "September"; *perşembe* for *četvŭrtŭk* "Thursday"). Both teenagers and middle-aged people consistently used the Bulgarian names for most countries, continents and other geographical features: e.g. *Ungarija* rather than *Macaristan* ("Hungary"). Combined with the overwhelming use of Bulgarian rather than Turkish technological and social terminology of the sort discussed in 5 and 6, this lack of knowledge of Turkish vocabulary could lead to great difficulty in communicating with Turks from Turkey – especially since young people were sometimes unaware of which words are Turkish and which not.

For the most part, speakers were aware of the differences between the two languages, however; in fact, code switching was sometimes used for rhetorical effect.[5] This was particularly prevalent in songs, as in the two examples in 12. The first example shows two lines differing in a single word; the second is a popular song about the army, whose chorus consists of one line in Turkish and a nearly identical one in Bulgarian.

(12a) Geldi zor   zaman. *Dojde* zor   zaman.
　　　 came hard time　 came hard time
　　　 "Hard times have come, hard times *have come*."

(12b) Yaktı   bütün gençleri. *Izjade vsičkite mladeži.*
　　　 it-burned all   youth   it-ate all   youth
　　　 "It burned up all the youth, *It ate up all the youth*."

Even in everyday speech language switching was sometimes used consciously for comic effect. My sister Durdugül said (13) to her husband, who had just finished helping her chop cabbage for dinner, and both laughed at the unexpected predicate.

(13) Senin şimdi başka işin   *njama*.
　　　your now   other work there-isn't
　　　"Now *there isn't* any more work for you."

---

[5] This is a traditionally popular device in Bulgarian folk songs as well, where phrases like *ovčarče mlado çobançe* "shepherd, young shepherd" are not uncommon; *ovčarče* is Bulgarian, and *çobançe* Turkish for "shepherd".

We turn now to brief discussion of written language. Although fluency in spoken Turkish was essentially universal in Polyanovo and among Turks of Bulgaria in general, literacy in Turkish was far from universal. As we have already mentioned, Turkish-language instruction in the schools was eliminated by 1970, so those who began school after 1970 were taught to read and write only in Bulgarian. Turkish-language publications became unavailable at the same time. Many Turks who were over twenty-five could write in both Bulgarian and Turkish, although those between twenty-five and thirty years old, who were began their schooling during the years when Turkish instruction was being phased out (1960s), had minimal reading and writing skills in Turkish. For most of those under twenty-five, literacy was exclusively in Bulgarian. Thus my twenty-year-old nephew, who had recently immigrated to the United States, wrote to and received letters from his friends back in Polyanovo in Bulgarian, although they would normally speak to each other in Turkish. This was true in spite of the fact that they do know the Roman alphabet (having studied French in school, and now English) and in spite of their anti-Bulgarian feelings resulting from the recent wave of official repression of the Turkish minority in Bulgaria.

A few of the Polyanovo children learned to write Turkish during the 1980s, probably as a direct result of the anti-Turkish policies. When the Turkish language became an overt political issue, some parents were motivated to teach their children to read and write at home. My niece Sevinç, who was about eleven at the time, wrote the message in 14 in a 1986 postcard; the few errors are not surprising considering that she was just learning to write Turkish at the time.

(14) Yaz   mevsiminda bir hatra.
     summer   season-at   a   souvenir
     "A souvenir of the summer."
     (correct: Yaz mevsiminden bir hatıra)

A different approach to Turkish literacy is exemplified in 15, the text of a card written to us in 1987 by my then nine-year-old niece Selime. With the exception of the first line, which is a formulaic greeting in Bulgarian, the entire note is in Turkish, but is written in the Cyrillic Bulgarian alphabet (Turkish is normally written in Roman letters). The transcription is phonemically correct except for **ч** instead of the more accurate **дж** in **йенгечим** (*yen-gecim* "my auntie").

(15) 1987 **година да ви честита.**
Селям Сизлере. Йени йълънъз кутлу олсун абейим ве йенгечим
гьондерен Селиме. Хошчакалън.
(Turkish) transliteration: 1987 godina da vi čestita.
Selâm Sizlere. Yeni yılınız kutlu olsun abeyim ve yengecim.
gjonderen Selime. Hoşçakalın.
translation: Happy New Year 1987.
Greetings to you. May your new year be happy uncle and
auntie.
sent by Selime. Goodbye.

Since children knew both spoken Turkish and the Cyrillic alphabet, such phonetic spelling was probably felt to be relatively easy to learn. The efforts at teaching the children to write Turkish by either method may have been short-lived, though; these same nieces later reverted to writing to us in Bulgarian.

The difference in orthography is a frequent source of errors in written Turkish, even for adults who write both languages. We often noticed spelling errors clearly resulting from Cyrillic interference. A few representative examples from letters written by people aged between twenty and forty are shown in 16. Especially typical is the spelling *dc* instead of *c* for /dž/, presumably as a calque on Cyrillic **дж**. Confusion of *d* and *g*, *c* and *s*, *p* and *r*, and so on is also common, for similar reasons.

(16) Güldcan (for *Gülcan* (a girl's name))
deredceyle (for *dereceyle* "by degrees")
gerhal (for *derhal* "immediately")
gakika (for *dakika* "minute")
bykagarla (for *bukadarla* "with this much")
ceviyorum (for *seviyorum* "I love")

After 1989, the restrictions on religious, educational, and personal rights of minorities imposed by the communist regime were lifted. Issues which had been taboo for decades, such as free choice of names, classes in minority languages in state schools, freedom of worship and so on could be discussed freely. The reintroduction of Turkish-language classes in state schools was high on the MRF agenda. Between June 1990 and the end of 1991 when the government was dragging its feet on the issue of Turkish-language instruction, finally prohibiting it altogether on 1 October 1991, the MRF established a special corner in its newspaper *Hak ve Özgürlük* devoted to practical lessons on Turkish. The topics of the corner alternated weekly between Muharrem Tahsin's "Çğdaş Türkçemiz," (Our Contemporary Turkish), and Kazim Memiş's "Evinizde Dil Dersleri" (Language Lessons in Your Home). Under "Çağdaş Türkçemiz" the author alerted readers to the many Bulgarian words in common use in spoken and written Turkish, suggested proper Turkish words to replace these, and illustrated the use of the Turkish words in one or more sample sentences. Under the byline "Evinizde Dil Dersleri" the author presented practical lessons in Turkish syntax and morphology. The second part of the byline gave examples illustrating some of the typical "mistakes" made in spoken and written Turkish due to interference from Bulgarian, explained the specific reasons for these "mistakes", and gave examples showing how these could be corrected.

Before discussing the examples below it is necessary to enter an important caveat here. It is true that many of the "mistakes" illustrated by the following examples are due to interference from Bulgarian. It is also true that these constructions have become part of Turkish colloquial usage and to Turkish speakers in Bulgaria the meaning of these words or constructions is clear. They are "mistakes" only within the context of the syntax and morphology of standard literary Turkish. The editors address the question of what kind of Turkish the children should be taught in public schools. To the editors of *Hak ve Özgürlük*, the only correct Turkish is the standard literary form and it is this that should be used in everyday speech, in writing, and in schools. In discussing the examples that follow this caveat should be kept in mind.

Sentences under 17a illustrate a typical nonstandard usage due to the literal translation of the Bulgarian phrase "ot imeto na" into Turkish. In Bulgarian "ot imeto na" means 'in the name of". When the phrase is translated into Turkish literally, it means "from the name of ". The sentences under 17b illustrate correct usage.

(17a) —Siz kimin ad*ından* konuşuyorsunuz?
     (From whose name are you talking?)

–Biz bütün seçmenlerin adından konuşuyoruz.
(We are talking from the name of all voters.)

(17b) –Siz kimin ad*ına* konuşuyorsunuz?
(In whose name are you talking?)
–Ben bütün seçmenlerin ad*ına* konuşuyorum.
(I am talking in the name of all voters.)

The mistake in sentences under 18a is due to translating Bulgarian "s" (with) into Turkish "ile". The sentences under 18b illustrate standard usage.

(18a) –Yavu, ne oluyor siz*inle?*
(Hey, what's happening with you?)
–Biz*imle* ne olacak şimdi?
(Now what is going to happen with us?)

(18b) –Yavu, ne oluyor siz*e?*
(Hey, what is happening to you?)
–Biz*im* halimiz ne olacak şimdi?
(Now, what is going to happen to us?)

The sentences under 19a illustrate a different type of confusion with "with". The correct usage is shown under 19b.

(19a) –Kitapları kim*den* yolladınız?
(From whom did you send the books?)
–Kitapları da, defterleri de Yusuf*'tan* yolladık.
(We sent both the books and the notebooks from Yusuf.)

(19b) –Kitapları ki*minle* yolladınız?
(With whom did you send the books?)
–Kitapları da, defterleri de Yusuf*'la* yolladık.
(We sent both the books and the notebooks with Yusuf.)

The example under 20a again illustrates typical "mistakes" in spoken and written Turkish due to literal translation of Bulgarian words into Turkish. Here the Bulgarian "pribra se" – went/came home, came back, returned – is translated as *toplandı*. The verb *toplanmak* is often used in a nonstandard way by Turkish speakers as result of interference from Bulgarian. In Turkish, the verb *toplanmak* means to be gathered, or to be collected. The use of *toplandı* in 20a is wrong. The correct word should be *geldi* (came) or *döndü* (returned) as in 20b.

(20a) – Arkadaşım dün çok geç toplandı.
(Yesterday my friend gathered home very late.)

(20b) – Arkadaşım dün eve çok geç döndü/geldi.
(Yesterday my friend returned/came home very late.)

In the sentences under 21a the words *kaldırdılar* and *kaldırılan* are nonstandard. The writer expresses the opposite of what she wants to say. The mistake is due to Bulgarian interference in Turkish. It is a literal translation of "izdigam" – to build, to erect. In Turkish *kaldırmak* means to lift up, to do away with. The writer should have said to erect (*dikmek*) or to build (*inşa etmek*) as illustrated under 21b.

(21a) – Meydanlığa büyük bir anıt kaldırdılar.
(They raised a big monument in the public square.)
– Kaldırılan binalar hep sekiz katlı.
(The buildings that were raised are all eight floors.)

(21b) – Meydanlıkta büyük bir anıt diktiler.
(They erected a big monument in the public square.)
– İnşa edilen binalar hep sekiz katlı.
(All the buildings that were built have eight floors.)

In sentences under 22a the word *hesabına* is a literal translation of Bulgarian "za smetka na" – to the detriment of something or someone. However, in standard Turkish the word *hesabına* means to the benefit of something or someone. The examples under 22a express the opposite of what the writer wants to say. The writer should have used the word *zarar/zararına* instead of *hesabına* as illustrated under 22b.

(22a) – Hızlı çalışmak kalitenin hesabina oluyor.
(Speedy work improves quality.)
– Bulgaristan ile Yunanistan arasında varılan anlaşma öteki komşuların hesabına değil.
(The agreement reached between Bulgaria and Greece is not going to benefit their neighbors.)

(22b) – Hızlı çalışmak kalitenin zararina oluyor/kaliteye zarar getiriyor.
(Speedy work harms quality/brings harm to quality.)
– Bulgaristan ile Yunanistan arasında varılan anlaşma, öteki

komşuların zararına değil
(The agreement reached between Bulgaria and Greece is
not going to harm their neighbors.)

The example in 23a is taken from a conversation about a
soccer game between Çavdar and Dunav teams. A Turk who
doesn't know Bulgarian would find it impossible to figure out
from 23a that the game ended in favor of Dunav. Examples
under 23b clarify the meaning:

(23a) –Maç nasıl bitti?
(How did the game end?)
–Üç bir Dunav için. . .
(Three one for Dunav. . .)

(23b) –3-1 Dunav yendi.
(Dunav won 3-1.)
Or
–Çavdar, Dunav'a 1-3 yenildi.
(Çavdar lost to Dunav 1-3.)
Or
–Dunav: 3, Çavdar:1.
(Dunav 3, Çavdar 1.)

The sentence under 24a is grammatical but the suffix -çı, -ci
is not standard Turkish. The proper suffix here is -lı, -li as illustrated
under 24b.

(24a) –Ben Dunav'cıyım, eşim Spartak'çı, oğlum da Levski'ci . . .
(I'm Dunavist, my wife is Spartakist, my son is Levskiist. . .)

(24b) –Ben Dunav'lıyım, eşim Spartak'lı, oğlum da Levski'li . . .
(I'm a Dunav fan, my wife is a Spartak fan, my son is
a Levski fan . . .)

In example 25a the word *paylaştı* is considered inappropriate
and unnecessary because in standard Turkish the word *paylaşmak*
refers to something which is shared among two or more people.
Here we see the interference of the Bulgarian word "spodelyam"
–share, partake of, participate in, which always requires a com-
plement. Instead of *paylaştı* the appropriate word is *söyledi* or *dedi*
as in example 25b. Examples under 25c illustrate the correct
usage of the word *paylaşmak*.

(25a) Genç öğretmen:
       –Köyde bunlar görülmüyor ki, diye paylaştı.
       (The young teacher:
       Shared, saying, "in the village these things cannot be seen.")

(25b) Genç öğretmen:
       –Köyde bunlar görülmüyor ki diye söyledi/dedi.
       (The young teacher:
       Said, "these things cannot be seen in the village.")

(25c) –Topladığımız cevizleri akşamsı arkadaşlaria paylaştık.
       (In the evening we distributed the walnuts that we had
       collected among friends.)
       –Kendisiyle sevinç ve kederimi paylaşabileceğim yakın bir
       dosta ihtiyacım var.
       (I need a close friend with whom I can share my joys
       and sorrows.)
       –Sen bu kadınla kaderini paylaşmaya hazırmısın?
       (Are you ready to share your destiny with this woman?)
       –Ayni otelin ayni yatağını bir bayanla paylaştı.
       (He shared the same bed in the same hotel with a woman.)

Sentence 26a is constructed according to Bulgarian grammatical
rules. It is a literal translation of "Az ne sŭm sŭglasen s vas." The
Bulgarian word "sŭglasen" – in agreement with – is translated as
razı. Instead of saying "I disagree with you", the writer is saying
"I'm not satisfied with you." In Turkish *to agree* or *not to agree*
with someone is phrased differently than in Bulgarian. Examples
under 26b better express what the writer is trying to say. Of
course it is possible to form different sentences using the words
razı – willing, ready – and *nza* – consent, assent, approval – in the
form of *nzasını almak* – to get (someone's) consent; *razı etmek* – to
get someone to agree to something/do something; *razı olmak
(gelmek)* – to agree to, consent to, as illustrated under 26c.

(26a) –Ben siz*inle* razı değilim!
       (I'm not willing/ready with you.)

(26b) –Ben bu görüşte değilim.
       (I do not agree with your point of view.)

−Ben sizinle hemfikir değilim.
(I am not of the same opinion as you.)
−Ben bu düşüncenizi desteklemiyorum.
(I do not support your idea/opinion.)

(26c) −Benim rızamı almadan bu işi yapamazsın.
(You cannot do this work without my consent/agreement.)
−Ben buna rıza gösteremem.
(I cannot consent/agree to this.)
−Kim razı oldu, kim razı geldi?
(Who agreed to this, who consented to this?)
− Kadın geri dönmeye razı olmuyor.
(The woman does not agree to return.)

The "mistake" in sentences under 27a is not due to interference from Bulgarian. It is the result of perpetuating "incorrect" usage in colloquial speech most likely due to ignorance of "proper" grammatical rules. Examples under 27b illustrate standard usage. The same rules apply when using *buluşmak* (to come together), *görüşmek* (to meet, converse), *karşılaşmak* (to run into), *rastlaşmak* (to meet by chance), and so on.

(27a) −Bu akşam ner*eye* toplanacağız?
(To where will we meet tonight?)
−E, gene biz*e* toplanalım.
(Let's meet to our place again.)
−Mektep önün*e* toplansak olmazmı?
(Could we meet to the front of the school?)

(27b) −Bu akşam ner*de* toplanacağız?
(Where will we meet tonight?)
−E, gene biz*de* toplanalım.
(Let's meet at our place again.)
−Mektep önün*de* toplansak olmazmı?
(Could we meet in front of the school?)

The author notes that many mistakes in spoken and written Turkish are the result of thinking in Bulgarian, then trying to express the thought in Turkish. The author advises his readers that the Turkish version doesn't have to be a word for word translation from Bulgarian. It can take different forms as long as the thought is expressed clearly. These lessons continued until the end of 1991, when the government finally announced plans to reintroduce Turkish-language instruction in public schools acceptable to the Turkish community.

Over the past half century, the general trend was toward greater facility in Bulgarian by an ever greater proportion of the ethnic Turkish population. Nonetheless, even though most Turks in Bulgaria spoke Bulgarian quite comfortably, Turkish remained the primary language and was used almost exclusively at home. Many Turks, especially young ones, switched between the two languages many times a day, speaking Bulgarian in many public situations and even sometimes in private among themselves. In addition, as we have seen, Bulgarian loan words pervaded the spoken language, particularly of the young, and some minor grammatical effects of bilingualism were evident in spoken Turkish. Some more isolated Turkish communities had less Bulgarian influence, while Turks in larger cities had more. But to the best of our knowledge all Turkish communities in Bulgaria showed similar linguistic effects, differing only in degree.

As late as the end of the 1980s it looked as if the increasing use of Bulgarian, erosion of Turkish vocabulary, loss of Turkish literacy, and social advantages of speaking the majority language and being able to "pass" as Bulgarian would lead inexorably to accelerated changes in the Turkish spoken in Bulgaria, and perhaps even to significant numbers of Turks abandoning their ancestral language altogether within the next generation or two. The recent nationality policy zigzags have made this less likely.

The extreme anti-Turkish policies of 1984-90 had the unintended effect of strengthening Turkish ethnic identity. Speaking and writing Turkish became a political act of defiance. When speaking Turkish in public became an offense punishable by fines or imprisonment, parents were motivated to make the effort to teach their children to read and write the language, and children themselves became conscious of its importance to their cultural identity. Many Turks became more militantly Turkish than they had been previously. The liberalizing trend since the ouster of Živkov has lead to a revival of native-language instruction, access to Turkish periodicals, books, and radio and television broadcasts, and opportunities for travel to visit relatives in Turkey. The influence of all this on everyday speech is difficult to measure at this time. Our most recent observations suggest that Bulgarian influence on Turkish lexicon continues. However, Turkish speakers are more conscious of Bulgarianisms in their speech than in the recent past. The trend toward using only Bulgarian as a written language is being reversed. The influence of Buglarian on the Turkish lexicon will continue. However, increased exposure to standard Turkish will allow Turkish to resist massive influence as in the past.

Nationalism and language and cultural policies designed to create a nation-state with a single language and a homogeneous culture in Bulgaria failed. Attempts at forced assimilation of the Turkish minority into mainstream Bulgarian culture, instead of dissolving linguistic, ethnic and religious bonds, strengthened them. The opening up of the political process to many competing interest groups, including Turks, since 1989 and the general commitment of most political leaders to democracy and civic freedoms, should make a return to the authoritarian policies of the past difficult, if not impossible.

Unfortunately, authoritarian tendencies in Bulgarian political life remain. After the BSP victory in the 1994 elections, several draft laws were introduced in parliament, the primary aim of which is to restrict the rights of minorities in Bulgaria. What the communists failed to do through arbitrary police coercion, their successors are trying to do through legislative coercion. For example, a draft law on national radio and television would mandate broadcasting in Bulgarian only and would prohibit broadcasts in Turkish and other minority languages (Tatarlı 1995: 5). A more insidious draft law has the innocuous title, "On the Use and Protection of Bulgarian Language". This law would not only make Bulgarian the official language in all spheres of life except the home, but would impose exorbitant extra-judicial fines on violators. According to the preliminary version of the draft law, all contracts, whether between businesses or individuals, must be in Bulgarian; only Bulgarian must be spoken in government offices, courts, hospitals, schools, stores and restaurants, buses and trains, theaters and movie houses, on the streets, radio and television, and in political campaigns. The law would also prohibit the use of Turkish words or phrases in the print and broadcast media (Çavuş 1996: 1-2 Tatarlı 1996a: 5, 1996b: 3). A watered-down version of this draft law is likely to approved by parliament. The Bulgarian language does not need protection, nor are there disagreements among the citizens over the status of Bulgarian as the official language of the country. Such laws serve no other purpose beside fanning ethnic tensions unnecessarily. Policies designed to make Bulgarian the sole language of communication among Turks failed in the past. Such efforts will fail again and for the same reasons.

Several characteristics of the Turkish community in Bulgaria favor retention of the native language. First, the size of the ethnic Turkish community in the country. The Turks make up close to 10 per cent of the Bulgarian population. Linguists have noted that "[t]he larger the community of speakers of a given [minority] language, the longer the language is likely to be retained" (Chaika 1989: 312). Second, most Turks in Bulgaria live in ethnically homogeneous communities and neighborhoods. In such environments their most intensive contacts are with other Turks. Turkish is used as the primary medium of communication and major social activities are carried out in that language. Chaika (1989: 312) points out that a minority language is most likely to survive "where people are somewhat isolated physically or psychologically from the mainstream." In addition to the physical separation noted above, the trauma of the recent forced assimilation campaign has increased the psychological distance between Turks and Bulgarians. To a greater degree than in the past, Turks try to restrict their contacts with Bulgarians to official encounters and the workplace.

Attempts to restrict the use of Turkish would compound the psychological trauma of recent assimilation campaigns, increase ethnic tensions in the country, set back the integration of citizens of Turkish origin into Bulgarian society, and diminish Bulgaria's prospects of taking her rightful place within the community of European nations. That would indeed be a tragedy.

6

POST-1989 POLITICS AND MUSLIM MINORITIES

Bulgaria is the only formerly communist East European country that has a constitutional ban against the formation of political parties on exclusively ethnic or religious bases. Although Article 11(1) of the constitution adopted on 12 July 1991 states that "Politics in the Republic of Bulgaria shall be founded on the principle of political equality", paragraph 4 of the same article states in unequivocal terms, "There shall be no political parties on ethnic, racial or religious lines . . ." (Sofia Press Agency 1991: 6). This ban contradicts Article 6 (2): "There shall be no privileges or restriction of rights on the grounds of race, nationality, ethnic self-identity, sex, origin, religion, education, opinion, political affiliation, personal or social status or property status" (Sofia Press Agency 1991:6). Nevertheless, over the last several years the constitutional ban against the formation of political parties on ethnic and religious bases has been used by nationalists within and outside of government in attempts to disenfranchise minority groups who tried to form their own political parties. However, with the end of totalitarianism and one-party rule, controlling or stifling political dissent became more difficult. As Bates (1994: 202) observes:

> Prior to 1990, the minority populations themselves had no public voice, no organizational infrastructure, few shared visible symbols of community and history; the past four years have seen the emergence and empowerment of an ethnic political movement, the rise of politicized Turkish ethnicity, and the construction of a sense of a national Moslem community.

The forced assimilation campaign against Muslim minorities during the 1971-84 period supplied these groups,

> . . . . with a shared interest, the security of person and property;

167

religion, language, and a sense of shared experience of exclusion furnished the affect. The result has been the emergence of a highly politicized, ethnically constructed opposition; just like the "nation", Turkish and Moslem minorities have come to see themselves as a community, to call up shared symbols and texts, set limits to their identity, and use appeals to shared history and struggle to mobilize politically (Bates 1994: 203).

One of the most important, and most successful so far, organizations formed to mobilize Turks and other Muslims and to articulate their interests and concerns is the Movement for Rights and Freedoms (MRF). It has successfully withstood several challenges to its legitimacy. The MRF was officially founded in January 1990 to represent the interests of Muslims and other minorities in future multi-party elections. When the Movement attempted to register as a political party before the 1990 elections, Bulgarian nationalists mounted a court challenge to declare it illegal on the grounds that the Political Party Act of 1990 prescribed the formation of parties exclusively on ethnic or religious grounds. First the Sofia City Court, then the Supreme Court denied permission to the MRF to register. Finally, bowing to international pressure, the Central Electoral Commission granted permission to the MRF to register on 26 April 1990, less than two months before the elections. Anguelov (1990: 28) observes:

> Despite the brief span of the campaign, ostracism by officials and opposition activists, and the lack of a newspaper or other propaganda materials, the Movement for Rights and Freedoms, succeeded in winning a surprise 23 seats in Parliament (from 98 candidates). This [made] it the third political force [after the Bulgarian Socialist Party (formerly communist), which won the election, and the anti-communist coalition, the Union of Democratic Forces] in the country – ahead of the Bulgarian Agrarian Union (BAU), the traditional second-place party.

After the 1990 elections the nationalists tried to prevent the seating of MRF deputies during the symbolic opening of the Grand National Assembly in Veliko Tŭrnovo on 11 July by blocking the doors to the building. When this failed and the MRF deputies

> . . . . were seated in Parliament, another round of nationalist strife was stirred up . . . Instead of immediately electing a

president and appointing a government to deal with the out-
standing economic questions facing the country, the National
Assembly was forced to debate illegal and contrived demands
[from representatives of two nationalist parties] to oust the
Turkish representatives from Parliament on the grounds that
the MRF [was] unlawful under the constitution (Anguelov
1990: 28).

The second multi-party elections for parliament, along with
the first regional and local elections, were held on 13 October
1991. Only three parties were able to overcome the 4 per cent
threshold and elect deputies to parliament. The anti-communist
opposition represented by the UDF scored a narrow victory over
the BSP, electing 110 deputies to the 240 member parliament
to 106 deputies for the BSP. The MRF increased its support
from 6 per cent in the 1990 elections to 7.5 per cent, electing
twenty-four deputies to parliament. On 8 November 1991, with
the support of the MRF, the UDF was able to form Bulgaria's
first non-communist government since 1944, forcing the BSP
(ex-communists) into opposition. For the first time since Bulgarian
independence from Ottoman rule in 1878, a Turk was elected
Vice-President of parliament. A number of MRF deputies were
appointed as vice-presidents at several ministries. The MRF also
did extremely well in the regional and local elections in 1991,
electing 653 village headmen, twenty-seven municipal mayors,
and 1,144 representatives to municipal councils. Two back-to-back
successes established the MRF as the third political force in the
country after the UDF and the BSP (see Bates 1993).

In 1991 nationalists made another attempt to disenfranchise
the MRF. Several Bulgarian socialist deputies filed a complaint
at the Bulgarian Constitutional Court, claiming that the MRF
violated Article 11 (4) of the Constitution banning the formation
of political parties on ethnic or religious bases and Article 44 (2)
which prohibits the establishment of organizations that threaten
the sovereignty and territorial integrity of the country or foment
ethnic or religious enmity. The petitioners argued "that the MRF
[was] founded along ethnic and religious lines; that the Movement
us[ed] the Turkish language; and the MRF favor[ed] a policy of
ethnic assimilation of Bulgarian Moslems to the Turkish minority
and thus promot[ed] ethnic and religious confrontation within
the population." On the basis of these arguments the court was

asked to declare the MRF unconstitutional and its deputies in parliament "unelectable". On 22 April 1992, the Court, by the narrowest of margins, rejected the petitioners' claims and left the MRF free to function (*East European Constitutional Review* 1992: 11).

Having failed to ban the MRF through legal means, the nationalists resorted to new tactics in 1993 and 1994. They began to exploit the divisions within the leadership of the Movement and the Muslim community. They encouraged the formation of splinter parties among Turks and other Muslims in an attempt to divide the community, to weaken the MRF politically and, if possible, to shut it out of parliament altogether. Simmering disagreements within the Movement over tactics and goals and the make-up of the top leadership broke through the surface. Several high profile MRF members from southeastern Bulgaria left in protest against the dominance of Turks from northeastern Bulgaria who were accused of compromising the principles of the Movement in order to remain in power. Mehmed Hoca, a leading member of the MRF and Chairman of the Parliamentary Human Rights Commission left to form a new party, the Party of Democratic Changes. Another party, the Democratic Party of Justice, was formed by the former Chief Mufti Nedim Gencev, who had been relieved of his duties in 1992.

Even though the supporters of both parties were almost ex-clusively Turkish and/or Muslim, no questions were raised about their constitutionality and both were allowed to register as legitimate political parties. Both parties fielded candidates during the national elections in 1994 and in regional and local elections in 1995. In 1994 neither party was able to overcome the 4 per cent threshold necessary to elect deputies to parliament but they were able to take enough votes away from the MRF to reduce its representation in the current parliament to fifteen deputies, nine fewer than in the previous parliament. The BSP government rewarded Nedim Gencev for his effort by reinstating him into his former position as Chief Mufti over the objections of the majority of Muslims in Bulgaria. In the 1994 elections, the BSP won an absolute majority in parliament with 125 deputies. The UDF coalition fell apart before the elections and its representation was reduced from 110 deputies in the previous parliament to sixty-nine in the newly-elected one:

Table 6.1. ELECTION RESULTS, 1990, 1991 AND 1994:
REPRESENTATION OF POLITICAL PARTIES IN PARLIAMENT

	1990 seats	*1991* seats	*1994* seats
Bulgarian Socialist Party	211	110	125
Union of Democratic Forces	144	106	69
Movement for Rights and Freedom	23	24	15
Bulgarian Agrarian National Union	16	–	–
People's Union	–	–	18
Bulgarian Business Block	–	–	13
Others	6	–	–
Totals	400	240	240

Source: Troxel 1993: 408, 423; *East Europe Newsletter* 1995: 2.

Since 1990, the BSP has increasingly resorted to nationalism as a strategy to maintain itself in power. *Duma*, the official newspaper of the party, constantly harps on about the "Turkish threat" to the unity and the stability of the nation, and about the "unconstitutional" character of the MRF. During the Presidential elections in 1992, national elections in 1994, and regional and local elections in 1995, the BSP resorted to a blatant nationalist and anti-Turkish campaign, accusing the MRF and others of encouraging ethnic separatism. It courted the most militantly nationalist parties and groups to join its ranks. To the BSP, Bulgaria is a single-nation state, and therefore everyone in Bulgaria should be required to speak Bulgarian and to have Bulgarian names. After the 1994 elections, the BSP used its absolute majority in parliament to pass laws, most of them constitutionally suspect, to limit the powers of mayors from opposition parties and to more easily challenge electoral results that it did not like.

By 1995 clear electoral patterns had emerged. The BSP remained strong in rural areas; the UDF had established a strong constituency among the educated and urban population, especially in the larger towns and cities, while the MRF had a stable constituency among Turks and other Muslims. In preparation for the 1995 regional and local elections, the BSP used its parliamentary majority to amend existing electoral laws and to pass new ones to improve its own electoral prospects. The BSP amended the Local Self Government Act by creating the office of a government-appointed

"'Sofia Regional Governor' whose sole purpose [was] to curb the power of the mayor. Also, the powers of the mayors of the three largest cities, Sofia Plovdiv, and Varna, where the BSP anticipated the electoral victory of the opposition, were diminished through the establishment of popularly elected 'municipal district mayorships' "(*East European Constitutional Review* 1995: 6). Control over a few of these mayorships would give the BSP leverage to influence the implementation of local politics in large cities. The power of local councils was increased so that these councils could dismiss a mayor by a two-thirds majority, or call a referendum for dismissal by a simple majority. The BSP captured 194 municipal mayorships during the 1995 regional and local elections, demonstrating its strength in rural areas and small towns. All other parties were far behind the BSP, the MRF with twenty-six, the UDF/PU coalition with fifteen, and independent candidates with eighteen mayoralties. As expected, the UDF/PU coalition captured the mayorships of Sofia, Plovdiv, and Varna and held the majority in local councils in Bulgaria's big cities.

Prior to the 1995 elections the BSP also passed a new electoral law introducing several changes pertinent to local elections. The new law allowed three (instead of two) candidates to participate in run-off elections, which was designed to split the opposition vote, thus enhancing the chances of BSP candidates. Moreover, the new law expanded "the jurisdiction of regional courts to consider petitions contesting election results . . . BSP swiftly utilized this new weapon" (*East European Constitutional Review* 1995: 6). Rasim Musa, the MRF candidate, was elected mayor of Kŭrdžali by 658 votes over the BSP candidate. The Central Electoral Commission and the Kŭrdžali Municipal Council confirmed that the elections were legal. Immediately upon the announcement of election results the BSP filed a suit at the Municipal Court demanding that the electoral results be annulled on the grounds that 731 people from neighboring constituencies had voted illegally in Kŭrdžali. While the decision of the court was pending, the government-appointed governor of the Haskovo province, within which Kŭrdžali is located, refused to call a meeting of the new mayor and the newly elected municipal council. Finally, on 5 February 1996, the Kŭrdžali Municipal Court declared the elections to the municipal council and for mayor invalid. New elections were called for May. On 17 February, 6,000 ethnic Turks demonstrated against the court decision (*OMRI Daily Digest* 1995, 1996a). On 15 April 1996, the Bulgarian Supreme Court overruled the decision of the Kŭrdžali Municipal Court and reinstaled Rasim Musa as mayor of Kŭrdžali. The Supreme Court noted that the "irregularities" claimed by the Bulgarian Socialist Party in its original appeal to the Municipal Court were "insignificant" and did not affect the outcome of the elections (*OMRI Daily Digest* 1996b).

Of all the political parties in Bulgaria today, the MRF stands out with the civility of its discourse. The general aim of the MRF, as spelled out in its platform, is "to contribute to the unity of the Bulgarian people and . . . an unequivocal compliance with the rights and freedoms of mankind and of all ethnic, religious, and cultural communities in Bulgaria" (Engelbrekt 1991: 6-7). The leaders of the MRF have done their utmost to calm fears by categorically distancing themselves from "terrorism, chauvinism, revanchism, Islamic fundamentalism, nationalism, and the striving for autonomy" (Engelbrekt 1991: 7). They have acted very prudently by neutralizing extremist elements in their ranks and have shied away from inflammatory statements and unreasonable demands. Since its founding in 1990, the MRF has been consistent in its advocacy of the legal protection of minorities in Bulgaria in conformity with national and international laws; in its demand that the Muslims "be provided with the means to restore their cultural and religious identity" through restoration of Turkish-language instruction and instruction in Romany in state schools in ethnically mixed areas as well as reopening Islamic schools; and its insistence that those implicated in the forced assimilation campaign against Turks and other Muslims during the 1970s and 1980s be brought to justice (Engelbrekt 1991: 7). Unfortunately, these reasonable demands have been interpreted by Bulgarian nationalists as indications of Turkish nationalism or Islamic fundamentalism and a threat to the sovereignty and integrity of the Bulgarian state.

The more immediate objectives of the Movement are concerned with the specific situation of Turks and other Muslims in Bulgaria.. Engelbrekt (1991: 7) summarizes the most important points in the 1990 MRF platform:

> All Turks who fled communist oppression in 1989 to have their property returned and their jobs restored; the optional teaching of Turkish, three or four hours a week, in Bulgarian

schools to pupils who are ethnic Turks; the optional teaching of Islamic theology in Bulgarian schools to pupils who are ethnic Turks; the restoration of regional cultural and ethnic institutions, such as Turkish theaters, folklore ensembles, cultural clubs, and regular radio and television broadcasts in Turkish; the restoration of mosques in Kyustendil, Plovdiv, and elsewhere; permission to construct Islamic prayer houses if Moslem congregations wish to do so; the lifting of the ban on publishing Islamic literature, including the Koran; the introduction of Ramadan and Kurban as national holidays for Moslems, the lifting of bans on religious rites; for example, in connection with burials; and the return of property belonging to Islamic communities that was nationalized by the communist party.

To date, most of these problems have been addressed adequately, although several problems, such as the restoration of property and jobs of Turks who emigrated to Turkey in 1989 and subsequently returned to Bulgaria, Turkish-language programs on the national radio and television, reopening of professional Turkish and Gypsy theaters, return of mosque and *vakf* properties, and so on remain unresolved. Also worrisome are the debates in the current parliament that aim to restrict the rights of Turks and other minorities through legislative means.

The deteriorating economic conditions in Turkish and Pomak areas in the Rhodopes are especially problematic for the MRF. The collapse of markets for Bulgarian tobacco in Eastern Europe and the former Soviet Union after 1989 has led to serious economic problems in Muslim areas, especially in the Rhodopes. The unemployment rate has skyrocketed to more than twice the national average, forcing many Turks to emigrate to Turkey and Pomaks to leave their native communities in search of jobs in the cities. The BSP has used the power of the purse to withhold economic aid from areas where the MRF enjoys widespread support, while disingenuously blaming the MRF for the economic plight of the people.

The nationalist efforts to ban or to fragment the MRF have failed so far. Since its founding in 1990 the constituency of the Movement has remained remarkably stable. Turks make up 90 per cent of its membership; the rest include Pomaks, Gypsy Muslims, Tatars and a small number of Bulgarians. Over 90 per cent of Turks have voted for the Movement's candidates in three national and two local elections. Two splinter parties, Hoca's Party of Democratic Changes and Gencev's Democratic Party of Justice, ran candidates during the 1994 and 1995 elections, but have not gained a wide following. The voting patterns among Pomaks and Gypsy Muslims are mixed. The Pomaks living in Turkish areas, fearing assimilation by Turks, have generally voted for the BSP, while those living in Bulgarian areas, fearing assimilation by Bulgarians, have voted for the MRF. Most of the Gypsies, on the other hand, have generally voted for the BSP. Under communist rule they depended on government services to a greater degree than other groups and have suffered greater economic hardships under the transition. The BSP has effectively manipulated Gypsy fears by promising them to slow down economic reforms and to maintain government services.

The Movement has done quite well in the three multi-party elections and the two local elections since 1989. However, its influence at the national level has been limited. The MRF has been politically isolated in parliament. Even after the 1991 elections when it theoretically held the balance of power in parliament, its nominal ally, the UDF, often joined the BSP to block initiatives introduced by the MRF. Nevertheless, it remains a potent political force at the local level, especially in ethnically mixed regions of the country. The continuing economic stagnation in Muslim areas may prove the Achilles heel of the Movement. If the BSP could overcome its nationalist rhetoric and use its power of the purse to rejuvenate the economies of the Rhodopes and northeastern Bulgaria, it could gain the support of large numbers of Muslims and weaken the MRF considerably. So far there are no indications that the BSP is contemplating such a course.

EPILOGUE

For most of the post–Second World War period, especially during the 1970s and 1980s, the policy of the communist regime toward minorities in Bulgaria can be described as nothing short of an attempt at cultural genocide defined as a "coordinated plan of different actions aimed at destruction of the essential foundations of the life of national groups . . . The objective of such a plan [was the] disintegration of the political and social institutions, of culture, language, national feelings, [and] religion . . . of individuals belonging to such groups" (Lemkin 1994: 79). Serious attempts were made to destroy the unique cultural traditions of Turkish and other Muslims and to impose the Bulgarian cultural pattern upon them.

Some concrete examples of this attempt at cultural genocide in Bulgaria included the destruction or prevention of use of mosques, defacement or destruction of Muslim gravestones with Turkish or Arabic inscriptions on them, elimination of separate Muslim cemeteries, replacement of traditional religious rituals associated with important life-cycle events such as birth, marriage and death with so-called "socialist" rituals, banning the circumcision of Muslim boys and the wearing of traditional clothes by Muslim women, banning the celebration of major Muslim religious holidays, prohibition of publication of basic religious texts within Bulgaria as well as the importation of such texts from outside, and so on. For Turkish Muslims and other Turkish speakers, additional measures were taken in an attempt to extinguish important aspects of their cultures. These included elimination of Turkish-language instruction, and between 1985 and 1989, prohibition of the use of Turkish in daily intercourse, banning the printing and circulation of publications in Turkish, confiscation and destruction of books in Turkish, including those which had been published in Bulgaria by the government publishing house, Narodna Prosveta. This prohibition against the use of Turkish in daily intercourse was expanded to listening to Turkish music over the radio or cassette players as well as watching broadcasts from Turkey on television.

The efforts of the communist regime in Bulgaria to eradicate the social, cultural, and religious heritage of Muslims in its attempt to create a homogenous, single-nation state had the opposite effect to the one desired. Such policies not only failed to unify the nation, but heightened the differences between Christians and Muslims. Instead of weakening ethnic and religious cleavages, the assimilation campaigns strengthened the identity and separateness of Bulgarians, Turks, Gypsies, and Pomaks. Group exclusivity, which had always existed in Bulgaria, was exacerbated.

Under the transition from communism to post-communism a new set of problems have emerged. The certainties of communist ideology about the inexorable march of history toward a brighter future have disappeared. The liberalizing trends initiated by the transition have given a new dimension to ethnic conflict. Politicized ethnic identities have become instruments of contestation for political power. What the outcome of such a contestation will be cannot be predicted with certainty. One would hope that the people will use the power granted them wisely to shape a better future for themselves and for their country.

In spite of serious problems in the areas of education, politics, religion, and the economy, most Muslims in Bulgaria today are more confident about themselves and feel greater pride in who they are when compared with the recent past. They have reclaimed most of their cultural and civil rights without the armed conflict that characterizes the relationship between ethnic groups in many multi-ethnic states, especially those in formerly communist societies who recently gained their independence. The catalyst for such a peaceful change has been the astute leadership of the MRF, which has demonstrated a sense of balance, moderation, perspective, pragmatism, and common sense. The leaders of the MRF have stressed the ideals of consensus and cooperation instead of confrontation to solve the pressing problems of the country. They have emphasized the integration of Muslim citizens of Turkish, Gypsy, and Bulgarian origin into Bulgarian society on an equal footing with Bulgarians. However, just below the surface a sense of unease and insecurity remains. Bulgarian nationalists within and outside government have used, are using, and will use scapegoating of Turkish and other Muslims to further their political and personal interests. Deteriorating economic conditions provide fertile ground for these reactionary forces to try to maintain an undefined "national unity" by keeping ethnic tensions close to the boil. Continued discrimination against Muslims, the persistence of economic inequalities between Bulgarian Christians and Muslims, and growing government interference in the religious and educational affairs of the Muslim community necessarily force Muslims to activate their unique linguistic, ethnic, and religious support systems in attempts to maintain their identity and integrity.

In Anderson's apt phrase, nations indeed are imagined communities. However, the leaders of Bulgaria today, to paraphrase Maybury-Lewis (1996: 250-1), need a leap of the imagination beyond lip service to democracy to imagine a pluralist nation within which diversity is not only tolerated but different cultural traditions are allowed to flourish. Only such conditions will inspire citizens from minority cultural traditions to commit themselves to building a transcendent imagined nation that serves the interests of all of its citizens.

APPENDIXES
A

LETTER ORDERING MUSLIMS TO DEFACE TOMBSTONES OF
THEIR RELATIVES WITH TURKISH OR ARABIC INSCRIPTIONS.

People's Republic of Bulgaria
Çernoočene Village System
Municipality

Date.....
Village Head's Office

Dear.....
.....Village

Pursuant to the recommendations of the "Commission for
Ceremonies" headed by Master Sergeant Mladenov you are required
to cover up with cement plaster whatever is inscribed on the tombstones of your relatives (father, mother, brother, and sister) by 30
May 1987; otherwise, you will be punished with payment of a
fine of 50 to 2000 Leva according to Items 31 and 32 of the Administrative Offenses Act and Penal Code.

In case you fail to comply with the above order within the specified
time, in addition to the fine you will be handed over to the Militia
authorities.

Village Elder: D. Iliev
Secretary: M. Aleksandrova

(*Official seal and signature*)

Source: Solidarity and Cultural Association of the Balkan Turks 1988: 45.

179

B(i)

ORDER PROHIBITING THE WEARING OF *SHALVARI*
(TRADITIONAL BAGGY TROUSERS WORN BY TURKISH
AND OTHER MUSLIM WOMEN) AND THE SPEAKING
OF TURKISH IN PUBLIC, AND AN ORDER PROHIBITING
THE USE OF TURKISH NAMES AND SPEAKING TURKISH

People's Communal Council of the Stambolovo Village System
Gledka Town Hall
Order no. 5
Gledka, 3 August 1984

On the basis of Regulation No. 1 of the People's Communal Council
and the order of the President of the People's Communal Council
concerning the wearing of *shalvari* by the Turkish population and
the use of the Turkish language

I PROHIBIT

the wearing of *shalvari* at any time in the street, offices or public
institutions. Those who wear *shalvari* or who speak Turkish in commercial premises will not be served.
  Only Bulgarian is to be spoken in kindergartens.
  Those who disobey will be sanctioned.

(*signed*) Mayor

Source: Amnesty International 1986: 8, 19.

B(ii)

In connection with the efficacy of the measures for the returning of forcibly Islamized Bulgarians

I ORDER

1. From 1 January 1985 attendance for work on form 76 be filled out with reconstructed Bulgarian names.
2. The same requirement will apply to the issue of travel cards, sick records and other administrative documents.
3. The use of the Turkish language in public and work places is to be stopped.
4. All those with Arabic names who do not produce the necessary documents for name-changing will not be admitted to work.

This order is to be brought to the attention of all collectives for information and implementation. I assign the responsibility for its implementation to the leadership of the workshops/departments.

(*signed*) Director

C

A FORM MUSLIM PARENTS WERE REQUIRED TO SIGN, PROMISING NOT TO HAVE THEIR YOUNG SONS CIRCUMCISED

DECLARATION

Persons whose signatures are found below......................................
(name and surname)
Identity card............No......... Place of issue....................................
Police Headquarters ....
Identity Card ....No.......... Place of issue....................................
Police Headquarters.....................With this declaration I promise not
to have my son..........................circumcised, because it is playing
with the life and health of my son.

I sign this statement knowing that in the event that I allow this
operation to be performed on my son, I am punishable according
to Paragraph 2 of Article 320 and Paragraph 3 of Article 20 of
the Penal Code.

I sign this declaration in front of the clerk on duty.

....
(name and surname of the clerk on duty)
Declarer. 1..............................

2...........................

....
City of Haskovo

Clerk on duty:...........................

Source: Korkud 1986a: 29.

D

DECLARATION OF THE BULGARIAN MUFTIS SENT TO THE BULGARIAN NEWS AGENCY AND PUBLISHED IN OTEČESTVEN FRONT, 26 MARCH 1985.[1]

The declaration was signed by the Chief Mufti and most of the regional muftis, except for the Mufti of the district of Kŭrdžali, with their Bulgarian names.

Over the past few days some of the leading news agencies in a number of western countries have been putting out reports to the effect that the names of Moslems in Bulgaria were being forcibly changed, that the normal performance of their religious rites was being hindered and that mosques and other sacred places of the Bulgarian Moslems were being destroyed. It was also reported that the ambassadors of the Islamic countries accredited to Ankara had been summoned to the Turkish Foreign Ministry, where they were told the same story. The Turkish side demanded that the Islamic countries intercede with the Bulgarian government for the Bulgarian Moslems.

We, the religious leaders of the Moslem community in the People's Republic of Bulgaria, cannot but promptly react to these untrue and slanderous assertions concerning the Bulgarian Moslems and our homeland, the People's Republic of Bulgaria.

We declare clearly and unambiguously that Moslems in Bulgaria enjoy complete freedom which is guaranteed by the Constitution and the country's laws. They can profess Islam and perform their rites with the same freedom enjoyed by all other religions in this country. All mosques in the country are open and the clergy regularly perform their religious rites and services. There have been no cases of preventing or in any way restricting Moslems from performing religious rites and services. There have been so cases of mosques or other Moslem shrines being desecrated.

We wonder who gave the Turkish Foreign Ministry the right to become a spokesman of Islam, and to judge and decide matters that are exclusively within the competence of the Bulgarian Moslems? Islam is a world religion and every Moslem is entitled to bear a name reflecting his national identity.

We appeal to our Moslem brothers all over the world not to allow the Moslem faith to be linked with the selfish political ends of a given

---

[1] Over the next two weeks *Otečestven Front* also published letters of district *imams* in support of the declaration of the muftis (Sofia Press 1985: 29-48).

183

state, not to allow the sacred feelings of millions of believers to be abused and manipulated.

We take this opportunity to express our gratitude to the Bulgarian socialist state for our guaranteed constitutional freedoms, for the financial support it gives us every year so that our creed and religious organizations can be maintained and function normally. We are also grateful for the concern the state has been showing for the restoration and preservation of cultural and historical Moslem monuments.

We kindly request you to inform the public opinion in foreign countries about this letter of ours, as well as about our categorical rejection of the slanders against our people and homeland, slanders aimed at discrediting the People's Republic of Bulgaria and hindering the development of its relations with states with a Moslem population.

Source: Sofia Press 1985: 27-8.

E

DECLARATION SIGNED BY A GROUP OF NATIVE TURKISH
INTELLECTUALS, REFERRED TO AS "BULGARIANS WHO
RESTORED THEIR BULGARIAN NAMES", IN SUPPORT OF
GOVERNMENT POLICIES PUBLISHED IN *OTEČESTVEN FRONT*
ON 26 JULY 1985

For a century now a revival process has been under way among the descendants of those Bulgarians who during the five-century-long Ottoman domination were subject to forcible Islamization and ethnic assimilation. Due to its objective and law-governed character, this process gathered momentum, made way for itself and unfolded and reached completion in the years of people's rule.

Profound economic, social, political and cultural changes have taken place in modern Bulgarian society. True equality of rights of its citizens in all spheres of life has been established. This provides the basis for the promotion of a historical way of thinking which makes one realize the truth about the progress of the Bulgarians as a people and a nation.

The process of revival in our history is a vivid example of how the Bulgarians, despite the vicissitudes of their historical destiny, remained true to the logic of their 13 centuries-long existence. Essentially, this is a revolutionary act which erases one of the deepest scars left from the time of the Ottoman domination.

Many and undoubted are the facts which prove our Bulgarian ethnic character. We ourselves established the truth on the basis of irrefutable facts from our material and spiritual culture, from our mentality and traditional lifestyle, customs, rites and mores still alive in the memory of our mothers and fathers leaving deep traces in our way of life.

All the more so as there are many and well-known authors in the world, including Turkish ones, who have proved that the Ottoman conquerors carried out a systematic and consistent policy of assimilation as regards the enslaved peoples.

Within the borders of our country there is not a square foot of foreign land or foreign population.

Deeply rooted in the Bulgarian land, the honest and hard working people, the Moslemized Bulgarians subjected to ethnic assimilation at the time of the Ottoman domination, remain organically linked with the historical destiny of their people.

Reactionary circles in Turkey, however, do not take into consideration this fact. The mass media, the interested political circles in Bulgaria's southern neighbour, spread lies and slander about an alleged forcible

"Bulgarization of Turks" in Bulgaria. The new anti-Bulgarian propaganda campaign is built entirely upon unprecedented fabrications about thousands of murdered and wounded, about raped women and girls, about destroyed mosques, etc. They are increasingly trying to foist their absurd allegation to the effect that Turkey is the symbol of Islam, that in Bulgaria everything that is Islamic is Turkish and all Moslems are Turks.

It is true that in Bulgaria there are people who profess Islam, just as there are others who profess East Orthodox, Catholic and other religions. In this country religious sentiments and rights are under the protection of the law. But this is no reason for anyone to lay ethnic claims on the believers.

Turkish nationalists have subjected to persecution more than 12 million Kurds and other ethnic communities of non-Turkish origin, living on land of their own within the borders of Turkey. According to the Constitution of the Republic of Turkey, every citizen of that country is a Turk regardless of his or her ethnic or religious affiliation. Even the mentioning of the existence of national minorities in Turkey is prohibited by law. No other language except Turkish can be taught as a mother tongue at educational and training establishments in the country. Raising high our voice in defense of the truth and denouncing firmly the incredible lies and slanders, we declare:

– We the Bulgarians have one and the same national destiny, one and the same national character, one and the same goals and aspirations, irrespective of the religion professed by our grandfathers and grandmothers, fathers, and mothers. We are all offspring of the Bulgarian nation, we are the master of this land, and our paradise is here. There is no, and there cannot be any other, paradise for us!
– Yes, we are Bulgarians who gave up voluntarily, fully consciously and with conviction that the names were alien to our Bulgarian national roots. The Bulgarian name is for us a pledge of historical continuity and an invincible spiritual stronghold of our progress. We are proud of our Bulgarian names and we shall bear them with dignity, serving our socialist homeland loyally and with devotion.
– We consider every attempt to twist the essence of this fully natural historical process, which is an expression of our reborn Bulgarian national spirit, to be a crude and inadmissible encroachment upon our national dignity and human rights.
– We decisively oppose the attempt of Turkish reactionary circles to speculate with the so-called emigrants' question. They should grasp the truth that it is neither logical nor admissible for Bulgarians who have made their historical choice of nation and homeland, to emigrate to a

country which is foreign to them. This will never be! The choice has been made, it is final and irrevocable!

We desire peace, cooperation and good neighbourly relations with the Republic of Turkey. We believe that the honest Turkish intellectuals and sober-minded public figures want the same. In the name of this goal we appeal for an end to be put to the hostile anti-Bulgarian propaganda campaign, launched by Turkish nationalists and actively supported by their patrons.

We request the Bulgarian News Agency (BTA) to bring this declaration of ours to the knowledge of the Bulgarian and the world public.

Source: Sofia Press 1985: 13-19.

F

A DOCUMENT OF ADMINISTRATIVE VIOLATION ISSUED TO A TURK FOR SPEAKING TURKISH

People's Municipal Council
District of Kŭrdžali
Statement No....

For determining administrative violation

On 2-18-1985 in city/village Kŭrdžali
the undersigned Angel Radev Hristov
in the presence of witnesses: Stoyan Georgiev Dobrev
                              and Dimitŭr Ivanov Topalov
drew up this statement against Sasho Yordanov Stoyanov from the city of Kŭrdžali who resides at Georgi Dimitrov Street, Block 90, Apt. 3, retired due to illness, 54 years old

for the following: speaking Turkish

This is a violation of Article 2, paragraph A of decree No. 1. Therefore, in compliance with article 36, paragraph 1 of the law on administrative violations and penalties I drew this document for determining administrative violation.

Witnesses: 1. (signature)
            2. (signature)

Official: (signature)

Source: Korkud 1986b: 16–17.

188

G

CONVICTION OF TURKS WHO HAD COMPLAINED ABOUT
THEIR PLIGHT IN LETTERS TO THEIR RELATIVES IN TURKEY

People's Republic of Bulgaria
High Court of Justice
Date.....
No.......

The Central Committee of the Communist Party of Bulgaria,
Department of "Private Letters"

Copy......
Ref.......
Accused......

....The accused and his family members have acccepted their Bulgarian
names with their free will in the course of the Rebirth Process.
However, the accused, influenced by domestic vacillations and foreign
propaganda, has lately taken negative stance against the Rebirth Process.
His letter ... addressed to one of his relatives in Turkey contains
slanders about the manner of adopting Bulgarian names, and about
public attitude towards the citizens whose names have been changed.
He wrote a similar letter to his cousin...... on ..... His slanders suggest
that the citizens belonging to the minority community do not enjoy
equal rights, that MVR (Bulgarian Ministry of Home Affairs) applied
pressure, that doctors refused medical help, that prisons are filled
with "Turkish" youth. He has enclosed in his letter to his cousin
another letter, containing similar slanders, to be conveyed to Radio
Voice of Germany.

Both the letters, in addition to slanders, contain appeal for in-
tervention for restoration of the old situation.

.......on account of his deeds stated above he is found guilty and
is convicted for a prison term of 3 years and 6 months.

Petition of the accused to court of Appeal relevant to ..... criminal
case ..... verdict of ..... court is rejected according to the court verdict
No..... dated .....

The term of imprisonment approved is commensurate with the
offense committed.

The lower court, while deciding on the term of imprisonment
has duly taken into account the particular conditions relevant to

Appendixes

the nature of the case as well as to the difficult family situation and ill health of members of his family. Therefore, the accused is penalized at average level of punishment stipulated in the law. The lower court has correctly assessed the great danger posed by the action the accused had attempted.

The punishment ordered is just. There is no need to resume hearing.

Chairman
High Court of Justice
People's Republic of Bulgaria

(Seal and Signature)

Source: Solidarity and Cultural Association of the Balkan Turks 1988: 46-9.

H

MEASURES AGAINST THE TURKISH SELF-IDENTIFICATION
OF GYPSIES, BULGARIAN MUSLIMS (POMAKS) AND TATARS
APPROVED BY THE POLITBURO, APRIL 1962

In its policies toward the national minorities the BCP (Bulgarian Communist Party) has always been guided by the Marxist-Leninist theory on the national question. Securing the complete political and social equality of rights to all working people with no difference as to language, religion, or nationality, the Party and the government of the people have taken a number of special measures for the quick liquidation of the great economic and cultural backwardness of the Turkish and Gypsy population. The victory of 09.09.1944 opened new bright perspectives for the economic and cultural development of the Bulgarian Muslims as well. This correct policy of the Party has given its positive results. Almost all capable workers from this part of our people participate in the construction of socialism, their material status is improving quickly, their culture is rising, a local intelligentsia is created, the children go to school, they are entitled to free medical services etc.

But in the process of successful realization of the cultural revolution some negative tendencies can be noticed which hamper its development, create difficulties for the strengthening of the moral and political unity of the people, and serve as an instrument of the propaganda of the enemy. A considerable part of the Gypsies, the Tatars, and the Bulgarian Muslims still tend to affiliate with the Turks under various forms, a tendency which is especially helped by the Muslim religion and the Turkish and Arabic names. Stimulated by the Turkish reactionary propaganda and religious fanaticism, and helped by the incorrect activities of a number of bodies of the people's government, more than 130,000 Gypsies and tens of thousands of Tatars and Bulgarian Muslims in many parts of the country have registered themselves as Turks.

The families of Bulgarian Muslims move from the Rhodopes region to villages with Turkish populations and register themselves there as Turks. The intermarriages between Bulgarian Muslim women and Turks and vice versa are used for the "acquisition" of a Turkish nationality both for the spouses and their children.

This tendency to affiliate with the Turks was objectively aided in certain towns and villages by the teaching of the Turkish language to the children of Tatars, Bulgarian Muslims and Gypsies in classes together with Turkish children.

The religious services for the believers among the Gypsies and the Tatars conducted by imams and Turks also help the tendency towards affiliation with the Turks.

The gathering of the young Gypsies, Tatars, and Bulgarian Muslims with young Turks in common military companies and platoons and labor units also has a harmful effect on their national and patriotic education.

In order to stop these negative tendencies for affiliation with the Turks, which are in fact leading to the assimilation of the Bulgarian Muslims, the Gypsies, and the Tatars by the Turkish influence, and in order to strengthen their patriotic education even more, the Politburo of the CC of BCP

DECIDED:

(1) The party committees and organizations, the committees and organizations of the Fatherland Front, the Komsomol, the trade unions and other social organizations, the bodies of the ministries, the administration, the people's councils, and the economic Organization in the places with Gypsies, Tatars, and Bulgarian Muslims should take as one of the major tasks in their political and ideological work among this population systematic and diligent activities for the enhancement of the political consciousness and labor activity, for the raising of its culture, for the gradual overcoming of the tendency to affiliate with the Turks by leading a systematic ideological and political struggle against the Turkish religious and chauvinistic propaganda and its pan-Turkish and pan-Islamic aims and aspirations.

(2) The ministry of Justice together with the Department for the People's Councils at the Council of Ministers on the basis of the constitution and the legislation of the country must work out instructions for the application of art. 16 of the regulations on maintaining registers on the civil status, in which to give detailed instructions on the process of registration of the population. The instructions must especially point out that religion and personal names are not criteria for nationality. It must also be made clear that intermarriage does not lead to change of nationality of the spouses. The children of the intermarried couple can be registered as Bulgarians completely voluntarily and with the explicit agreement of both parents.

The instructions must elucidate the rights of the citizens of non-Bulgarian descent, who in accordance with their internal conviction and openly declared personal desire can register themselves and their families as Bulgarians, can change their names without asking for permission from the people's court but by making a written application to the respective people's councils. It must also be included in the instruction that the same right to a simplified procedure for the change of their names is given to the Bulgarian Muslims.

The enforcement of the instructions must be accompanied by a large and systematic popular persuasion, and by no means should any form of violence or administrative force be used. The regional committees of the Party and the other bodies and organizations of the Party as well as the bodies of government which are in charge of these questions must take all the necessary measures against the violation of the laws and regulations and the possible perversions which might occur in the registration of the citizens of non-Bulgarian descent and the Bulgarian Muslims.

(3) The party committees and organizations and the people's councils must carry out a large campaign of public persuasion among the Tatars, the Gypsies, and the Bulgarian Muslims, who are registered as Turks according to Letter no. 5-434 from 11 May 1950 by the Civil Status Department of the Ministry of the Interior or for other reasons, so that these people should be registered with their real nationality according to the Law of Civil Status and the instructions for the application of this law, with the exception of those who have already registered themselves as Bulgarians. Measures must be taken during the registration not to allow perversions, pressure or administrative force.

(4) The people's councils must not allow Bulgarian Muslims and Gypsies to move to villages or towns with compact Turkish populations.

(5) The Ministry of Education and Culture and the regional people's councils must take measures so that the Turkish language is not taught to the children of Gypsies, Tatars, and Bulgarian Muslims. These children must be taught in Bulgarian. The appointment of Turkish teachers at schools where the children of Gypsies, Tatars and Bulgarian Muslims predominate must be avoided. The children of Bulgarian Muslims and Gypsies must not be allowed to live in hostels or to study in the same groups with Turkish children wherever this is possible.

(6) The Ministry of the People's Defense and the Chief Headquarters of the Labor Services must ensure favorable conditions for the correct education of the young Bulgarian Muslims, Gypsies or Tatars. The

Chief Political Department of the Ministry of the People's Defense and the Political Department of the Chief Headquarters of the Labor Services must strengthen the educational and political work for the national awareness, the communist and patriotic education of the young servicemen and members of the labor corps of Gypsy, Tatar or Bulgarian descent, who tend to affiliate with the Turks.

(7) The Committee on the questions of the Bulgarian Orthodox Church and the Religious Cults at the Ministry of Foreign Affairs must take measures for the correct explanation of the Bulgarian-Muslim, Gypsy, and Tatar questions to the Muslim clergymen; should see that the imams comply with the socialist legislation and should not allow them to carry out any reactionary propaganda in favor of the affiliation with the Turks, especially through religious services; should not permit the appointment of Turkish clergymen in the villages with compact Gypsy and Tatar population and among Bulgarian Muslims.

(8) The Bulgarian Academy of Sciences must send complex expeditions of historians, ethnographers, philologists, etc. for the comprehensive study of the national origins and the nationality of the population in the respective regions of the country; the expeditions should establish especially the ethnic origin and the national peculiarities of Turks. Tatars, Gypsies who live in Bulgaria. The study of the historic past of the Bulgarian Muslims in the Rhodopes, the Lovech region and other parts of the country must continue in order to make further discoveries about the historical truth about the results of the assimilation policies of the Turkish oppressors, about the mass and individual conversions to Islam.

A special section must be set up at the Institute for the History of Bulgaria at the Bulgarian Academy of Sciences for the study of the historic past of the Bulgarian Muslims.

(9) At the Propaganda and Campaigning Department of the Central Committee of the BCP a committee must be formed to study the problems and to design activities for the national awareness and the communist education of the Bulgarian Muslims. For this purpose an instructor for the work among Bulgarian Muslims must be appointed by the department.

Source: Helsinki Watch 1991: 69–73.

I

PARTIAL LIST OF TURKISH WORDS AND THEIR BULGARIAN EQUIVALENTS[1]

Turkish	Bulgarian	English translation
albay	polkovnik	captain
algılamak	vuzpriemane	to perceive
araç	sredstvo	means (vehicle, tool)
arıza	povreda	defect, failure
bağışıklık	imunitet	immunity
bakan	ministır	state secretary
baskan	predsedatel	president
bayındırlık	blagoustroystvo, blagoustroeno	development, developed
beğeni	vkus	taste
bursburs	stipendiya	stipend
evren	horizont	horizon
dernek	krıjok	association
dilekçe	molba	petition
dönem	period	era
dümen	kormilo	steering wheel
ebe	akuşerka	midwife
edebiyat	literatura	literature
eğilim	sklonnost, tendentsiya	tendency, inclination
eleştiri	kritika	criticism
emekli	pensioner	retired
endişe	agrijenost, grija	anxiety, worry
gerilim	naprejenie	tension
gezmen	pıteşestvenik	traveler, tourist
gözlem, gözlemci	nabludenie, nabludatel	observation, observer
günlük	dnevnik	daily register
hemşire	sestra	nurse
ihtar	preduprejdenie	a warning
işgal, istila	okupatsiya, zaviadyavane	occupation, invasion
iştirak	uçastie	participation

[1] The transliteration of Turkish and Bulgarian words is as given in the original sources.

195

ihracat	iznos	export
itiraf	priznanie	confession, admission
ithalat	vnos	import
itki	impuls	impulse
kalite	kaçestvo, kaçestveno	quality, of good quality
kanun	zakon	law
katkı	prinos	contribution, assistance
kaza	a) okoliya, b) katastrofa	a) province, b) accident
kınamak	osıjdam, poritsavam	to condemn, censure
kütüphane	biblioteka	library
maaş	zaplata	salary
mağaza	sklad	warehouse
makbuz	kvitantsiya	receipt (for payment)
malzeme	material	material, supplies
mefküre	ideya	idea
mermi	patron	bullet
mevki	klasa, obştestveno polojenie	rank, social status
mezun	abiturient	a graduate
muhasebe	sçetovodstvo	accounting, bookkeeping
muhteşem	velikolepno	splendid
mukavele	dogovor	contract
musluk	kran	faucet
mutabakat	suglasie	mutual agreement
müdahele	namesa	interference
okuma yurdu	çitalişte	community reading room
öneri	predlojenie	proposal
öngörmek	predvijdane	to forsee, to anticipate
özbilinç	samosıznanie	self-consciousness
özerklik	avtonomiya	autonomy
sağduyu	blagorazumie, zdravomisleşt	common sense, sensible
sanık	obvinaem, podsıdim	accused, defendent
saydam	prozraçno, prozraçnost	transparent
serüven	priklüçenie, prejivyavane	adventure
sınav	ispit, izpitanie	test, examination
sipariş	ponçka	order (things for purchase)
sırnaşık	lepkav, nahalen	pertinacious, impudent
somut	konkretno	concrete
soyut	abstraktno	abstract
subay	ofitser	commissioned officer

şikayet	oplakvane, jalba	complaint
şirket	kompanya, sdrujeniye	company, association
taburcu	ispisvane, osvobojdavane	discharged, dismissed
talep	iskane, iziskvane	demand, formal request
temas	kontakt	contact
trafik	dvijenie, transport	traffic
uydu	spıtnik, satelit	satelite
uyruk	podanstvo, grajdanstvo	citizenship
veli	nastoynik	guardian
veri	danni	datum
yatırım	investitsiya	investment
yedek	rezerv	spare part
yenilikçi	ratsionalizator	advocate of change
yoğun	intenzivno, kompaktno	intensive, dense
yorum	komentar	commentary
zam	uveliçenie, povişenie	price increase
zorunlu	nasilstveno, prinuditelno, zadıljitelno	forced, compulsory, obligatory

Source: Çavuş 1988: 67, Tahsin 1991.

BIBLIOGRAPHY

Ayata, Sencer (1996), "Patronage, party, and state: the politicization of Islam in Turkey", *Middle East Journal*, 50 (1): 40-56.

Acaroğlu Türker (1992), "Bir Bulgar profesörün 'itirafları', *Türk Dünyası Tarih Dergisi*, 70: 17-22.

Aliev, Ali (1980), *Formiraneto na Naučno-ateističen Mirogled u Bŭlgarskite Turci*, Sofia: Partizdat.

Amnesty International (1986), *Bulgaria: Imprisonment of Ethnic Turks – Human Rights Abuses during the Forced Assimilation of the Ethnic Turkish Community*, London.

Anguelov, Zlatko (1990), "The leader and his movement", *East European Reporter* 4 (3): 27-8.

Ashley, Stephen (1989), "Unrest among Bulgaria's Pomak community", *Radio Free Europe Research*, 1 September, 19-23.

—— (1990), "Ethnic unrest during January", *Radio Free Europe Research: Report on Eastern Europe*, 1 (6): 4-11.

Baest, Thorsten F. (1985), "Bulgaria's war at home: the People's Republic and its Turkish minority, 1944-1985", *Across Frontiers*, 2 (2): 18-26.

Bakoğlu, Naim (1993), "Türkçe öğretimine engellikler devam ediyor", *Hak ve Özgürlük*, 41:5.

—— (1995), "Türkçenin okunması bile bile engelleniyor", *Hak ve Özgürlük*, 18: 5.

Barkan, Ömer (1942), "Osmanli imperatorluğunda bir iskan ve kolonizasyon metodu olarak vakıflar ve temlikler", *Vakıflar Dergisi*, 2: 279-386.

—— (1949-50), "Les déportations comme méthode de peuplement et de colonisations dans l'Empire Ottoman", *Revue de la Faculté des Sciences Economiques de l'Université d'Istanbul*, 11: 108-19.

—— (1955), "Quelques observations sur l'organisation économique et sociale des villes Ottomanes des XVI et XVII siècles", *Recueils de la Société Jean Bodin* (Brussels) 8: 289-311.

—— (1970), "Research on the Ottoman fiscal surveys" in M.A. Cook, ed., *Studies in the Economic History of the Middle East from the Rise of Islam to the Present Day*, Oxford University Press, 163-71.

Bates Daniel G. (1993), "The ethnic Turks and the Bulgarian elections of October 1991", *Turkish Review of Balkan Studies* (annual), pp. 193-204.

—— (1994), "What's in a name? minorities, identity, and politics in Bulgaria", *Identities*, 1 (2-3), 201-25.

Beytulla, Mehmed (1993), "Türk dili öğretimi konusunda: biz ne istiyoruz, onlar ne veriyor", *Hak ve Özgürlük*, 26: 1, 7.

Bejtullov, Mehmed (1975), *Životŭt na Naselenieto ot Turski Proizhod v NRB*, Sofia: Partizdat.

Birge, John Kingsley (1937), *The Bektashi Order of Dervishes*, London: Luzac.

Bogoev, Goran (1993), "Contemporary religious changes in the life of the Mohammedan population in the eastern and western Rhodopes" in *The Ethnic Situation in Bulgaria (Researches in 1992)*, Sofia: Club 90 Publishers, 74-80.

Brisby, Liliana (1985), "Administrative genocide in the Balkans?", *The World Today*, 41 (4): 69-70.

Browning, Robert (1975), *Byzantium and Bulgaria: A Comparative Study across the Early Medieval Frontier*, London: Temple Smith.

Bŭlgarska Akademija na Naukite (1969), *Kratka Bŭlgarska Enciklopedija*, vol. 5, Sofia.

Cafer, Ayten (1992), "Nedim Gencev başmüftü görevinden alındı", *Hak ve Özgürlük*, 7:1-2.

Chaika, Elaine (1989), *Language: The Social Mirror*, New York: Newbury House.

Charanis, Peter (1955), "On the date of the occupation of Gallipoli by the Turks", *Byzantinoslavica*, 16: 113-17.

Crampton, Richard (1983), *Bulgaria, 1878-1918: A History*, Boulder, CO: East European Monographs.

—— (1990), "The Turks in Bulgaria, 1878-1944" in Kemal Karpat, ed., *The Turks of Bulgaria: The History, Culture and Political Fate of a Minority*, Istanbul: Isis Press, 43-78.

Cvetkova, Bistra (1983), "Ottoman *tahrir defters* as a source for studies on the history of Bulgaria and the Balkans", *Archivum Ottomanicum*, 8: 133-213.

Çavuş, Ismail (1996), "Yeni bir 'soya dönüş süreci' tezgahlanıyor," *Hak ve Özgürlük*, 3: 1-2.

Çavuş, Mehmet (1988), *20 Yüzyıl Bulgaristan Türkleri Şiiri: Antoloji*, Istanbul: Yaylacık Matbaası.

Çete, Mustafa (1993), "Türkçemizin öğretiminde engellikler", *Hak ve Özgürlük*, 40:5.

Dawkins, R.M. (1933), "The crypto-Christians of Turkey", *Byzantion*, 8, 247-75.

De Jong, Federik (1986a), "Notes on Islamic mystical brotherhoods in northeast Bulgaria", *Der Islam: Zeitschrift für Geschichte und Kultur des Islamischen Orients*, 63 (2): 303-8.

—— (1986b), "The Turks and Tatars in Romania: Materials relative

to their history and notes on their present-day condition", *Turcica*,
28: 165-89.

—— (1993), "Problems concerning the origins of the Qizibas in Bulgaria:
remnants of the Safaviyya?", *Accademia Nazionale dei Lincei* (Rome),
25: 203-15.

Denich, Bette (1993), "Unmaking multi-ethnicity in Yugoslavia: meta-
morphosis observed", *Anthropology of East Europe Review*, 11 (1-2):
43-53.

Dimitrov, Strašimir (1965), "Demografski otnošenija i pronikvane na
isljama v zapadnite Rodopi i dolinata na Mesta prez XV-XVII v.",
Rodopski Sbornik, 1: 63-114.

—— (1982), *Balkanite: Politiko-Ikonomičeski Spravočnik*, Sofia: Partizdat.

Dimitrova, Donka (1994), "Ethnic scarecrows in the press and the traditional models of communication between Christians and Muslims
in Bulgaria" in *Relations of Compatibility and Incompatibility between
Christians and Muslims in Bulgaria*, Sofia: International Center for
Minority Studies, 331-43.

Dinev, Ljubomir and Kiril Mišev (1969), *Bŭlgarija: Kratka Geografija*,
Sofia: Nauka i Izkustvo.

Djurdjev, Branislav (1960), "Bosna", *Encyclopedia of Islam*, 1, 1261-75.

Donkov, Kiril (1994), "Etničeskijat sŭstav na naselenieto na Bŭlgarija",
Statistika, 36 (2): 34-46.

Džambazov, Ismail (1981), "Kakvo se krie zad 'reformata' na religioznoto
obrazovanie v Turcia?", *Ateistična Tribuna*, 6: 52-69.

East Europe Newsletter (1995), "Bulgaria", 9 (1): 1-2.

East European Constitutional Review (1992), "Turkish party in Bulgaria
allowed to continue", 1 (2): 11-12.

—— (1993-4), "Bulgaria", 2 (4)/3 (1): 4-5.

—— (1995), 'Bulgaria', 4 (4): 5-8.

East European Reporter (1989), "Stirrings in Bulgaria", 3 (4): 26-8.

Eminov, Ali (1983), "The education of Turkish speakers in Bulgaria",
Ethnic Groups 5 (3): 129-49.

—— (1986), "Are Turkish speakers in Bulgaria of ethnic Bulgarian
origin?", *Journal, Institute of Muslim Minority Affairs*, 7 (2): 503-18.

—— (1990), "There are no Turks in Bulgaria: rewriting history by
administrative fiat" in Kemal Karpat, ed., *The Turks of Bulgaria: The
History, Culture and Political Fate of a Minority*, Istanbul: Isis Press,
203-22.

Engelbrekt, Kjell (1991), "Nationalism reviving", *Report on Eastern Europe*,
2 (48): 1-6.

Eren, Hasan (1986), "The Bulgarians and the Turkish language" in *Turkish
Presence in Bulgaria*, Ankara: Turkish Historical Society, 1-14.

Eroğlu, Hamza (1986), "The question of Turkish minority in Bulgaria from the perspective of international law" in *The Turkish Presence in Bulgaria: Communications*, Ankara: Turkish Historical Society.

Fine, John (1983), *The Early Medieval Balkans: A Critical Survey from the Sixth to the Late Twelfth Century*, Ann Arbor: University of Michigan Press.

Gellner, Ernest (1993), *Nations and Nationalism*, Ithaca, NY: Cornell University Press.

Georgeoff, John (1978), *The Education System in Bulgaria*, Washington DC: HEW.

Georgieva, Ivanička, ed. (1991), *Bŭlgarskite Aliani: Sbornik Etnografski Materiali*, Sofia: Universitetsko Izdatelstvo "Sv. Kliment Oxridski".

Gökbilgin, Tayyib (1957), *Rumelide Yürükler, Tatarlar ve Evladi-i Fatihan*, Istanbul: Osman Yalçın.

Goodwin, Godfrey (1994), *The Janissaries*, London: Saqi Books.

Gradešliev, Ivan (1993), *Gagauzite*, Dobrič: Biblioteka "Dobrudža".

Gradeva, Rossitsa (1994), "Ottoman policy towards Christian church buildings", *Etudes Balkaniques*, 30 (4): 14-36.

Grannes, Alf (1978), "Le redoublement Turc à M-initial en Bulgare", *Linguistique Balkanique*, 21 (2): 37-50.

—— (1990), "Turkish influence on Bulgarian" in Kemal Karpat, ed., *The Turks of Bulgaria: The History, Culture and Political Fate of a Minority*, Istanbul: Isis Press, 223-39.

Grekova, Maja (1992), "Otnošenijata Bŭlgari-Turci" in *Etnokulturnata Situacia v Bŭlgarija*, Sofia, 68-80.

Güngör, Harun and Mustafa Argunşah (1991), *Gagauz Türkleri*, Ankara: Kültür Bakanliği Yayinlari.

—— (1993), *Dünden Bugüne Gagauzlar*, Ankara: Elektronik Iletişim Ajansı Yayınları.

Gürün, Kamuran (1981), *Türkler ve Türk Devletleri Tarihi*, vol. 1, Ankara: Karacan Yayınları.

Gyuzelov, Vasil (1976), *The Adoption of Christianity in Bulgaria*, Sofia: Sofia Press.

Hafız, Nimetullah (1987) *Bulgaristan'da Çağdaş Türk Edebiyatı Antolojisi: 1944-1984*, 2 vols, Istanbul: Kültür ve Turizm Bakanlığı.

Hak ve Özgürlük (1995), "Bulgaristan Müslümanlarının ulusal konferansı yasaldır", 10: 2.

Halaçoğlu, Ahmet (1994), *Balkan Harbi Sırasında Rumeli'den Türk Göçleri (1912-1913)*, Ankara: Türk Tarih Kurumu Basımevi.

Hasluck, F.W. (1921), "The crypto-Christians of Trebizond", *Journal of Hellenic Studies*, 41: 199-202.

—— (1929), "Haji Bektash and the Janissaries" in *Christianity and Islam under the Sultans*, vol. 2, Oxford: Clarendon Press, 483-93.

—— (1948), "Firman of A.H. 1013-4 (A.H. 1604-5) regarding Gypsies in the Western Balkans", *Journal of the Gypsy Lore Society*, 27: 10-11.

Helsinki Watch (1986), *Destroying Ethnic Identity: The Turks of Bulgaria*, New York: Human Rights Watch.

—— (1987), *Destroying Ethnic Identity: The Turks of Bulgaria, An Update*, New York: Human Rights Watch.

—— (1989), *Destroying Ethnic Identity: The Expulsion of the Bulgarian Turks*, New York: US Helsinki Watch Committee.

—— (1991), *Destroying Ethnic Identity: The Gypsies of Bulgaria*, New York: Human Rights Watch.

—— (1993), *Bulgaria: Police Violence against Gypsies*, New York: Human Rights Watch.

—— (1994), *Bulgaria: Increasing Violence against Roma in Bulgaria*, New York: Human Rights Watch.

Hoffman, Stanley (1993), "The passion for modernity", *Atlantic*, August, 101-8.

Höpken, W. (1987), "Modernisierung und Nationalismus: Sozialges- chichtliche Aspekte der Bulgarischen Minderheitenpolitik gegenüber den Türken" in R. Schönfeld, ed., *Nationalitätenprobleme in Südosteuropa*, Munich: Oldenbourg, 255-303.

Hristov, Hristo (1980), *Bulgaria 1300 Years*, Sofia: Sofia Press.

Hupchick, Dennis (1983), "Seventeenth century Bulgarian Pomaks: forced or voluntary converts to Islam?" in Stevan and Agnes Vardy, eds, *Society in Change: Studies in Honor of Bela K. Kiraly*, Boulder CO: East European Monographs, 305-14.

Ilchev, Ivan and Duncan M. Perry (1993), "Bulgarian ethnic groups: politics and perceptions", *RFE/RL Research Report*, 2 (12): 36-7.

Iliev, Chavdar L. (1989), "The Bulgarian nation through the centuries", *Journal, Institute of Muslim Minority Affairs*, 10 (1): 1-20.

Iljazov, S. (1981), "Isljamŭt i turskiyat buržoazen nacionalizm", *Ateistična Tribuna*, 5:22-7.

Inalcik, Halil (1954), "Ottoman methods of conquest", *Studia Islamica*, 1: 103-29.

—— (1965), "Dobrudja", *Encyclopedia of Islam*, 2: 610-13.

—— (1973), *The Ottoman Empire: The Classical Age, 1300-1600*, London: Weidenfeld and Nicolson.

—— (1976), "The rise of the Ottoman Empire" in M.A. Cook, ed., *A History of the Ottoman Empire to 1730*, Cambridge University Press, 10-53.

—— (1991), "The status of the Greek Orthodox Patriarch under the Ottomans", *Turcica: Revue d'Etudes Turques*, 21-3: 407-36.

International Center for Minority Studies (1994), *Relations of Compatibility and Incompatibility between Christians and Muslims in Bulgaria*, Sofia.

Ipek, Nedim (1994), *Rumeli'den Anadolu'ya Türk Göçleri (1877-1890)*, Ankara: Türk Tarih Kurumu Basımevi.

Jelavich, Barbara (1983), *History of the Balkans: Eighteenth and Nineteenth Centuries*, Cambridge University Press.

Kafesoğlu, Ibrahim (1983), "Türk-Bulgar'ların tarih ve kültürüne kısa bir bakış", *Güneydoğu Avrupa Araştırmalan Dergisi*, 11-12: 91-123.

Karpat, Kemal (1976), "Gagauz'ların tarihi menşei üzerine ve folklorundan parçalar" in *I. Uluslarası Tük Folklore Kongresi Bildirileri*, c. 1, Ankara, 163-77.

—— (1978), "Ottoman population records and the census of 1881-82, 1893", *International Journal of Middle East Studies*, 9: 237-74.

—— (1984-5), "Ottoman urbanism: the Crimean Tatar emigration to Dobruca and the founding of Mecidiye, 1856-1878", *International Journal of Turkish Studies*, 3 (1): 1-25.

—— (1985), *Ottoman Population, 1830-1914: Demographic and Social Characteristics*, Madison: University of Wisconsin Press.

Karpat, Kemal, ed. (1990), *The Turks of Bulgaria: The History, Culture and Political Fate of a Minority*, Istanbul: Isis Press.

Kertikov, Kiril (1991), "The ethnic nationality problem in Bulgaria (1944-1981)", *Bulgarian Quarterly*, 1 (3): 78-87.

Kiel, Machiel (1985), *Art and Society of Bulgaria in the Turkish Period*, Assen: Van Gorcum.

—— (1990), "Urban development in Bulgaria in the Turkish period: the place of Turkish architecture in the process" in Kemal Karpat, ed., *The Turks of Bulgaria: The History, Culture and Political Fate of a Minority*, Istanbul: Isis Press, 79-158.

—— (1991), "Hrazgrad-Hezargrad-Razgard: the vicissitudes of a Turkish town in Bulgaria", *Turcica: Revue d'Etudes Turques*, 21-3: 495-563.

King, Robert R. (1973), *Minorities under Communism: Nationalities as a Source of Tension among Balkan Communist States*, Cambridge, MA: Harvard University Press.

Kinross Lord (1977), *The Ottoman Centuries: The Rise and Fall of the Turkish Empire*, New York: Macmillan.

Kohn, Hans (1973), "Nationalism," in Philip P. Wiener, ed. *Dictionary of the History of Ideas*, vol. 3. New York: Charles Scribner's Sons, 324-39.

Konstantinov, Yulian, Gulbrand Alhaug and Birgit Igla (1991), "Names of the Bulgarian Pomaks", *Nordlyd*, 17: 8-118.

Korkud, Refik (1986a), *Bulgaristan Şövenist Politikasını Sürdürüyor*, Ankara: Türkiye Fikir Ajansi.

—— (1986b), *Bulgarian Administration and Historical Myth*, Ankara: Türkiye Fikir Ajansi.

Kosev, Dimitür., Xristo Xristov, Dimitür Angelov (1966), *Kratka Bŭlgarska Istorija*, Sofia: Nauka i Izkustvo.

Kowalski, T. (1933), *Les Turcs et la Langue Turque de la Bulgarie du*

Nord-Est, Crakow: Polska Akademija Umieyetnosci, Mémoires de la Commission Orientaliste, 16.

—— (1938), "Les éléménts ethniques turcs de la Dobrudja", *Rocznik Orientalistyczny*, 66-80.

Kostanick, Huey (1957), *Turkish Settlement of Bulgarian Turks, 1950-1953*, Berkeley: University of California Publications in Geography, 8, 2.

Kŭnev, Krasimir (1992a), "Etničeskite predrasŭdŭci i etnokulturnata situacija" in Krasimir Kŭnev, ed., *Etnokulturnata Situacija v Bŭlgarija*. Sofia, pp.44-50.

—— (1992b), "Socialna distancija" in Krasimir Kŭnev, ed., *Etnokulturnata Situacija v Bŭlgarija*, Sofia, pp. 51-8.

Lehiste, Ilse (1988), *Lectures on Language Contact*, Cambridge, MA: MIT Press.

Lemkin, Raphael (1944), *Axis Rule in Occupied Europe*, Concord, NH: Carnegie Endowment for International Peace/Rumford Press.

Lewis, Flora (1985), "Bulgaria's image problem", *New York Times*, 31 May, p. 23.

Lewis, Stephen (1994), "Muslims in Bulgaria", *Aramco World*, 45 (3): 20-9.

Lopasic, Alexander (1979), "Islamisation of the Balkans: some general considerations" in Jennifer M. Scarce, ed., *Islam in the Balkans:Persian Art and Culture of the 18th and 19th Centuries*, Edinburgh: Royal Scottish Museum, 49-53.

Lory, Bernard (1985), *Le Sort de l'Héritage Ottoman en Bulgarie: L'Exemple des Villes Bulgares, 1878-1900*, Istanbul.

Lunt, Horace G. (1986), "On Macedonian nationality", *Slavic Review*, 95 (4): 729-30.

Madjarov, Djeni (1993), "Adaptation – reality and image" in *The Ethnic Situation in Bulgaria (Researches in 1992)*, Sofia: Club '90, pp. 104-21.

Malcolm, Noel (1994), *Bosnia: A Short History*, London: Macmillan.

Mancev, Krastjo, (1992), "National problem in the Balkans until the second world war" in Krastjo Mancev, Zhorzheta Chakurova, and Boby Bobev, eds, *National Problems in the Balkans: History and Contemporary Developments*, Sofia: Arges Publishing House, 9-57.

Markov, Julian G. (1971), "Razvitie na obrazovanieto sred Turskoto naselenie v Bŭlgarija (1944-1952)", *Istoričeski Pregled*, 27 (1): 69-79.

Marushiakova, Elena (1993), "Relations among the Gypsy Groups in Bulgaria" in *The Ethnic Situation in Bulgaria (Researches in 1992)*, Sofia: Club '90 Publishers, 7-16.

—— (1995), 'Inter Group Self-Government of Bulgarian Gypsies', paper presented at V World Congress for Central and East European Studies, Warsaw.

Marushiakova, Elena and Veseling Popov (1993), *Ciganite v Bŭlgarija*, Sofia: Izdatelstvo Klub '90.

—— (1995), *Ciganite v Bŭlgarija – The Gypsies of Bulgaria*, Sofia: Club '90 Publishers.

Maybury-Lewis, David H.P. (1996), "A new world dilemma: the Indian question in America" in William A. Haviland and Robert J. Gordon, eds, *Talking About People: Readings in Contemporary Cultural Anthropology*, 2nd edn, Mountain View, CA: Mayfield Publishing Co., 241-51.

Memišev, Juseyin (1977), *Učastieto na Bŭlgarskite Turci v Borbata protiv Kapitalizma i Fašizma, 1914-1944*, Sofia: Partizdat.

Memişoğlu, Hüseyin (1991), *Pages of the History of Pomak Turks*, Ankara: H. Memişoğlu.

Mishkova, Diana (1994), "Literacy and nation-building in Bulgaria, 1878-1912", *East European Quarterly*, 29 (1): 63-93.

Mitev, Petar (1994), "Relations of compatibility and incompatibility in the everyday life of Christians and Muslims in Bulgaria (sociological studies)" in *Relations of Compatibility and Incompatibility between Christians and Muslims in Bulgaria*, Sofia: International Centre for Minority Studies, pp. 179-230.

Mizov, Nikolai (1965), *Isljamŭt v Bŭlgarija*, Sofia: Izdatelstvo na BKP.

—— (1989), *Isljamŭt i Isljamizacijata*, Sofia: Voenno Izdatelstvo.

Monov, Cvetan (1972), "Prosvetnoto delo sred Bŭlgarite s Mohamedanska vjara v Rodopskija kraj prez godinite na narodnata vlast", *Rodopski Sbornik*, 3: 9-50.

Moškov, Mosko (1985), *Borbata protiv Čuždite Dumi v Bŭlgarskija Knižoven Ezik*, Sofia: BAN.

Moškov, V. (1904), *Tureckija Plemena na Balkanskom Poluostrove*, Moscow: IIRGO, 11: 418-19.

Mutafchieva, Vera (1994), "The Turk, the Jew and the Gypsy" in *Relations of Compatibility and Incompatibility between Christians and Muslims in Bulgaria*. Sofia: International Center for Minority Studies, pp. 5-63.

—— (1965), "Kŭm vŭprosa za statuta na bŭlgarskoto naselenie v Čepinsko pod osmanska vlast", *Rodopski Sbornik*, 1: 115-27.

Mutlu, Mustafa (1993), "Yeni ders yılında Türk dili öğretimine hazır mıyız?", *Hak ve Özgürlük*, 37: 1, 5.

Nacionalen Statističeski Institut (1993a), *Religijata i Pŭlnoletnoto Naselenie (Sotsiologičesko Izsledvane*, Sofia.

—— (1993b), *Demografska Xarakteristika na Bŭlgarija (rezultati ot 2% izvadka). Prebrojavane na Naselenieto i Žilišcnija. Fond kŭm 4 Dekemvri 1992 Godina*, Sofia.

Negencov, K. and I. Vanev (1959), *Obrazovanieto v Iztočna Rumelija, 1879-1885*, Sofia: BAN.

Newsletter of the East European Anthropology Group (1988), "Racism in Bulgaria", 7 (1-2): 16-17.

Nitzova, Petya (1994), "Islam in Bulgaria: a historical reappraisal", *Religion, State and Society*, 22 (1): 97-108.

Norris, H.T. (1993), *Islam in the Balkans: Religion and Society between Europe and the Arab World*, London: Hurst.

Obolenski, Dimitry (1971), *The Byzantine Commonwealth: Eastern Europe, 500-1453*, New York: Praeger.

Omarčevski, Stoyan (1992), *Otčet na Dejnosta na Ministerstvoto ot 20 maj 1920 god do 1 Juli 1922*, Sofia: Državen Vestnik.

OMRI Daily Digest (1995), "Continued tension over ethnic Turkish mayor in Bulgaria", 236, part II, December 6.

—— (1996a), "Bulgarian ethnic Turks protest annullment of Kurdzhali elections", 35, part II, February 19.

—— (1996b), "Bulgarian Supreme Court confirms elections in Kurdzhali", 83, part II, April 26.

Ömer, Fevzi (1995), "Müslümanlar arasında yapamacık gerginlik", *Hak ve Özgürlük*, 7: 2.

Özbir, Kamuran (1986), *Bulgar Yönetimi Gerçeği Gizleyemez*, Istanbul: Başkent Gazetecilik.

Perry, Duncan M. (1991), "Ethnic Turks face Bulgarian nationalism", *Report on Eastern Europe*, 2 (11): 5-8.

Petkov, Krastju and Georgi Fotev, eds (1990), *Etničeskijat Konflikt v Bŭlgarija 1989 (Sotsiologičeski Arxiv)*, Sofia: BAN.

Petrov, Petŭr (1964), *Asimilatorska Politika na Turskite Zavoevateli: Sbornik ot Dokumenti za Pomohamedančvanija i Poturčvanija, XV-XIX v*, Sofia: Nauka i Izkustvo.

—— (1975), *Sŭdbonosni Vekove za Bŭlgarskata Narodnost Krajat na XIV vek – 1912 godina*, Sofia: Nauka i Izkustvo.

—— (1977), *Po Sledite na Nasilieto: Dokumenti za Pomohamedančvanija i Poturčvanija, XIV-XIX v*, Sofia: Nauka i Izkustvo.

—— (1981), "Bulgaria on the geographical map" in Georgi Bokov, ed., *Modern Bulgarian History, Policy, Economy, and Culture*, Sofia: Sofia Press, 128-54.

Pinson, Mark (1972a), "Russian policy and the emigration of Crimean Tatars to the Ottoman Empire", part 1, *Güneydoğu Avrupa Araştırmaları Dergisi*, 1: 7-55.

—— (1972b) "Ottoman colonization of the Circassians in Rumili after the Crimean War", *Etudes Balkaniques*, 3: 71-85.

—— (1974) "Russian policy and the emigration of Crimean Tatars to the Ottoman Empire", part 2, *Güneydoğu Avrupa Araştırmaları Dergisi*, 2-3: 101-14.

Piroğlu, Ali (1993), "Türkiye'ye giden gençlerimize uğurlar olsun", *Hak ve Özgürlük*, 28: 1, 3.

Pitcher, D.E. (1968), *A Historical Geography of the Ottoman Empire*, Leiden: E. J. Brill.

Popov, Veselin (1993), "Bulgarian Gypsies (ethnic relations)" in *The*

Ethnic Situation in Bulgaria (Researches in 1992), Sofia: Club '90 Publishers, 17-26.

—— (1995), "Gypsy Nomads in Bulgaria–Traditions and Contemporary Dimension", paper presented at V World Congress for Central and East European Studies, Warsaw.

Popovic, Alexandre (1986a), *L'Islam balkanique. Les musulmanes du Sud-Est Européen dans la periode post-ottomane.* Berlin: Osteuropa Institut.

—— (1986b), "Les ordres mystiques musulmans du sud-est européen dans la période post-Ottomane" in A. Popovic and G. Veinstein, eds, *Les Ordres Mystiques dans l'Islam. Cheminements et Situations Actuelles.* Paris: EHESS, 63-99.

Poulton, Hugh (1993), *The Balkans: Minorities and States in Conflict*, 2nd edn, London: Minority Rights Publications.

Rabotničesko Delo (1971), April 29.

—— (1977), November 22.

—— (1979), April 28.

Radio Free Europe Research (1985), "Officials say there are no Turks in Bulgaria", *Bulgarian Situation Report* 26, March 28, 3-8.

Rajkin, Spas (1990), *Politiceski Problemi pred Bŭlgarskata Obšcestvenost v Čuzbina*, vol. 4, ed. Milka Ruseva, Tŭrnovo: DE "Abagir".

Reid, Alastair (1994), "The Scottish Condition", *Wilson Quarterly*, 18 (1), pp. 50-8.

Rudin, Catherine and Ali Eminov (1990), "Bulgarian Turkish: the linguistic effects of recent nationality policy", *Anthropological Linguistics*, 32 (1-2): 149-62.

—— (1993), "Bulgarian nationalism and Turkish language in Bulgaria" in Eran Fraenkel and Christina Kramer, eds. *Language Contact – Language Conflict.* New York: Peter Lang, 43-71.

Runciman, Steven (1930), *A History of the First Bulgarian Empire*, London: G. Bell and Sons.

Savory, R.M. (1980), "Kizil-bash", *Encyclopaedia of Islam*, 5: 243-5.

Seypel, Tatjana (1989), "The Pomaks of northwestern Greece: an endangered Balkan population", *Journal, Institute of Muslim Minority Affairs*, 10 (1): 41-9.

Shaw, Stanford J. (1976), *History of the Ottoman Empire and Modern Turkey: The Rise and Decline of the Ottoman Empire, 1280-1808*, Cambridge University Press.

Shaw, Stanford J. and Ezel K. Shaw (1977), *History of the Ottoman Empire and Modern Turkey: The Rise of Modern Turkey, 1808-1975*, Cambridge University Press.

Shoup, Paul S. (1981), *The East European and Soviet Data Handbook: Political, Social and Developmental Indicators, 1945-1975*, New York: Columbia University Press.

Silverman, Carol (1984), "Pomaks" in R. Weeks, ed. *Moslem Peoples:*

A World Ethnographic Survey, 2nd edn, Westport, CT: Greenwood Press, 612-16.

— (1986), "Bulgarian Gypsies: Adaptation in a Socialist State", *Nomadic Peoples*, 21-2: 51-62.

— (1989), "Reconstructing folklore: media and cultural policy in Eastern Europe", *Communication*, 11: 141-60.

Skendi, Stavro (1967), "Crypto-Christians in the Balkan area under the Ottomans", *Slavic Review*, 26 (2): 227-46.

Snegarov, Ivan (1958), *Turskoto Vladičestvo Prečka za Kulturnoto Razvitie na Bŭlgarskija Narod i Drugite Balkanski Narodi*, Sofia: BAN.

Sofia News (1985a), "No part of our people belongs to any other nation," April 3, pp. 1, 12.

— (1985b), "Bulgaria has no spare citizens", May 1, p. 3.

— (1985c), "Lessons in religious tolerance", April 10, p. 9.

Sofia Press (1971), *The Constitution of the People's Republic of Bulgaria.*

— (1985), *Who Worries about Moslems in Bulgaria and Why?*

— (1990), *Bulgaria on the Road to Democracy: Law on the Names of Bulgarian Citizens.*

Sofia Press Agency (1991), *Constitution of the Republic of Bulgaria.*

Solidarity and Cultural Association of the Balkan Turks (1988), *Bulgarian Oppression*, Ankara.

Spiridonakis, G.G. (1977), *Essays on the Historical Geography of the Greek World in the Balkans during the Turkokratia*, Thessaloniki: Institute for Balkan Studies.

Stavrianos, L.S. (1958), *The Balkans since 1453*, New York: HRW.

Sugar, Peter (1969), "External and domestic roots of Eastern European nationalism" in Peter Sugar and Ivo Lederere, eds, *Nationalism in Eastern Europe*, Seattle: University of Washington Press, 3-54.

— (1977), *Southeastern Europe under Ottoman Rule, 1354-1804*, Seattle: University of Washington Press.

— (1978), "Major changes in the life of the Slav peasantry under Ottoman rule", *International Journal of Middle East Studies*, 9 (3): 297-305.

Südost-Europa (1985a), "Von bulgarischen Türken und 'getürken' Bulgaren", 6 (34), 359-67.

— (1985b) "Aubenpolitische Aspekte der Bulgarischen 'Türkenpolitik' ", 9, (34), 477-87.

Szaykowski, Bogdan and Tim Niblock (1993), "Islam and ethnicity in Eastern Europe", *Balkan Forum*, 1 (4): 167-87.

Şahin, Ilhan, Feridun M. Emecen and Yusuf Halaçoğlu (1990), "Turkish settlements in Rumelia (Bulgaria) in the 15th and 16th centuries: town and village population" in Kemal Karpat, ed., *The Turks of Bulgaria: The History, Culture and Political Fate of a Minority*, Istanbul: Isis Press, pp. 23-42.

Şimşir, Bilal (1966), *Contribution à l'Histoire des Populations Turques en Bulgarie, 1876-1880*, Ankara: Türk Kültürünü Araştırma Enstitüsü.

—— (1986a), *Glimpses on the Turkish Minority in Bulgaria*, Ankara: Directorate General of Press and Information.

—— (1986b), *Turkish Minority Education and Literature in Bulgaria*, Ankara: Ministry of Foreign Affairs Press.

—— (1986c), *The Turkish Minority Press in Bulgaria: Its History and Tragedy 1865-1985*, Ankara: Ministry of Foreign Affairs Press.

—— (1988), *The Turks of Bulgaria (1878-1985)*, London: K. Rustem and Bro.

—— (1989), *Rumeli'den Türk Göçleri*, 3 vols, Ankara: Türk Tarih Kurumu Basımevi.

Tahsin, Muharrem (1991), "Çağdaş Türkçemiz", *Hak ve Özgürlük*, nos 7 and 9, p. 9; nos 20, 24, 26, 28, 30, 32, 34, 38, and 40, p. 5.

Tatarlı Ibrahim (1993), "Bulgaristan'da demokrasiye geçiş döneminde (1990-1993): Latin alfabesi ve Türk dili ve edebiyati öğrenimiyle ilgili bazi sorunlar", *Hak ve Özgürlük*, 44: 5.

—— (1995), "Herkesin mensubiyetine uygun olarak dendi kültürünü geliştirmeye hakki vardir", *Hak ve Özgürlük*, 44: 5.

—— (1996a), "Avrupa'ya girmek için Avrupa'ya benzemek gerek", *Hak ve Özgürlük*, 1: 5.

—— (1996b), "Ikinci Bulgarlaştırma süreci geliyor", *Hak ve Özgürlük*, 3: 3.

Thirkell, John (1979), "Islamization in Macedonia as a social process" in Jennifer M. Scarce, ed., *Islam in the Balkans: Persian Art and Culture of the 18th and 19th Centuries*, Edinburgh: Royal Scottish Museum, 43-7.

Todorov, Nikolaj (1963), "Sur quelques aspects du passage de féodalisme au capitalisme dans les territoires Balkaniques de l'Empire Ottomane," *Revue des Etudes Sud-Est Européennes*, 1 (1-2): 103-36.

—— (1969), "The Balkan town in the second half of the 19th century", *Etudes Balkaniques*, 2: 31-50.

—— (1983), *The Balkan City, 1400-1900*, Seattle: University of Washington Press.

Todorova, Maria (1992), *Language in the Construction of Ethnicity and Nationalism: The Case of Bulgaria*, Berkeley: University of California, Center for German and European Studies, Working Paper 5.5.

Tomova, Ilona (1992a), "Gypsy-bashing: palpable frustration, if not outright contempt", *The Insider*, 1: 20-1.

—— (1992b), "Etničeskite stereotipi" in Krasimir Kŭnev, ed., *Etnokulturnata Situacija v Bŭlgarija*, Sofia, 26-43.

Tomova, Ilona and Plamen Bogoev (1992), "Minorities in Bulgaria: A Report of the International Conference on the Minorities", *The Insider*, (Bulgarian Digest Monthly), Rome 1991, 2: 1-15.

Topçiev, Mehmed M. (1992), "Nedim Gencev bilmelidir: yalancının mumu yatsıya kadar yanar", *Hak ve Özgürlük*, 10: 8.

Triska, F. Jan, ed. (1968), "Bulgaria" in *Constitutions of the Communist Party States*, Stanford: Hoover Institution, pp. 151-79.

Troxel, Luan (1992), "Bulgaria's Gypsies: numerically strong, politically weak", *RFE/RL Research Report*, 10 (March 6).

—— (1993), "Socialist persistence in the Bulgarian elections of 1990-1991", *East European Quarterly*, 26 (4) 407-30.

Tunalı, Hüseyin M. (1993), "Türkçemiz okul programlarına girmelidir: anadilimiz zorunlu ders bilimi oluncaya kadar direneceğiz", *Hak ve Özgürlük*, 40: 5.

Ülküsal, Müstecib (1966), *Dobruca ve Türkler*, Ankara: Türk Kültürünü Araştırma Enstitüsü.

Vasileva, Darina (1992), "Bulgarian Turkish emigration and return", *International Migration Review*, 26 (2): 342-52.

Vrančev, Nikolaj (1948), *Bŭlgari Mohamedani (Pomaci)*, Sofia: Biblioteka Bŭlgarski Narod.

Vryonis, Speros (1971), *The Decline of Medieval Hellenism in Asia Minor and the Process of Islamization from the Eleventh through the Fifteenth Centuries*, Berkeley: University of California Press.

—— (1972), "Religious changes and patterns in the Balkans, 14th-16th centuries" in H. Birnbaum and S. Vryonis, eds., *Aspects of the Balkans*, The Hague: Mouton, 151-76.

—— (1975a), "Byzantine and Turkish societies and their source of manpower" in V.J. Parry and M.E. Yapp, eds. *War, Technology and Society in the Middle East*. Oxford University Press, pp. 125-52.

—— (1975b), "Religious change and continuity in the Balkans and Anatolia from the fourteenth through the sixteenth century" in S. Vryonis, ed., *Islam and Cultural Change in the Middle East*, Wiesbaden: Otto Harrassowitz, 127- 40.

Vucinich, Wayne S. (1969), "Islam in the Balkans" in A.J. Arberry, ed. *Religions in the Middle East: Three Religions in Concord and Conflict*, vol. 2. Cambridge University Press, 236- 52.

Wittek, Paul (1952), "Yazijioghlu 'Ali on the Christian Turks of Dobruja", *Bulletin of the School of Oriental and African Studies*, 14: 639-68.

—— (1953), "Les Gagaouzes les gens de Kaykaus", *Rocznik Orientalistyczne*, 28: 12-24.

Woolard, Kathryn A. (1989), *Double Talk: Bilingualism and the Politics of Ethnicity in Catalonia*, Stanford University Press.

The World Today (1951), "The expulsion of the Turkish minority from Bulgaria", 7 (1): 30-6.

Xristov, Xristo, ed. (1989), *Stranici ot Bŭlgarskata Istorija Očerk za Isljamiziranite Bulgari in Nacionalnovŭzroditelnija Process*, Sofia: BAN.

Yankov, Georgi, ed. (1989), *Aspects of the Development of the Bulgarian Nation*, Sofia: BAN.

Zajaczkowski, Wlodzimierz (1965), "Gagauz", *Encyclopedia of Islam*, 2: 971-2.

—— (1974), "K etnogeneuz Gagauzow", *Folia Orientalia*, 15: 77-86.

Željazkova, Antonina (1990a), "The problem of the authenticity of some domestic sources on the Islamization of the Rhodopes, deeply rooted in Bulgarian historiography", *Etudes Balkaniques*, 4: 105-11.

—— (1990b), *Pazprostranenie na Isljama v Zapadnobalkanskite Zemi pod Osmanska Vlast XV-XVIII vek*, Sofia: BAN.

Živkov, Todor (1964a), *Bulgaristan Türkleri Sosyalist Vatanlarinin Aktif Kurucularidir*, Sofia: Narodna Prosveta.

—— (1964b), "Bulgaristan Türk ahalisi sosyalist cemiyette yaşadiğina iftihar eder", *Yeni Işik*, March 5, 1-2.

INDEX